PSYCHIATRIC CLAIMS IN WORKERS' COMPENSATION AND CIVIL LITIGATION

VOLUME 2

PSYCHIATRIC CLAIMS IN WORKERS' COMPENSATION AND CIVIL LITIGATION
VOLUME 2

HERBERT LASKY
Rancho Palos Verdes, California

Wiley Law Publications
JOHN WILEY & SONS, INC.
New York • Chichester • Brisbane • Toronto • Singapore

This text is printed on acid-free paper.

Portions previously published in *Guidelines for Handling Psychiatric Issues in Workers' Compensation Cases.*

Library of Congress Cataloging in Publication Data:

Lasky, Herbert.
Psychiatric claims in workers' compensation and civil litigation / Herbert Lasky.
p. cm. — (Personal injury library)
Includes index.
ISBN 0-471-58490-8 (set : acid-free paper). — ISBN 0-471-59437-7 (v. 1. : acid-free paper). — ISBN 0-471-59438-5 (v. 2 : acid-free paper)
1. Workers' compensation—Law and legislation—United States. 2. Forensic psychiatry—United States. 3. Psychiatric disability evaluation—United States. I. Title. II. Series.
KF3616.L37 1993
344.73'021—dc20
[347.30421] 92-41684

Printed in the United States of America

10 9 8 7 6 5 4 3 2 1

SUMMARY CONTENTS

VOLUME 1

VOLUME 2

DETAILED CONTENTS

VOLUME 1

VOLUME 2

Appendixes

CHAPTER 13

PSYCHIATRIC TREATMENT

Gregory J. Firman

§ 13.1 Introduction

Trying to summarize *psychiatric treatment* in one chapter of a book is almost as difficult as it would be to capsulize all of medical treatment in a similarly small space, especially given that a patient might have several overlapping psychiatric diagnoses or other complicating conditions. Further, two patients with the same psychiatric diagnosis might have significantly different personality structures, social support systems, body chemistries, and ongoing stressors, making their respective treatments quite different. Nevertheless, this chapter provides an overview of the various psychiatric treatments, divided into (1) the psychosocial therapies and (2) the biological therapies.

§ 13.2 Psychosocial Therapies

Psychotherapy is defined in the *Psychiatric Glossary* of the American Psychiatric Association as "a process in which a person who wishes to relieve symptoms or resolve problems in living or is seeking personal growth enters into an implicit or explicit contract to interact in a prescribed way with a psychotherapist."[1] It is also sometimes referred to as *talk therapy.* In this type of treatment, the patient and therapist talk about the experiences the patient is having, important relationships and future goals, and the feelings, thoughts, and behaviors they produce (Greist and Jefferson, 39).

According to Jerome Frank, the therapeutic process (that is, the therapeutic relationship, setting, rationale, and task taken together) influences patients in five interrelated ways, which seem necessary to produce attitude change and therapeutic benefits. All forms of psychotherapy

1. Provide the patient with new opportunities for learning, at both cognitive and experiential levels
2. Enhance the patient's hope of relief
3. Provide success experiences, which enhance the patient's sense of mastery, interpersonal competence, or capabilities
4. Help the patient overcome the demoralizing sense of alienation from others. The patient discovers that her problems are not unique and that others can understand them and do care about her behavioral change
5. Arouse the patient emotionally (emotional arousal being a necessary precondition to all attitudinal and behavioral change).

In sum, all successful forms of psychotherapy relieve dysphoric (unpleasant) feelings, give the patient hope, stimulate emotional arousal, increase the sense of

---

[1] American Psychiatric Ass'n, A Psychiatric Glossary (5th ed. 1980).

mastery over self and environment, and restore morale. As a result, the patient becomes able to tackle the problems she had been avoiding, with new and better ways of handling them.

The psychotherapies are generally further divided into three types:

1. Insight-oriented or psychodynamic
2. Supportive
3. Cognitive/behavioral/interpersonal.

§ 13.3 —Psychodynamic

As explained by Enelow (at 33ff), these therapies originated in Freud's methods of psychoanalysis. They seek to help the patient achieve greater awareness and understanding of how unconscious conflicts affect feelings and behavior and to increase the ability to put these insights into words.

Psychoanalysis and psychoanalytically oriented (psychodynamic) psychotherapy are theoretically quite similar, though there are some differences, such as in frequency and duration of treatment and the technical aspect of guiding and managing the insights obtained. In grossly oversimplified terms, psychoanalytically oriented psychotherapy seeks to change long-standing maladaptive behaviors, anxiety, and depression by means of intellectual insight, resumption of interrupted maturation, and healthier emotional experiences. Interpretation of dreams, free association, and exploration of the past (especially as applied to present relationships and role functioning) are important techniques in this type of treatment (Greist and Jefferson, 40–41).

In general, psychoanalytically oriented therapies are indicated for long-standing character problems (which used to be called *neuroses*), obsessive-compulsive symptoms, and certain sexual perversions. These conditions, in general, fall under the heading of what the American Psychiatric Association's *Diagnostic and Statistical Manual of Mental Disorders* (third edition, revised) (DSM-III-R) calls *Axis II disorders.* Therefore, they are not the type of problems that tend to be the result of industrial injuries.

Traditionally, psychoanalytically oriented therapies lasted several years. More recently, however, psychotherapy using the same underlying principles, but time-limited to an average of 10 to 20 sessions, has proven to be of comparable benefit in selected psychiatric conditions, especially depression (Stewart, 1331ff; Ursano and Hales, 1507–17).

§ 13.4 —Supportive

As its name suggests, supportive therapy focuses more on providing emotional support than on increasing intellectual insight and making unconscious conflicts accessible to the conscious mind. Ordinarily, it is more appropriate for dealing with industrial injury problems.

In supportive psychotherapy, the therapist does not attempt to provide insights, although the patient may learn something about aspects of her behavior or the impact of her behavior on others. Instead, the therapist generally suggests, advises, and directs, with the primary aim of helping the patient reestablish previously successful ways of coping with problems.

Another important aspect of supportive psychotherapy, especially with patients who have concurrent somatic problems, involves interpreting and explaining the relevant medical or surgical condition or treatment in a manner and at a pace that the patient can assimilate. The therapist also explains the course of the medical or psychiatric condition, monitoring changes and reassuring the patient that improvement should, in time, occur.

In the workers' compensation setting specifically, an important facet of supportive psychotherapy involves helping the patient understand the workers' compensation system itself. The psychotherapist is often the only person who takes the time to explore (and usually correct) the patient's expectations vis-à-vis the procedures, duration, and specific stages of her case and what she can expect in the way of symptomatic improvement, reemployment, vocational rehabilitation, and money.

Supportive psychotherapy has much in common with the help provided by clergymen, helpful teachers who counsel students, attorneys, and family physicians (Greist and Jefferson, 40; Enelow, 75–76; Stewart, 1331ff).

Ordinarily supportive therapy would not involve sessions more frequently than once a week. The usual program would be in the nature of weekly sessions for two to three months, tapering off to once per month over a period of another two months, with an overall treatment duration of approximately six months. This norm can, however, be complicated by continuing stressors or new and disturbing life events, such as family problems, medical problems, and the like.

§ 13.5 —Cognitive/Behavioral/Interpersonal

Cognitive therapy is based on the finding that some psychological disturbances stem from specific, habitual errors in thinking (cognition). For example, patients may reason on the basis of self-defeating assumptions, incorrectly interpret life situations, judge themselves too harshly, jump to inaccurate conclusions, or fail to generate adequate plans or strategies to deal with external problems.

For example, a patient might see an old friend cross the street and feel anxious. On examination of her semiconscious reactions, she is taught to realize that what went through her mind was, "If I say hello he may not remember me—he may snub me—he may not care to pick up the relationship—it's easier to walk on like I didn't see him." In another situation, the patient might be afraid to count her change in front of a cashier for fear of being insulted by the cashier. The patient is then helped to understand the unrealistic aspects of her thoughts and behavior and, through a combination of verbal procedures and behavior modification techniques, to deal more effectively with her problems. This leads to greater confidence and a sense of well-being (Beck, 1541ff).

Cognitive psychotherapy, like interpersonal psychotherapy, is one of the few types of psychotherapy to be systematically studied and might have significant advantages over medication treatment alone or psychodynamically oriented psychotherapy in nonpsychotic depressions, various anxiety disorders, and some addictions (Beck, 1541ff). Most of these conditions occur in the workers' compensation setting. The time frames for this type of treatment are comparable to supportive therapy.

Interpersonal psychotherapy has been applied most often to the treatment of various depressions. It is based on the evidence that "most clinical depressions—regardless of symptom patterns, severity, presumed biologic vulnerability, or personality traits—occur in an interpersonal context. Understanding and renegotiating the interpersonal context associated with the depression is important to the depressed person's recovery and to the prevention of possible future episodes." (Weissman and Klerman, 1863ff). Interpersonal therapy is time-limited, usually in the range of 12 to 16 weeks, once weekly, and is focused on improving the quality of the depressed patient's current interpersonal functioning. It can be used alone or in conjunction with pharmacologic approaches. Both interpersonal and cognitive therapies have approximately equal efficacy in the treatment of nonpsychotic depression (Elkin, 971ff). Both types of therapies have in common brief duration and access to manuals and explicit training programs (Klerman, 1732).

§ 13.6 —Behavioral Therapy

One of the core theoretical tenets of psychoanalytically oriented therapy is that ideas and feelings must change before any meaningful change can be brought about in behavior or mood. The behavioral therapist, in contrast, postulates that feelings and thoughts are just as often the result of problem behaviors, so that treating the behaviors themselves is the focus of this type of treatment. Key techniques in behavioral treatment include systematic desensitization and assertion training.

Systematic desensitization involves using a competitive (and incompatible) response (such as eating, relaxation, or conversation) to inhibit a previously learned anxiety response, such as fear of heights or closed spaces. To do so, an ascending hierarchy of progressively more intense fear-producing stimulus situations is used. For example, if the patient has a fear of elevators, she is first taught to relax completely and then is instructed to use this relaxation response in situations of increasing anxiety. These anxiety-producing situations may simply be visualized in the mind (*in vitro*) or may instead be conducted outside the therapist's office, at or around the feared place or situation (*in vivo*).

In the fear of elevators situation, for example, a male patient would be asked first to visualize in his mind standing outside a tall building that has elevators (the in vitro model) or he might actually be brought to that place (in vivo). Then he would learn to relax his body completely with that mental image or in that situation. As the next step, the patient would be brought into the lobby of the building (again, either by means of mental visualization or by actually going into the lobby) and would repeat this scene or behavior until he could do it while relaxed. Ultimately, the patient would be able to ride up and down in an actual elevator without paralyzing anxiety or panic.

Systematic desensitization (either alone or in conjunction with short-acting antianxiety medications) is the treatment of choice for various phobias, including those accompanying post-traumatic stress disorders. These problems are encountered frequently in the workers' compensation setting.

In *assertion training,* strong self-assertion is used as the competitive response to inhibit conditioned anxiety and fear in a way that parallels conceptually the use of relaxation in systematic desensitization. Clinically, assertion training is often helpful for individuals who characterologically fail to stand up for their own rights in a firm, effective, appropriate, but nonaggressive manner (again, a recurring theme in the workplace).

The following specific disorders are eminently treatable by behavioral methods: all types of phobias; obsessive-compulsive behaviors; lack of appropriate self-assertion; various tics; stuttering; various types of headaches; impotence; frigidity; vaginismus; premature ejaculation; and various maladaptive habits and addictive behaviors (Birk, 433ff).

The course of treatment is ordinarily not extensive. Effective results may be expected in from eight to fifteen treatments over a period of two to three months.

§ 13.7 Biological Treatments

Biological treatments include medication, electroconvulsive therapy (ECT), and some new and experimental interventions. In contrast to the psychotherapies, biological treatments work directly on the central nervous system.

§ 13.8 —Psychotropic Medication

It has been estimated that some 10 percent of Americans use psychotropic medications by prescription, and probably several times that number use nonprescription chemicals such as caffeine, nicotine, alcohol, and marijuana to "feel better" in various ways. Thus, psychotropic medication, in one form or other, is a part of everyday life.

The impact of modern psychopharmaceuticals on the practice of psychiatry in the 1950s and the 1960s, when they were introduced, has been compared with the impact of antibiotics on general medicine.

Statistics confirm the importance of antipsychotic and antidepressant drugs on hospital practice. In the United States, the number of hospitalized psychiatric patients reached a peak of close to 600,000 in 1955, with an initially rapid (and now slower) downward trend since then to about 200,000 in 1974, despite an increase in the total population.

Psychotropic medications are generally divided into the *antipsychotics* (also called *neuroleptics* or *major tranquilizers*), the *antidepressants,* the *antianxiety agents, lithium,* and some miscellaneous classes. Almost all of the psychotropic medications affect neurotransmitters, those chemicals that transmit electrical impulses between neurons in the brain and between the brain and tissue receptors in the peripheral nervous system.

Many psychiatric conditions have been shown to involve either an excess of one or more neurotransmitters in a given part of the brain, a deficiency of one or several neurotransmitters, or an imbalance between two or more neurotransmitters. Essentially, the various psychotropic medications are used to correct these abnormalities.

For example, Thorazine and related antipsychotic drugs (such as Haldol, Prolixin, Mellaril, and Stelazine) counter the effects of excessive dopamine (a neurotransmitter) in the brains of schizophrenics, moderating or stopping such uncomfortable and disabling phenomena as delusions, hallucinations, irrational anxieties, and violent behavior. Antidepressants (such as Tofranil, Elavil, Norpramin, Sinequan, Prozac, Parnate, and Nardil) probably work by increasing the amount of norepinephrine and serotonin (other neurotransmitters) in the brains of depressed people. The benzodiazepine antianxiety agents (such as Valium, Librium, Ativan, and Serax) act primarily on the neurotransmitter called *GABA* (gamma-aminobutyric acid). A new antianxiety agent, Buspar, is not a benzodiazepine and appears to act on different neurotransmitters, primarily serotonin. Buspar seems to be as effective as the benzodiazepines in the treatment of anxiety and has a significant advantage of having less addictive potential (Gorman and Davis, 1579). The mechanism of action for lithium is not yet clear, but its effectiveness as a mood stabilizer or supplemental antidepressant in appropriate cases (such as manic-depressive illness or treatment-resistant depression) is firmly established.

Some psychiatric conditions require the use of several different classes of medications. For example, severe or resistant depression might require trials of two different chemical types of antidepressant, lithium, stimulant medications (such as Dexedrine or Ritalin), thyroid hormone, and l-tryptophan (the latter an amino acid that is a building block for one of the neurotransmitters), or combinations of these agents (Baldessarini, 387ff; Goldsmith, 33–35; Greist and Jefferson, 52 and 60).

§ 13.9 —Electroconvulsive Therapy

In the experience and judgment of many psychiatrists, as well as patients with severe depressions who have received electroconvulsive therapy (ECT) and other antidepressant treatments, ECT is the single most effective treatment for severe depression.

ECT has a number of advantages over other treatments. For example, ECT works rapidly, so that patients can quickly return to productive living. It has a higher success rate for severe depression than any other single treatment approach. It is clearly the treatment of choice when a patient is making dangerous suicide attempts or when the patient has lost contact with reality and has delusions or hallucinations. Patients in a precarious medical condition usually tolerate ECT quite well, with fewer complications than those associated with antidepressant drugs.

ECT is administered after the patient is put to sleep with a short-acting anesthetic and after the patient's muscles are relaxed, so that muscle contractions from the treatment will not damage muscles or bones. A generalized seizure does not, in fact, occur because of the muscle relaxant given. Patients do not remember or feel the treatment.

Unfortunately, ECT has a "scary" name and negative associations in the public mind (from various popular movies as well as from a regrettable tendency for overuse in past years), and the psychiatric profession has not yet been able to counter these problems with the factual data very effectively (Greist and Jefferson, 63–65; Weiner, 1670ff).

§ 13.10 —New Biological Treatments

Among new biological treatments, partial sleep deprivation involves waking patients after they have had half a night of sleep, usually the first half, and keeping them awake the rest of the night. This is done two or three times a week. Sleep deprivation for this period of time sometimes results in an immediate and dramatic response in severely depressed patients, possibly by means of resetting the patient's "biological clock."

Exposure to bright white light for an extra four to six hours per day, over one or two weeks, is another new approach for treating certain types of depression, especially the recurrent or seasonal type.

Both of these treatment approaches are still in the experimental stage, and the specific treatment indications, methods, and long-term follow-up results are not yet established. However, they are exciting because both treatments are virtually without side effects (Kaplan and Boggiano, 1685–86; Akiskal, 22).

§ 13.11 Treatment of Major Psychiatric Conditions

Sections 13.12 through **13.18** discuss the treatment of major psychiatric conditions commonly seen in workers' compensation cases. Included are depression, post-traumatic stress disorder, post-concussive syndrome, chronic pain, generalized anxiety disorder, schizophrenia and manic-depressive illness, and conversion disorder.

§ 13.12 —Depression

Depression is not a homogeneous disorder, but instead is a spectrum of illnesses, including bipolar affective (manic-depressive) illness in the depressed phase; major depression, either single episode or recurrent; cyclothymic disorder in the depressed phase; dysthymic disorder (formerly called *depressive neurosis*); atypical depression; and adjustment disorder with depressive features.

Both psychotherapy and antidepressant medication should always be considered in the treatment of depression because these treatment modalities act on different parameters of the depression. That is, psychotherapy and medications are complementary treatments. For example, the antidepressant medications are most helpful in relieving the insomnia, anorexia, decreased sex drive, physical slowing, and sluggish thinking common to significant depressions, while the psychotherapies are most helpful vis-à-vis social and family functioning and depressive thoughts and behaviors.

Although mild (nondisabling) depression often disappears without treatment, it may resolve sooner with psychotherapy. Mild depression that is long lasting or unresponsive to psychotherapy may be helped by medication. Moderate and severe depressions usually require combined treatment with psychotherapy and antidepressant medications. There is some evidence that cognitive psychotherapy (see **§ 13.5**) combined with antidepressant medications may be more effective than either treatment alone for moderate depression. Severe depression is not likely to respond to psychotherapy, but requires antidepressant medications, supplemented with psychotherapy and sometimes ECT.

No final evaluation of depression for permanent disability purposes (or indeed for treatment planning purposes) should be made without an appropriate trial of medication. This should be conducted by a physician trained in the administration of such therapy. Common errors include inadequate dosage due to unfamiliarity with the course of the disease and failure to select the appropriate antidepressant for the individual (thus producing avoidable side effects).

It is important for the patient first to have a full course (at least six weeks) of an adequate dosage of one antidepressant, with the adequacy of the dosage preferably confirmed by plasma levels. If this is not effective, the first antidepressant should be stopped, and a similar course of a second, chemically distinct antidepressant should be tried. If the second trial is not effective, then various other medication combinations and ECT should all be tried (Akiskal, 22; Greist and Jefferson, 43–44; Jacobson and McKinney, 184ff).

§ 13.13 —Post-traumatic Stress Disorder

The treatment of post-traumatic stress disorder (PTSD) may consist of behavior techniques, medications, and various forms of psychotherapy.

Behavioral techniques may be of value when anxiety and phobic symptoms are prominent. Relaxation therapy (discussed in **§ 13.6**) may be useful in decreasing anxiety and inducing sleep. Progressive desensitization may be used to overcome various phobic symptoms.

Regarding medications, antianxiety agents such as Valium or Librium may be helpful, for short-term use. Imipramine (Tofranil), alprazolam (Xanax), fluoxetine (Prozac), and certain of the MAO (monoamine oxidase) inhibitors (Parnate, Nardil) may be useful, especially in decreasing phobic or depressive symptoms.

Psychotherapy may be used either alone or in conjunction with behavioral treatment methods or medication. Milder or more acute (recent) cases of PTSD will often respond to supportive psychotherapy. More chronic or severe cases will usually require modes of psychotherapy that add insight and ventilate emotion. Psychotherapy should be initiated as early as possible and at the same time kept as brief as possible to minimize the risks of dependence and chronicity (Andreasen, 918ff). A condition that could be treatable in two to three months (eight to twelve sessions) may become chronic if neglected.

§ 13.14 —Post-concussive Syndrome

This entity refers to a complex of somatic and emotional symptomatology following a significant head injury. The most common symptoms include headaches (often exacerbated by physical exertion), tenderness over the scalp, lightheadedness, irritability, intolerance for such sensory stimuli as light and noise, easy fatigability, insomnia, decreased auditory and visual acuity, photosensitivity, blurred vision, tinnitus, difficulty with concentration and memory, decreased tolerance to alcohol, and diminished interest and spontaneity, sometimes with marked social withdrawal.

It is important to note that post-concussive symptomatology can arise even when there is no clear or prolonged loss of consciousness. It is commonly seen in severe whiplash-type injuries or in closed-head trauma in which the patient is only dazed or stunned briefly.

This syndrome lies in the "borderland" between neurology and psychiatry. The consensus of most authors is that the symptomatology is due to a combination of organic, emotional, and social factors, the latter two becoming more operative with the passage of time. The DSM-III-R does not contain this term, but includes it under the general rubric of *organic brain syndrome,* with the appropriate adjectives used to describe the most salient clinical features.

Some authors have found the prolongation of post-concussive symptoms to be more marked in patients who are somehow seeking financial compensation, whereas others have not found any empirical support for this hypothesis. Generally, routine neurological examination, electroencephalograms (EEG's), and computerized axial tomography (CAT scans) are negative in this syndrome. Sleep EEG studies, however, often show a pathognomonic finding of periods of rapid eye movement (REM) sleep on the EEG tracing itself without the normal concomitant eye movements on electromyography. The sleep EEG tracings often show other abnormalities as well, such as elongated sleep spindles and disruption of the normal progression of the sleep stages.

In a good number of patients, BEAM (brain electrical activity mapping, or a computer-analyzed EEG), electronystagmography (ENG), and brainstem-evoked potential studies yield the only positive diagnostic data. Specialized neuropsychological testing also shows diffuse functional deficits, the latter generally improving with time.

The symptom duration is from several months to many years, with median duration of three to four years. Younger patients tend to recover more quickly than older ones. Some clinicians feel that significant preexisting personality pathology predisposes a patient to a longer clinical course, though this is by no means clear.

Note that neurologists often refer to the post-concussive syndrome as a *post-traumatic syndrome.* This designation often causes confusion with the psychiatric entity of *post-traumatic stress disorder,* discussed in § **13.13**, which does not involve actual (physical) head trauma.

Important features of treatment of post-concussive syndrome include explanation of the symptoms to the patient and the patient's family, so that the ongoing symptoms are understood and validated rather than serving as a focus for recriminations, guilt, and unrealistic expectations of recovery; niacin or vitamin B-6 for the hearing difficulties and tinnitus; symptomatic treatment of the dizziness and vertigo; stimulants in small doses, particularly for the memory and concentration problems and irritability; and separate treatment of the pain and the anxiety and depression, if these are prominent in the overall clinical picture (Siegler and Murrow, 26ff; Wells, 877ff; Pincus and Tucker, 262–63; Alexander, 219–49; Strub and Black, 272–78; Trimble, 129–137; Hanley; Kwentus, 8–17; Stuss, 41–47).

§ 13.15 —Chronic Pain

The treatment of chronic pain problems is neither simple nor uniform. The incidence of depression in chronic pain patients varies between 10 and 85 percent, depending on the patient group studied and the diagnostic criteria utilized.

There is also a growing consensus that psychiatrists and other mental health professionals should be involved from the outset of treatment, whether or not there is "real" organic pathology as the basis for the pain. Even if a patient does not meet DSM-III-R criteria or Research Diagnostic Criteria (RDC) for major depression, antidepressant medications are often helpful in moderating pain.

An excellent summary of this problem is found in Lindsay and Wyckoff, "The Depression-Pain Syndrome and Its Response to Antidepressants." (*Psychosomatics* 22(7):571–77 (July 1981)). In this article, the authors report on a study of 300 patients at the Pain Center of the University of Washington in Seattle. Two hundred sixty-one (87 percent) of these patients, referred by their physicians for diagnosis and treatment of their pain syndrome (and not involved in litigation) met rigid clinical criteria for depression, similar to those found in DSM-III-R. In another study of 197 private patients with depression, 116 (59 percent) also had recurring benign pain. When this latter group was treated with antidepressant medications, 83 percent "obtained significant relief of their pain syndrome." The authors stated, "The frequency with which antidepressants can significantly alleviate pain associated with depression highlights the importance of the link between pain and depression."

Several factors are probably operative in this frequent association between pain and depression. Anyone with a tendency to see herself as industrious and productive tends to feel depressed when she is physically disabled for any reason. The depression, in turn, worsens the pain and disability for several possible reasons. First, depression tends to accentuate the affective (mood) component to pain. Second, the depression might actually lower the pain threshold of the central nervous system, possibly because pain and depression share some of the same neural pathways and neurotransmitters. More recently, there is also suggestive evidence of the effect of depression (and antidepressants) on the enkephalins and prostaglandins, the latter, in turn, having an important role in chronic and acute pain. Third, the disabled patient tends to live a constricted life, with an increased focus inward and upon somatic symptoms. The magnified pain and disability, then, tend to make the depression worse . . . and so on, in a vicious cycle. This mutual exacerbation is even more notable in patients who have little psychological insight and who tend to focus on somatic problems even when not depressed.

Two articles in the psychiatric literature sum up the pain-depression link:

> Chronic pain is the single predominant problem in the rehabilitation of disabled workers. Settling for compensation payments and finally for a disability pension may be unavoidable in many cases, but is obviously an undesirable solution for individuals without significant physical impairment who are in the midst of their best earning years and whose working capacity has been their strength. Joint efforts of physicians, rehabilitation specialists, and the employer may be required, and time is an important factor. Like the soldier with battle-fatigue who has been moved too far from action for too long and will not be able to return to the front line, the previously overachieving worker with the pain complaints will

> find it very difficult to function at work again if he has been away from his job for a long time. In the meantime, his position in the family as the respected breadwinner may crumble and much discontent if not open strife set in. Diminished activities and social life can result in a monotony which further increases the depression. The individual may become a permanent victim of work fatigue. . . . Pain-prone patients can be maintained at work if they are promptly and properly treated. (Blumer, 179–94).

Two authors have also noted an intimate relationship between self reports of depression and disability and suggest that levels of disability may have more to do with the depression than the physical illness involved. "In view of findings such as the marked improvement in memory function after antidepressant therapy . . . the identification and treatment of disability-associated depression should be given serious consideration in public health, industrial health and vocational rehabilitation programs." (Craig and Van Natta, 598–601).

A word about the DSM-III diagnostic entity of *psychogenic pain disorder,* now called *somatoform pain disorder* in DSM-III-R: The key diagnostic features of this condition are persistent complaints of severe and prolonged pain, in the absence of validating physical findings, and in association with evidence of the causal role of psychological factors. In practice, the treatment of patients showing this relatively narrowly defined syndrome and the mixed pain/depression picture described is essentially the same.

Some clinicians have noted the reluctance of pain patients to accept treatment that is labeled *psychiatric* and suggest that such patients are better treated in a multidisciplinary chronic pain program. At the present time, the treatment of choice for chronic pain syndromes involves the use of antidepressants and comprehensive, multifaceted, inpatient treatment programs. It is not at all clear what is "curative" about either of these approaches, and further research is indicated. Furthermore, it is not clear whether chronic pain is best treated by a primary care physician, the specialist (psychiatrist, anesthesiologist, neurologist, surgeon), or by the new specialist—the *algologist,* who is trained to treat all of the facets of chronic pain. The fact that such a subspecialty is endorsed by many clinicians now active in the field indicates the future significance of this area.

Treatment in a multidisciplinary pain program can be valuable by:

1. "Legitimizing" the role of the psychiatrist and allowing the patient to view psychologic aspects of chronic pain within the context of medical illness
2. Providing the psychiatrist with thorough knowledge of the patient's physical condition
3. Allowing integrated treatment planning, which alleviates the feeling on the part of the patient that psychiatric treatment is an "afterthought"
4. Allowing integrated multidisciplinary treatment
5. Resulting in more effective treatment. Psychological intervention within a multidisciplinary framework seems to be much more effective than if given

> outside such an integrated program. The outcome statistics of multidisciplinary inpatient programs, which incorporate a variety of psychological interventions, support this (Getto and Ochitill, 277–86).

A note of caution is necessary, however. Such programs can be extremely expensive. Prospective patients should be screened for motivation because the patient whose conscious or unconscious desire is not to return to work obviously will not be a good candidate. Also, the patient's progress in treatment should be carefully monitored. A program that does not show significant progress within six to eight weeks should be questioned.

§ 13.16 —Generalized Anxiety Disorder

Interestingly, although generalized anxiety disorder has been well known and studied for decades, there is but little evidence in the psychiatric literature that psychotherapy of any type (psychodynamic/psychoanalytic, cognitive, or behavioral) is of much value, though these psychotherapies do result in a slightly better outcome than no treatment at all.

The most commonly used therapeutic intervention for generalized anxiety disorder is the prescription of benzodiazepines (the chemical class name for most minor tranquilizers, such as Valium, Librium, Tranxene, Xanax, Zerax, and Ativan), or buspirone (Buspar).

However, addiction to benzodiazepines may be a problem with prolonged use, and the beneficial effects of these medications may tend to wear off shortly after they are discontinued, unless the patient has made some major cognitive or behavioral changes in the interim.

The course of treatment usually involves an initial regimen of one session per week of psychotherapy, primarily supportive in nature, again tapering off after a month or two to less frequent sessions, the entire process (barring complications) not exceeding three to six months.

A related treatment issue is that the differentiation between anxiety and affective (mood) disorders, especially depression, is difficult. Lifetime occurrence studies indicate that generalized anxiety symptoms often occur in conjunction with panic disorder and major depression, and it is well known that generalized anxiety symptoms are a ubiquitous component of most psychiatric disorders. It may be, therefore, that what is referred to as generalized anxiety disorder is actually a prodromal, incomplete, or residual manifestation of other psychiatric disorders (Breier, et al.).

Because of this symptom overlap between anxiety and depression, some authorities recommend a trial of antidepressant medications in anxious patients, especially those with depression and anxiety symptoms coexisting (Marks, 261ff; Breier et al., 787–97).

§ 13.17 —Schizophrenia and Bipolar Affective (Manic-Depressive) Illness

Schizophrenia and bipolar affective (manic-depressive) illness are considered here together for two reasons. First, there is often significant symptom overlap between these two conditions, as well as with schizoaffective illness. Second, these conditions are primarily genetic/biochemical in etiology and not caused by environmental stressors (including job stress), although such stressors may precipitate or exacerbate them. Yet another similarity is that medications (primarily the antipsychotic agents in schizophrenia, lithium in bipolar affective illness, and either or both in schizoaffective illness) are the most important facet of treatment.

Psychotherapy, whether psychodynamic, supportive, or cognitive-behavioral, is probably important in these conditions only insofar as it helps build a rapport with the treating psychiatrist, hospital, or clinic, so that increased medication compliance results (Jacobson and McKinney, 184ff; Simpson and May, 143ff).

In general, the prognosis for diagnosed schizophrenia is poor. The disease is progressive and most commonly results in total disability from a labor market standpoint. However, proper medication may still be successful in ameliorating such symptoms as delusions and hallucinations, thus enabling an individual to carry on basic living activities without being institutionalized.

With manic-depressive illness the picture is different. This disease is essentially completely controlled by appropriate medication so that the individual's occupational functioning is not impaired. There is one important caveat, however: this prognosis depends on the individual's adhering to the medication schedule. Sometimes, if the manic phase is not caught in time, the individual avoids taking medication, not wanting to come down from "the top of the world."

§ 13.18 —Conversion Disorder

Like psychogenic pain disorder, conversion disorder (previously denominated *hysterical neurosis, conversion type*) is essentially a diagnosis of exclusion. That is, "real" or organic pathology must be excluded before the diagnosis can be made.

This diagnostic entity is quite difficult to distinguish in clinical practice from early symptoms of various neurological conditions (especially multiple sclerosis), psychophysiological (psychosomatic) symptoms, hypochondriasis, schizophrenia, and malingering.

The treatment of (confirmed) conversion disorders generally involves psychotherapy, either of the psychodynamic or the supportive type, and often includes hypnosis. Medications have not been found effective for conversion symptoms themselves, though they might be helpful for the anxiety and depression that sometimes accompany these problems (Barsky, 1009–1017).

In general, the treatment regimen is similar to that indicated with respect to depression and anxiety. See **§§ 13.12** and **13.16**. If the patient appears to be responding after two or three months of treatment, up to another two or three months may be advised (though not if the initial period of treatment appears unsuccessful). The same approach would apply to "psychological factors affecting physical condition" (DSM-III-R 316.00), although here medical treatment would also be required.

§ 13.19 Treatment Parameters

Regardless of the specific psychiatric "prescription," it is important for attorneys, insurance carriers, and judges to insist that certain treatment parameters be addressed by the treating psychiatrist (or other mental health professional), as well as by treating physicians in general, whatever the specialty involved. The therapist/physician should:

1. Render a diagnosis using the DSM-III-R criteria
2. Translate the DSM-III-R diagnosis into specific impairments in functioning (primarily in occupational functioning)
3. At the outset of treatment, clearly identify which symptoms or impairments are the focus of the treatment, what are the specific (and concrete) treatment goals, what treatment interventions are proposed (including frequency of psychotherapy or other office visits), and its estimated duration and cost
4. Report on the patient's progress, generally every two or three months, and reassess the then-current treatment regimen, if the patient's progress (especially related to returning to work) is slower than expected.

As a very rough rule of thumb, both the patient and the psychiatrist should be able to see significant improvement within two to three months of starting treatment. If either or both do not, it is incumbent on the latter to discuss the probable reasons for the lack of improvement and to propose specific changes in the treatment regimen. It is also important for the patient to understand, at the outset, that the goal of treatment within the workers' compensation system is to help her improve to the point that she can return to work, even if she is not yet "completely well." By the same token, all parties to the treatment (including the applicant attorneys, the carrier, and the Workers' Compensation Appeals Board personnel) should recognize that the psychiatric treatment might well have to continue, either for some months after the patient returns to work (to consolidate and build on the earlier gains), or, in some instances, indefinitely.

Closely related to the foregoing are issues of cost-effectiveness and communication and coordination between and among the various components of the workers' compensation system. Both of these parameters are discussed more fully in following sections.

§ 13.20 Types of Therapists

There is a great deal of confusion among people outside the mental health field regarding the terms *psychotherapist, psychiatrist, psychoanalyst, psychologist,* and *counselor.*

The terms *psychotherapist* and *counselor* are generic. That is, these are general terms, referring to someone who does psychotherapy or counseling, but not indicating that person's formal credentials or licensure status. Although many informal types of counselors exist (including substance abuse counselors, school counselors, and clergy), §§ **13.21** through **13.24** deal with those mental health professionals who hold specific degrees and licenses.

A psychotherapist may be a psychoanalyst, a psychiatrist, a nonpsychiatric physician, a licensed psychologist, a psychiatric social worker, a marriage and family counselor, or a mental health nurse practitioner.

The scope of practice depends on the type of practitioner. This can become an issue in a case, both from the standpoint of whether a claimant has had proper treatment so as to be considered medically stable and, sometimes, in determining the practitioner's right to reimbursement.

§ 13.21 —Psychiatrists

A psychiatrist must be a licensed physician because psychiatry is a medical specialty. The majority of psychiatrists have had four years of postgraduate training, after medical school, and most are board certified by the American Board of Psychiatry and Neurology.

However, a state license as a physician does not limit the licensee to the practice of any specific medical specialty, and there is no legal bar to a licensed physician claiming to be a specialist of any type. For example, though the author has not had a single day of training in neurosurgery, it would not be legally prohibited (though certainly not ethical) for him to represent himself as a neurological surgeon. However, the public safety is protected by the fact that the author could not qualify for surgical privileges at any hospital. Such is not the case with nonsurgical specialties. Thus, it is important for every patient to make sure that a physician who claims to be a psychiatrist has, in fact, completed an approved residency in psychiatry and, preferably, has been board certified.

Most, but not all, psychoanalysts are psychiatrists who have had several years of training (in addition to the psychiatric residency) in a psychoanalytic institute. This training involves seminars, readings, and at least two supervised analyses, in addition to the candidate's personal analysis.

§ 13.22 —Psychologists

Aside from psychiatry, the other mental health disciplines are more rigidly defined by legal and licensure criteria. The consumer can be fairly certain that a psychotherapist represented as a "licensed psychologist" is, in fact, so licensed, as this licensure status can be easily checked with the appropriate state agency.

In California, a licensed psychologist must hold a Ph.D. from an approved university and must complete a required number of hours of supervised clinical experience before passing a two-part (written and oral) state examination. Some psychologists are also diplomates of the American Board of Professional Psychology, which requires several years of additional clinical practice and another certification examination.

§ 13.23 —Licensed Clinical Social Worker

A licensed clinical social worker (LCSW) must hold a master's degree in social work from a recognized university, have required hours of supervised clinical practice, and pass a state examination.

§ 13.24 —Licensed Marriage and Family Counselor

A licensed marriage, family, and child counselor (MFCC) must hold a master's degree in counseling or psychology from a recognized university, have required hours of supervised clinical practice, and pass a state examination.

§ 13.25 —Criteria for Choosing Type of Specialist

It is often difficult for the consumer or third-party payer to know whom to choose as a psychotherapist.

In the author's opinion, a psychiatrist is the mental health professional best qualified to make an initial assessment and formulate a treatment plan and is often the best person to act as the psychotherapist. Specifically, the psychiatrist is the only mental health professional who is also a licensed physician and who thus has the expertise to assess such important parameters as the possible contribution of somatic conditions to the presenting emotional symptoms.

Specific medical conditions that frequently present with psychiatric symptoms include hyper- and hypothyroidism, hyper- and hypoparathyroidism, adrenal cortical hyperfunction and insufficiency, porphyria, pernicious anemia, various tumors, multiple sclerosis, systemic lupus erythematosus, certain infectious diseases (including infectious mononucleosis, hepatitis, encephalitis, and malaria), alcoholism, organic brain dysfunction, congestive heart failure, and myocardial infarction (Lipkin, 1280ff).

The psychiatrist is also the only mental health professional with the education and training necessary to assess the importance of such important historical parameters as prior physical trauma and medical illnesses; occupational toxin exposure; and the effects of medications, drugs, and alcohol. The psychiatrist is able to weigh the risks and benefits of the addition of somatic treatments (such as psychotropic medications, ECT, and the like) to the psychotherapy and to prescribe these treatments. Finally, the psychiatrist is uniquely qualified to understand and interpret to the patient any concurrent somatic illness or treatments, such as diagnostic and surgical procedures, the likely course of an illness, and the reasons for prescriptions of various medications. Moreover, although patient education is theoretically an integral part of any physician-patient relationship, many primary care physicians and specialists do not deal adequately with a patient's questions, fears, and concerns because the physician is too rushed, because the patient is too intimidated to ask a question or too anxious or depressed to assimilate the answer, or because of some combination of these factors.

A psychiatrist functioning as a psychotherapist is also in an ideal position to deal with questions and concerns about the patient's somatic (physical) problems. The psychiatrist should be able to relay a question she cannot answer to the treating specialist and then communicate the answer back in a manner the patient can assimilate.

If the psychiatrist determines that somatic treatments are not necessary or are not an important focus of the patient's concerns, she might refer the patient to another mental health professional, such as a psychologist or psychiatric social worker. In this case, the referral is usually based on the psychiatrist's personal knowledge of other mental health professionals in the community, and specifically who has the right combination of personality, training, and expertise to handle the presenting problem (Frances et al., 109–13).

In other cases, the psychiatrist will work concurrently with another psychotherapist, managing the somatic aspects of psychiatric treatment and leaving the psychotherapy to the other professional.

A word about cost-effectiveness. There is some evidence that patients who suffer from concurrent physical and emotional disorders (a group overrepresented in the workers' compensation setting) tend to reduce their use of expensive medical-surgical services with psychotherapy more quickly than patients with the identical physical disorder alone. There are also data suggesting that the use of "psychologically informed" mental health services with surgical or coronary patients tends to reduce their required period of hospitalization.

Thus, there is some accumulating evidence that attending to the psychological needs of the patient may reduce the inappropriate use of medical care facilities and may also shorten the period of use of such services (Parloff, 6–7; Ursano and Hales, 1507–17).

§ 13.26 Special Problems in Implementing Psychiatric Treatment in Workers' Compensation Setting

Treatment in the workers' compensation system is often fraught with difficulties that are not seen in the private (or even public) sectors.

The space here is too limited to explore these difficulties in detail, but they should be mentioned, if only to raise the consciousness of everyone involved in the process: psychiatrists, other psychotherapists, patients, attorneys, claims and vocational rehabilitation personnel, and judges (Brodsky, 49ff).

One problem is that the patient and the psychotherapist often do not share the same goals. For example, the psychotherapist may make the assumption that the patient wants to get better and get back to work as soon as possible, whereas the patient might have a completely different agenda: having a period of "excused" time off work; securing funding for vocational rehabilitation; "getting back" at an employer who the patient perceives has harmed or abandoned her; or lengthening the period of disability to try to get a higher permanent disability rating and a larger settlement.

A related issue is that a patient might have one or several "advisers" as well as an attorney. These advisers might be counseling such courses of action as not going back to work until the case is settled or asking for additional medical examinations, both in the (often mistaken) belief that these maneuvers will increase the amount of the ultimate settlement. In many of these cases, not only the psychotherapist, but also the patient's own attorney, is left "in the dark."

Another issue is that the psychotherapist might never have explicitly clarified to the patient that she should return to work as soon as she is able to do so and not wait until the symptoms are gone. Sometimes the patient postpones returning to work, or seeking alternative work, in the belief that she must be "all better" before doing so.

Yet another difficulty in rendering psychiatric treatment within the workers' compensation system is the fact that there are "too many cooks" involved, often with no communication between them. For example, the psychotherapist and patient might both agree that the patient is now ready to return to work or enter a vocational rehabilitation program. However, long delays at each step might ensue, such as the patient being unable to contact her attorney, or the attorney being unable to arrange the appropriate conditions for return to work or for the initiation of the vocational rehabilitation process, or to settle the case, if necessary. Sometimes many months elapse between the time the patient is able to return to work or start a vocational rehabilitation program and the actual implementation of one or the other, by which time the patient's overall condition might have deteriorated significantly. The whole process then starts again.

Another problem is confidentiality. That is, it is often a surprise to the patient (though it should not be, if the attorney properly informs the patient) that the psychiatrist's evaluation and treatment records (just like orthopedic records) are not confidential and instead are public records. This situation often leads to significant guardedness on the patient's part, especially regarding materials she thinks will prejudice the case. The "psychotherapy to an audience" that results is often a waste of time and money for everyone involved. (The workers' compensation judge does have the power to seal a medical file, on the motion of either party or on the judge's own motion, though this power is only infrequently invoked.)

Finally, meaningful improvement in symptoms is difficult to bring about when significant environmental stressors are continuing, such as ongoing pain, financial problems, secondary substance abuse and family difficulties, marital separation, lack of a job to return to, and an ever-hardening "adversary" stance between the employee, on one hand, and the employer and insurance carrier, on the other.

An important point is that litigation itself, for most patients, acts as an ongoing stressor to fix or prolong symptoms. A recent follow-up study of litigants used standardized interviews and rating scales to clarify the course of post-accident psychological symptoms after resolution of a lawsuit, and also the factors that are associated with good and bad outcomes. The authors concluded, inter alia:

> This study suggests that factors associated with a better outcome of psychological symptoms after an accident and resulting litigation include a longer time after resolution of litigation and a shorter time between injury and litigation. Although the correlational design of this study precludes causal inferences, one hypothesis which could explain this result is that the stress of the litigation process itself maintains or exacerbates psychological symptoms. If the plaintiff has a shorter time to endure the stress of litigation, the outcome is better. In addition, as more time passes after litigation is finalized, the plaintiff has more time to recover from the psychological stress of the accident and the litigation. It is interesting that the important factor is not the amount of time after injury but, rather, the amount of time relative to the settlement of the lawsuit. To our knowledge, this is the first study to show this finding.
>
> Plaintiffs who had the most psychological symptoms after their injuries had the worst outcome on follow-up. Hence, severity of plaintiff's initial psychological symptoms appears to be a risk factor in terms of the likelihood of having a poor outcome.
>
> There are several potential limitations to this study, including small sample size, lack of a control group of accident victims who did not bring lawsuits (although in our litigious world, this group may be hard to find), and use of a cross-sectional assessment that relied on subjects' recollections of symptom course. In addition, the subjects were recruited from one center in England. The results may not be generalizable to other groups of litigants, but they are sufficiently promising to warrant further prospective studies with larger groups of plaintiffs [Binder et al., 1073–75].

Some of the difficulties mentioned are inevitable in such a complex treatment setting, but others are not and could be minimized (or even obviated) by a more thoughtful and caring approach on the part of all concerned. For example, many patients in treatment in the workers' compensation setting complain that no one from their company management, or even any of their coworkers, called or wrote after they left work on disability, even though they might have been with the company for 20 years. A helpful outreach approach from the employer may be enough to make the company a helper, not an enemy, in the patient's perception.

The applicant attorney would do well to acquaint the client with what is likely to happen in the course of a workers' compensation case, just as a physician is obligated to explain the risks and benefits of any proposed treatment. This explanation should include a briefing on confidentiality (or, more accurately, the lack of it) and the rights of the insurance carrier and its representatives, such as to subpoena medical records going back to the patient's childhood, to depose the patient, or to conduct sub-rosa (secretive) surveillance.

The attending physician or mental health professional should keep in mind that the goal of treatment is to return the patient to productive employment as soon as possible, even if the patient is not yet fully "cured" and even if the medical or psychological treatment must continue for a period of time after the patient's return to work. The insurance carrier and defense attorneys, reciprocally, should avoid gratuitously harassing or badgering an applicant and should provide ordered services and benefits promptly.

The writer realizes that some of these recommendations are often difficult to implement in the "real world." However, it is important that all the participants in the workers' compensation system at least be aware of the potential difficulties caused or exacerbated by the medical-legal setting, in order itself to avoid as many of these pitfalls as possible.

References

Akiskal, Hagop S. "The Clinical Management of Affective Disorders," *in* Michels, R. et al., eds. *Psychiatry.* Vol. I, Ch. 61. Philadelphia: J.B. Lippincott, 1986.

Alexander, M.P. "Traumatic Brain Injury," *in* Benson, D.F., and D. Blumer, eds. *Psychiatric Aspects of Neurologic Disease.* Vol. II. New York: Grune and Stratton, 1982.

Andreasen, Nancy C. "Post-traumatic Stress Disorder," *in* Kaplan, Harold I., and B.J. Sadock, eds. *Comprehensive Textbook of Psychiatry.* 4th ed. Baltimore: Williams and Wilkins, 1985.

Baldessarini, Ross, J. "Chemotherapy," *in* Nicholi, Armand M., ed. *The Harvard Guide to Modern Psychiatry.* Cambridge, Mass.: Belknap Press of Harvard University Press, 1978.

Barsky, Arthur J. "Somatoform Disorders," *in* Kaplan and Sadock. *Textbook of Psychiatry.* 5th ed.

Beck, Aaron T., and A. John Rush. "Cognitive Therapy," *in* Kaplan and Sadock. *Comprehensive Textbook of Psychiatry.* 5th ed. Baltimore: Williams and Wilkins, 1989.

Binder, Renee L. et al. "The Course of Psychological Symptoms After Resolution of Lawsuits." *American Journal of Psychiatry* 148(8):1073–75 (Aug. 1991).

Birk, Lee. "Behavior Therapy and Behavioral Psychotherapy," *in* Nicholi. *Harvard Guide.*

Blumer, D. "Chronic Pain as a Psychobiologic Phenomeon: The Pain-Prone Disorder," *in* Benson, D.F., and D. Blumer, eds. *Psychiatric Aspects of Neurologic Disease.* Vol. II. New York: Grune and Stratton, 1982.

Breier, Alan, Dennis S. Charney, and George R. Heninger. "The Diagnostic Validity of Anxiety Disorders and Their Relationship to Depressive Illness." *American Journal of Psychiatry* 142-7:787–97 (1985).

Brodsky, Carroll M. "Factors Influencing Work-Related Disability," *in* Meyerson, Arthur T., and Theodora Fine, eds. *Psychiatric Disability: Clinical, Legal, and Administrative Dimensions.* Washington, D.C.: American Psychiatric Press, 1987.

Craig, T.J., and P.A. Van Natta. "Disability and Depressive Symptoms in Two Communities." *American Journal of Psychiatry* 140(5):598–601 (May 1983).

Elkin, Irene et al. "National Institute of Mental Health Treatment of Depression Collaborative Research Program: General Effectiveness of Treatments." *Archives of General Psychiatry* 46(11):971ff (Nov. 1989).

Enelow, Allen J. *Elements of Psychotherapy.* New York: Oxford University Press, 1977.

Frances, Allen et al. "A Practitioner's Guide to Treatment Selection in Psychiatry." *Western Journal of Medicine* 146(1):109–113 (1987).

Frank, Jerome D. *Persuasion and Healing.* New York: Schocken Books, 1974.

Getto, Karl J., and Herbert Ochitill. "Psychogenic Pain Disorder," *in* Greist, John H., James W. Jefferson, and Robert L. Spitzer, eds. *Treatment of Mental Disorders.* New York: Oxford University Press, 1982.

Goldsmith, William. *Psychiatric Drugs for the Non-Medical Mental Health Worker.* Springfield, Ill.: Charles C. Thomas, 1977.

Gorman, Jack M., and John M. Davis. "Antianxiety Drugs," *in* Kaplan and Sadock. *Textbook of Psychiatry.* 5th ed.

Greist, John H., and James W. Jefferson. *Depression and Its Treatment.* Washington, D.C.: American Psychiatric Press, 1984.

Hanley, J. Personal communication with author.

Jacobson, Andrea, and William T. McKinney. "Affective Disorders," *in* Greist, Jefferson, and Spitzer. *Treatment of Mental Disorders.*

Kaplan, Peter M., and William E. Buggiano. "Anticonvulsants, Noradrenergic Drugs, and Other Organic Therapies," *in* Kaplan and Sadock. *Textbook of Psychiatry.* 5th ed.

Klerman, Gerald L. "Introduction to Mood Disorders," *in Treatment of Psychiatric Disorders: A Task Force Report of the American Psychiatric Association.* Washington, D.C.: American Psychiatric Association, 1989.

Kwentus, J.A. et al. "Psychiatric Complications of Closed Head Trauma." *Psychosomatics* 26(1):8–17 (Jan. 1985).

Lipkin, Mack Jr. "Psychiatry and Medicine," *in* Kaplan and Sadock. *Textbook of Psychiatry.* 5th ed.

Marks, Isaac. "Anxiety Disorders," *in* Greist, Jefferson, and Spitzer. *Treatment of Mental Disorders.*

Parloff, Morris. "Psychotherapy Outcome Research," *in* Michels. *Psychiatry.* Ch. 11.

Pincus, J., and G. Tucker. *Behavioral Neurology.* 2d ed. New York: Oxford University Press, 1978.

Siegler, Dewey K., and Richard W. Murrow. "Headache," *in* Joynt, Robert J., ed. *Clinical Neurology.* Vol. 2, Ch. 13. Philadelphia: J.B. Lippincott, 1990.

Simpson, George M., and Philip R.A. May. "Schizophrenic Disorders," *in* Greist, Jefferson, and Spitzer. *Treatment of Mental Disorders.*

Stewart, Robert L. "Psychoanalysis and Psychoanalytic Psychotherapy," *in* Kaplan and Sadock. *Textbook of Psychiatry.* 4th ed.

Strub, R.L., and F.W. Black. *Organic Brain Syndromes.* Philadelphia: F.A. Davis, 1981.

Stuss, D.T. et al. "Subtle Neuropsychological Deficits in Patients with Good Recovery After Head Injury." *Neurosurgery* 17:41–47 (1985).

Trimble, M.R. *Neuropsychiatry.* Chichester, England: John Wiley and Sons, 1981.

Ursano, Robert J., and Robert E. Hales. "A Review of Brief Individual Psychotherapies." *American Journal of Psychiatry* 143(12):1507–17 (Dec. 1986).

Weiner, Richard D. "Electroconvulsive Therapy," *in* Kaplan and Sadock. *Textbook of Psychiatry.* 5th ed.

Weissman, Myrna M., and Gerald L. Klerman. "Interpersonal Psychotherapy," *in Treatment of Psychiatric Disorders: A Task Force Report of the American Psychiatric Association.* Washington, D.C.: American Psychiatric Association, 1989.

Wells, Charles E. "Other Organic Brain Syndromes," *in* Kaplan and Sadock. *Textbook of Psychiatry.* 4th ed.

CHAPTER 14

DEPOSITION OF CLAIMANT

Herbert Lasky

§ 14.1 Introduction

The content of the claimant's deposition is formulated by asking questions derived from the basic approach of this book:

1. Does the claimant have a mental disorder?
2. Was the mental disorder caused by defendant?
3. Is or has claimant been disabled as a result of the mental disorder?
4. Did claimant have any preexisting disability because of a preexisting mental disorder?
5. Has claimant's medical treatment been appropriate?

In other words, we want to know what the claimant is doing and feeling now, the claimant's recent past feelings and activities since the injury, and a detailed background history covering family, social life, education, occupations, military involvement, involvement with the law, recreational and nonvocational interests, and personal relationships; in short, all the matters that would be covered in the examining psychiatrist's history.

Ordinarily, the acts of which the claimant is complaining on the part of the defendant should be taken up after all this preliminary information has been ascertained. The claimant's functioning and relationships on his current job should be covered as part of the general occupational history.

Remember that the deposition is essentially the first day of trial. The more information you have before the deposition, the more specific you can be, the more you will find out (see **Appendix C**), and the better your tactical approach will be. Your deposition will probably be reviewed by one or more medical experts. You cannot assume that they understand what is legally and strategically relevant the way you do. Therefore, your deposition will be a basic guideline for your medical expert.

Try not to accept vague answers; continue to probe until you are satisfied you have learned all there is in any specific area of inquiry. A good method for avoiding objections for redundancy in a deposition is to summarize all the witness has said in a particular area as a preface for the question, "Is that all you can tell me about . . . ?" You can follow this up by specifically establishing, item by item, what the witness cannot remember. This can be valuable if at trial the witness, as a result of prompting, comes up with additional information that represents a significant variance from the previous testimony.

At the outset of the deposition, the author has often asked whether the claimant is presently working and, if so, has immediately gone into great detail about the nature of the claimant's duties, responsibilities, relationships, and whether he is happy, that is, whether he is getting along with the supervisor and experiencing success on the job, shown by means of promotions, performance ratings, and the like. It has been not uncommon to "sew up" a case with information obtained in this way.

§ 14.2 Structure and Content

Establish the current symptomatology very early in the deposition. In this connection, remember the basic rules applicable to all depositions. The ideal deposition question, as distinct from a trial question, is open ended; do not suggest answers to the deponent until you are certain you have exhausted all the information he can give without prompting. For example, you might ask, "Do you have any emotional problems today that impair your ability to work?" If the answer is yes, get a list. If the answer is no, ask if the witness ever had any such problems. If the answer is still no, you might ask why the claim had been filed.

Witnesses sometimes claim they do not understand what you mean by "emotional complaints." There are several ways to handle this:

1. Ask, "Are you working? Why can't you work?"
2. "Do you have any complaints of any kind that affect your ability to work?" If the answer involves physical and emotional complaints, you may want to follow up to find the relative importance of the physical as distinguished from the emotional complaints.
3. "You have filed a claim alleging psychiatric injury. Is there something about the way you feel that leads you to believe that you have a psychiatric

injury?" Note that at this point the witness is likely to refer to whatever it is that he is complaining about on the part of the defendant. That is not a responsive answer; emphasize that what you want to hear from the witness is about his feelings. Be careful to avoid suggesting symptoms to a deponent.

Having elicited specific complaints, go through each individually and make sure you have the claimant's idea of what he is complaining about. Do not accept general statements such as, "I feel depressed." One way to ferret out more specific information is a question such as, "Is anything else bothering you that you think was caused by your treatment by defendant?"

Go through the list of symptoms again and find out when each individual symptom arose. After you have the timeframe, ask if the witness saw a doctor for the symptom and whether the witness told anyone or did anything about the symptom. Remember to deal with one symptom at a time.

If claimant continued to work after any symptom arose, ask if it affected his ability to do the job. Next, ask whether each symptom related ever occurred before the events about which claimant is now complaining. At this point, your prior knowledge of occupational history or medical history can be helpful in suggesting possible specific questions if you have evidence that indicates such preexisting symptoms. If reference to physical complaints has been made that are relevant to a psychiatric claim, you can repeat the above process as to those. Physical symptoms that may be produced by a psychological condition include stomach trouble, headaches, and asthma.

This is usually an appropriate stage at which to go into the issue of nonoccupational stressors. These usually involve two aspects: trying to find out whether some events in the witness's personal life are responsible for the complaints, and making use of any specific information you have on the subject. There is no point in trying to withhold such information for "surprise" purposes. Your own expert's report will have to refer to such matters. If it does not, they cannot be used as a basis for his opinion.

In terms of the general investigational approach, you could ask a question such as, "Earlier, you indicated you began experiencing difficulties with sleep around the beginning of such and such a time. Was there anything that occurred about this time that you thought was making you have such feelings?" You have nothing to lose with the question and sometimes you will be surprised by what you gain.

Next, it is appropriate to go into the detailed background information that will generally appear to the deponent to be relatively innocuous. The following is a checklist:

____ A. Family matters

  ____ 1. Addresses. Who do you live with? Relationships

  ____ 2. Family health

  ____ 3. Number of marriages

____ 4. Separations, deaths
____ 5. Antisocial behaviors of family members
____ 6. Mental disease, psychological problems in family. Be sure to follow up on anything that appears significant
____ 7. Upbringing. Repeat 2. through 6.

____ B. Medical history (complete)
____ 1. Hospitalizations
____ 2. Health plans
____ 3. Prior injuries
____ 4. All past treators
____ 5. Psychologist/psychiatrist/counselor
____ 6. Treatment, fever, head injury, thyroid, drug reaction, and so forth
____ 7. Medications
____ 8. Entries on medical records may be further inquired about at this point.

____ C. Military
____ 1. Denied entry into service for any disability
____ 2. Length of service and nature of assignments
____ 3. Highest rank obtained. Rank on discharge
____ 4. Honorably discharged
____ 5. Any service-connected disability applied for or received
____ 6. Treatment at any VA facility.

____ D. Education
____ 1. Why dropped out of any school
____ 2. Trade or specialized school
____ 3. Academic performance
____ 4. If dropped, what did witness do?
____ 5. Did the witness like school, and why or why not?

____ E. Occupational history
____ 1. Location of employer
____ 2. Name of superior
____ 3. Job description, promotions, job changes
____ 4. Any problems, reason for leaving
____ 5. Unemployment benefits, disability benefits between jobs
____ 6. Lengths of time between jobs and why (important)
____ 7. Any stress on previous jobs, problems with anyone
____ 8. Any symptoms similar to those claimant presently has.

____ F. Financial

- ____ 1. Current earnings
- ____ 2. Source of present income, present liabilities, any hardships
- ____ 3. Any bankruptcies, any history of being dunned by creditors
- ____ 4. Effects of any past or present financial hardship on witness.

____ G. Legal history

- ____ 1. Criminal; note that you are not restricted to asking about felonies because this is a psychiatric case, and anything indicative of psychiatric problems is relevant
- ____ 2. Civil litigation, including workers' compensation claims
- ____ 3. Grievances: labor, fair housing, and the like.

____ H. Drugs and alcohol usage, if not previously elicited.

____ I. Prescription medications

- ____ 1. What are you taking now? When was it prescribed and by whom?
- ____ 2. Ever prescribed before?
- ____ 3. Have there been any changes in the medication since the symptoms arose?
- ____ 4. What medications were taken for any prior symptoms?

____ J. Medical-legal evaluation and treatment for this injury

- ____ 1. Name and description of everyone the witness saw on first visit
- ____ 2. How long did witness spend with each, and what did each specifically do when arrived for appointment? When left? How much time spent waiting for the therapist?
- ____ 3. Did witness fill out forms? Did anyone assist? How did they assist?
- ____ 4. Was an interpreter used?
- ____ 5. Protocol of interviews: Did doctor just read from forms and confirm information?
- ____ 6. If questioner already has report, find out whether doctor asked about anything that was left out of the report that you feel is important
- ____ 7. Did the doctor take notes? What kind of notes?
- ____ 8. Psychological testing?
  - ____ a. Where were tests taken?
  - ____ b. Did anyone help out and how did they help?
  - ____ c. Manner in which the test was supervised, if supervised.

____ 9. Nature of therapy. See **Chapter 13**.
 ____ a. Credentials and qualifications of the therapist; see any diplomas?
 ____ b. Physical description of therapist
 ____ c. Length and frequency of sessions
 ____ d. What did you talk about? Ever talk about any critical information left out of written reports?
 ____ e. History of medications during treatment
 ____ f. Did therapist take notes?
 ____ g. Did the therapist give any advice; if so, what, and was the advice followed?
 ____ h. Has the therapy helped? Try to get specific answers. Do not settle for, "It made me feel better."
 ____ i. If therapy continued, find out why. Did the therapist at any time say the witness was cured? It is important to know what was said at the last session, particularly at the end.

____ K. Social and recreational activities: postinjury and present
 ____ 1. What organizations does claimant belong to: religious, social, civic, etc.?
 ____ 2. Activities in any of these organizations
 ____ 3. Favorite recreational activities
 ____ 4. Sports and/or hobbies
 ____ 5. Educational or training courses, whether vocational (introduction to computer basics) or recreational (basket weaving, ceramics, etc.). Remember that one of the important diagnostic criteria of depression is loss of interest in pleasurable activities.

Having gone through the background information, attempt to correlate with anything that did not show up when questioning about the nature and time of specific symptoms. For example, "Didn't your husband's death in 1988 cause you to become sad?"

This is the point at which to ask the claimant about his specific complaints about the events that allegedly caused the current symptoms. Of course, if we are talking about a single event such as a car accident or explosion, this would be a reasonably straightforward type of question. If the situation is a pattern of harassment at work or sexual harassment or a continuous period of stress from other reasons, the inquiry is not as simple.

First, by open-ended questions, the claimant's account of what happened should be elicited. The questioning can then become more specific if appropriate investigation has given the questioner the basis for such questioning. Thus, any information the questioner has about employment events from the employer's standpoint should be explored at this point.

Be as specific as possible. For example: "I have your attendance records here. I have a total of 45 tardies and 98 sick leave days, and 10 unexcused absences in the last three years. You think what I have just told you was accurate? Here, I'll show you the records. Why did you have such trouble getting to work on time?" and so forth. Do not allow vague answers. The attendance example was used purposely. Very often, poor attendance reflects alcohol or substance abuse. This might be an appropriate point at which to go into such information.

§ 14.3 Case of the Resentful Hotshot

The claimant said she was fired because she asked her boss for pregnancy leave. She claimed that during the approximately year and a half she worked for him, she was under constant stress due to overwork.

She was diagnosed by her psychiatrist as having a depressive disorder not otherwise specified (n.o.s) with a slight to slight to moderate disability.

Her first answer on the subject of her current activities led to testimony that eliminated any basis for any claim of permanent disability. She was an independent life and business insurance agent, had taken training courses, which she successfully completed, and was a self-starter who composed her own advertising for marketing purposes and liked being her own boss. In short, in terms of the Department of Labor's temperaments, she would have had a perfect score. See **Chapter 7**.

As to the job stresses, she revealed that she had no intention of quitting when she was terminated because the job had future potential.

On the issue of mental disorder, her comfortable relationship with her boyfriend was not consistent with the major depression criteria of the American Psychiatric Association's *Diagnostic and Statistical Manual of Mental Disorders* (third edition, revised) (DSM-III-R). The claimant ultimately lost the case.

Following is a deposition excerpt concerning the claimant's pregnancy, relations with her employer, and her current occupation:

Q. When did you become pregnant?
A. Not the entire time. I became pregnant in September of '88—no, make that October of '88. Sorry.
Q. And then when did you have your child?
A. June 1st.
THE REPORTER: Excuse me, may I clarify something? I have here in my notes that you became pregnant in October of '88?
THE WITNESS: October of '87. Excuse me.
Q. Now, let's see, did you start working for ____________ in February of '87?
A. Yes.
Q. I'm sorry. Was it '87?

A. Yeah.
Q. Well, the application refers to a continuous trauma beginning 2-23-87.
A. Yeah, it was '87. That's correct.
Q. What was your job at that time?
A. Everything.
Q. What was it—what was your title?
A. Whatever they wanted to call me, office manager, secretary.
Q. When you were hired, what did they say? "You're going to be . . . ."
A. Office manager/secretary.
Q. What were you paid?
A. I was hired at 1850 a month, but shortly thereafter I went to 2150 and shortly thereafter I went to 2350.
Q. Well, you say "shortly thereafter." You mean like three months?
A. One month later I went to 2150 and four or five months later I went to 2350, plus bonus—plus I received bonuses.
Q. Did your duties involve any selling?
A. Initially, no.
Well, yes.
Q. Were the bonuses like commissions for selling?
A. No, bonuses for—personal money from ___________.
Q. Did you get any raises after that?
A. After—
Q. From what you said, it would be like—
A. 2350 a month?
Q. Well, you started in February and about six months later, say in around August or September of '87, you were getting 2350?
A. Correct.
Q. Were there any advances after that?
A. Only cash bonuses.
Q. Was there any kind of a regular basis for computing bonuses or would he give them to you whenever he felt like it?
A. Whenever he felt like it, usually once a week.
Q. How often?
A. Every other week, he'd give me, like, $200 on a Friday—a thousand dollar check he gave me once on a—
Q. Did you have any concept that this was related to anything—any particular thing or was it just a matter of how he was feeling and how business was?
A. How business was and the fact that he was happy with the work I was doing.
Q. I see. So you wouldn't have any way of computing when you were entitled to a bonus or how much you—
A. No. It was strictly at his own discretion.
Q. He seemed to be in a good mood for at least at the beginning?
A. Yeah. He was very—good mood one week, a bad mood the next week, depending on his own business.

* * *

Q. Are you working at the present time?
A. Yes.

Q. Where do you work?
A. ____________.
Q. Where are they?
A. ____________, Pasadena, 91101.
Q. Well, do you go there every day?
A. Just about.
Q. You mean you drive in from Victorville?
A. Yes.
Q. How long a drive is that?
A. About an hour and a half one way.
MR. LASKY: Off the record.

(Remarks made off the record.)

Q. **BY MR. LASKY:** What is your job there?
A. I'm an agent.
Q. Does that mean you sell?
A. Yes.
Q. How long have you worked there?
A. Since December 1988.
Q. What is your compensation?
A. Commission.
Q. Straight commission?
A. Yes.
Q. Do you get any draw?
A. No.
Q. What kind of insurance is that?
A. Life, health and disability. I also sell securities.
Q. Securities?
A. Mutual funds, investments.
Q. You said life, health and what was that?
A. Disability.
Q. Is any of your work involved with estate planning?
A. Yes.
Q. How much money have you been making lately?
A. Not enough.
Q. I knew that before you told me. However, please answer as accurately as you can.
A. You want a dollar amount?
Q. Well, let's say, could you tell me the total amount that you earned since you started work?
A. $5,000.
Q. What do you think the potential of the job is?
A. Good.
Q. Like, how much would you expect to make if it turns out good?
A. Depends on circumstances obviously, but I'm expecting to make between 30 and 40,000 annually by my second or third year.
Q. About how many hours a week do you work?
A. I'd say about 25 to 30.

Q. Did you have any training for this job?
A. Yes.
Q. When did you start your training?
A. December 1988.
Q. When did you complete the training?
A. Well, I completed it—the agency training session in March of 1989; however, I still go through ongoing training once a week or depending on . . .
Q. While you were in training, were you also selling?
A. Yes.
Q. Did they have a regular training course that you enroll in when you get the job?
A. Yes.
Q. And how long was that course supposed to last? Three months?
A. Two weeks, plus one day a week for the following nine weeks, plus independent study on computer, one hour a day.
Q. Have you gotten any kind of written grades or anything like that?
A. No. Certificates.
Q. One certificate?
A. Two.
Q. What are they called? What are they for?
A. One is for completing the agency training course, and the other one was for completion of the business insurance training course.
Q. What were you taught in the agency training course?
A. Everything from marketing technique to product knowledge.
Q. Any other subjects?
A. Those are both very general so I guess it's just those.
Q. Would you describe the marketing techniques that you learned.
A. Phone technique—telemarketing, I guess is a better word—sales prospecting. Usually through telephoning or referrals or targeting a market of certain business people, word, mouth to mouth, you know, just advertising.
Q. You don't have to advertise on your own, do you?
A. Yes, I do.
Q. You do? Do you have to pay for that?
A. Yes.
Q. How do you advertise?
A. At the present time, since I have to pay for it, I don't do a lot.
Q. When you do it—
A. Brochures, flyers.
Q. Do you compose the brochures?
A. Yes. They have to be approved by the company.
Q. How did you like the general agency training course?
A. It was satisfactory.
Q. Do you have any faults to find with it?
A. Some of it may have been repetitive due to my experience in the industry as more than just a beginning, but the course is designed for beginners in the industry.
Q. And the business insurance training course?
A. I found it to be—that was not—well, I guess it was a course.
Q. You said you got a certificate.

A. It was like once a week for every—that was very informative.
Q. You mean because that's something you didn't know before?
A. Didn't know as well as I do now.
Q. Is that what you referred to as learning about the products?
A. Products, but it entails marketing insurance agreements, finding buy-sell agreements, that type of thing.
Q. Do you find it interesting?
A. Yes, I do.
Q. Do you like this kind of work?
A. Yes, I do.
Q. Between the time that you last worked with the __________ and the time you went to work for __________ did you work anywhere?
A. No.
Q. Did you have some part-time work?
A. No.
Q. What was your reason for not working in that period?
A. There were several reasons. Mostly due to my mental state.

[The next part of the deposition covers the witness's complaints about her job and relations with her boyfriend.]

Q. Well, I wanted to know since you've said that you became unhappy with the job almost as soon as you started just what that meant in terms of how you were affected.
A. I was unaware of the tremendous volume of work. I thought I would be starting at a level where my daily responsibilities and duties would start when I started. However, there was a lot of catching up to do, work that had not been done previously—previous to my starting working for him.

Therefore, it took a lot more hours and it took a lot more of learning the various—it's a very—he functioned in a way where everything had to be done his way, so I had to be trained in how—in procedure, how he wanted things done.

So it was a matter of just trying to learn all of this and handle all of it at the same time.
Q. Were you dissatisfied with your compensation?
A. No.
Q. Did you feel from these frequent bonuses that he appreciated what you were doing?
A. Yes.
Q. Now, did anything else happen on the job? Like, you've mentioned—you've referred, I think, to broken promises and other things.

Did anything else happen on the job that you were dissatisfied with beyond what you've told me?
A. Lots of things happened on the job. There were incidences where the person that was hired to assist me spent a lot of time assisting him in his personal life matters.
Q. When did that start happening?
A. Almost immediately after she started working there.

Q. You mean like in March?
A. Yeah. He would call her out to drive him certain places where he didn't feel like driving, to babysit for his eight-year-old son, to take care of his wife while she was in the hospital or at home, which would place all of the duties that I had trained her to do right back on my shoulders.
Q. Did you look for work anywhere else?
A. No, I didn't.
Q. What was your reason for that?
A. I assumed that he would—well, I mean, I'm—I made a commitment to work for him. We had an agreement—we made an agreement in the fall that I would be assuming his business at his retirement; and at that point, the business would be 75 percent mine, 25 his. He was 64 years—65 years old.
Q. When did he say he was going to retire?
A. He didn't give a specific date. He just kept saying, "I can't do this for much longer." Approximation would be a year to two years.
Q. So you were figuring it was worth holding out for?
A. Exactly.
Q. If he hadn't had fired you, would you have stayed?
MR. ______: Objection; calls for speculation.
MR. LASKY: You can answer the question.
THE WITNESS: Can I answer the question?
MR. ______: I think I'm going to direct her not to answer that.
MR. LASKY: I'll ask the reporter to repeat the question to the witness.

(The requested portion of the record was read by the reporter.)

MR. LASKY: Now, are you stating that on advice of counsel—
You're directing her to refuse to answer the question; is that correct, Counsel?
MR. ______: Yes, I am.
Q. **BY MR. LASKY:** Immediately prior to his firing you, did you intend to leave him?
A. No.
Q. When did you become pregnant? I believe you said in October of '87?
A. That's correct.
Q. When did you tell him that you were pregnant?
A. In January.
Q. Did you say that you were going to have to lose some time from work?
A. Our discussion was that I would work throughout my entire pregnancy and take off three weeks, the time to have my baby. And his response was, "Three weeks is an eternity in our business."
Q. Did he fire you shortly after that?
A. I was terminated in February, so . . .
Q. How long—
A. About a month.
Q. Why did he tell you you were terminated?
A. Well, the way things happened at that time was one evening in February I was feeling extremely tired and I was having pains in my lower abdomen. I went to see my OB doctor, ____________, who informed me that I was—he thought that I was under a lot of stress and that I was having premature labor cramps,

and he advised me to take a disability—temporary disability for three weeks to get rest.

When I informed ___________ of that, he simply told me that if the job was too stressful for me that I shouldn't—I told him I would be back in three weeks. He said I couldn't come back at all. At that time he terminated me and didn't even give me a final payment.

Q. You mean he still owes you a final payment?
A. He owes me a final paycheck, plus vacation time, a couple of sick days.
Q. Did he give you any notice or did he just say—you mean he just said, "Get out."?
A. He just said, "Don't come back," yes.
Q. By whom had you become pregnant?
A. My boyfriend.
Q. What's his name?
A. ___________, as in ___________.
Q. I didn't catch that.
A. ___________.
Q. What's his first name?
A. That's his first name. His last name is ___________.
Q. Had you been living with him?
A. Off and on, yes.
Q. Did you share a residence?
A. Yes, at one time.
Q. When did you start to share a residence?
A. It was late 1985.
Q. When did you stop sharing a residence?
A. October 1987.
Q. What was the reason for stopping sharing the residence?
A. That was when our office moved to Rolling Hills and I had to take an apartment in Torrance because the commute was just becoming too much.
Q. Did you continue to see him after you moved to Torrance?
A. Yes.
Q. Do you still see him?
A. Yes.
Q. I mean, is this an exclusive relationship?
A. Yes.
Q. Why haven't you gotten married?
A. At this time I don't want to.
Q. Did you ever want to marry him?
A. No. I mean, I do, but not right now.
Q. Well, when you became pregnant, did you think about getting married?
A. No.
Q. Did he talk to you about getting married?
A. Yes.
Q. What did he say?
A. Just wanted to know how I felt about it. We both had reservations. But I'm a pretty independent person and my feeling was that with my independence and

my financial situation that I would be able to raise my daughter or my child and be able to be a career woman as well.

Q. Did he want to marry you when you told him about the pregnancy?

A. Yes. But he has had reservations, too. He wanted me to give up my—you know, like be a wife/mother and I wanted to be a career/mother.

§ 14.4 Case of the Not-So-Depressed Gambler

The claimant had begun complaining of stress to a private doctor sometime after a new supervisor had taken over his department. He negligently allowed some thefts to occur and as a result was fired. Four months later, he got a similar job, and about six months later he had to resign because of complaints about his performance.

A few months after that, he got a similar job in which he was performing successfully at the time of his deposition.

His medical-legal psychiatric diagnosis was depression; his internal medical diagnosis was gastrointestinal problems. The psychiatric disability was found to be slight or 20 percent by the rules of the jurisdiction. The internal medicine disability was found to require avoidance of stressful work.

The following deposition excerpt relates to the issue of the depression diagnosis and shows activities after discharge and before obtaining new employment that were incompatible with the major depression DSM-III-R diagnostic criteria.

The case was settled for a portion of the claimed temporary disability benefits.

BY MR. LASKY:

Q. MR. ______, you, sometime after March of 1986—did you try to get your job back with ____________ savings?

A. Yes, I did.

Q. Then, I assume that if they had offered it to you, you would have taken it?

A. Yes.

Q. Did you make any specifications as to where, or who you would work for?

A. No, I didn't.

Q. You just said that you'd like to have your job back?

A. There . . . I did not make personal contact. Was an attorney that wrote a letter, and the demands were—I mean, it wasn't a demand form. It was a request that I receive my salary back for the wrongful termination, and I did not state who I wanted to work for. But any branch would have been sufficient.

Q. All right.

Then not long after—then you filed for unemployment insurance and were turned down, and then after that, did you go on expensive trips?

A. Expensive—

MR. ______: Well, that's really more than one question.

The first question is:

Did you get your unemployment insurance?

THE WITNESS: Yes, I am.

BY MR. LASKY:

Q. Well, you did apply for unemployment insurance, did you not?
A. Yes, I did.
Q. You were turned down, weren't you?
A. Yes.
Q. Then, after that, did you go on expensive trips?
A. How soon after that are we talking of?
Q. Well, you told—you recall telling Dr. __________ when he examined you that sometime after that, you went on expensive trips?
A. I don't know.
I don't recall saying anything like that.
Q. You go on any trips sometime after you were turned down for unemployment insurance, and before you started working again?
A. The only trip I went on was my last vacation, since I lost my job, and that was . . . just in October.
Q. That was what?
A. October of '88 was the last vacation I had.
Q. Did you tell Dr. __________ that you blew a lot of money in __________?
A. Don't recall saying anything along that line.
Q. Did you go to Las Vegas?
A. Yes.
Q. Did you lose a lot of money?
A. No.
I didn't have a lot of money to lose.
Q. How much time did you spend in Las Vegas after you left __________ and before you went to work for, I believe, that was the __________.
A. I don't recall.
Q. Did you go on one, or more than one trip?
A. It was more than . . .
Q. More than one trip?
A. Yeah.
Q. Did you go more than two times?
A. I really don't recall—recall how many times I went there, made the trips up there.
Q. Did you lose an amount of money you considered significant?
A. No.
I wouldn't have took anything that was significant to lose in my condition. No.

(Brief pause.)

BY MR. LASKY:

Q. Did you take anybody along with you when you went to Las Vegas?
A. I really don't—I really don't recall any trips. I keep stating that. I . . .
Q. You mean, you don't remember going to Las Vegas at all?
A. I don't recall any trips. I don't—
Q. Are you saying that you didn't go to Las Vegas?
A. I already stated I did—I went.
Q. Yes.

[The next part of the deposition reviews the witness's divorce and new girlfriend.]

Q. Now, were you separated from your wife in 1982?
Is that right?
A. I believe, that's the date.
Q. About that time, or in 1982, did you start living with another lady?
A. At . . . probably, about a year . . . almost—a year to two years later.
Q. Did you tell __________ that you lived with a Mexican woman from 1982 to 1984?
A. I don't recall those dates. No.
Q. Do you recall talking to Dr. __________ about living with a Mexican woman?
A. I did live. So, I'm pretty sure I did tell him. She knows that.
Q. Did you know the Mexican woman before you separated from your wife?
A. No.
Q. Did you break up with the Mexican woman in 1984?
A. No.
Q. You did not?
A. I don't recall the date. I'm not sure.
Q. Are you living with her now?
A. No, I'm not.
Q. Do you still see her?
A. No.
Q. So, there was a time when you stopped living with her.
Is that—I assume?
A. Yes.
Q. That was around 1984? Possibly later?
A. I'm not sure of the date.
Q. It would have been 1984, 1985?
A. I—I'm pretty sure I seen her . . . I . . . we were together, probably, through the turmoil at __________. I'm—I mean, I'm not sure of the date, exact date, but I think we—I—our final breakup was around the same time that I lost my job, because I was involved with her then.
Q. Well—
A. Was—
Q. Were you living together in 1986?
A. No. No.
Q. You mean, after you stopped living together, did you keep on seeing her?
A. Yes.
We went steady.
Q. Why did you stop living together?
A. It was a mutual agreement. I—it was . . . more, or less on her—her family's acceptance of the—and, I guess, moral, the whole—before we were married. So, we decided to separate until we . . . get married.
Q. So, you mean, at that time when you stopped living together, it was still your intention to get married sometime?
A. Yes.

Q. But, I take it, a time came when that was no longer your intention?
A. My intentions to marry her was always there, but I . . . it was . . . I—I couldn't marry her under the conditions that—
I don't—I don't know what happened to them. I don't know what was going through my mind. But . . . I—I feel the marriage—it was her—she couldn't wait any longer. Let's put it that way.
Q. You mean she wanted to get married, and then at that time, didn't feel that you could get married?
A. I didn't feel I was ready.
I really don't know what I felt, to be honest.
(Brief pause.)

§ 14.5 Case of More Than Meets the Eye

The applicant quit work in 1988 because of stress due to a rude and inconsiderate boss. He allegedly overworked the applicant, unfairly denied her opportunities to attend conventions, and increased her burdens by being uncooperative. She said she left for good on the last day of work because of a particularly unreasonable deadline he gave her. On these facts, her psychiatrist diagnosed a severe general anxiety disorder.

A thorough investigation was obtained, including relevant court documents that disclosed additional facts about ongoing custody problems with her first husband, ongoing concerns about her parents' health, and an injury to her son that coincided with her leaving her job.

Q. Within the last ten years, have you had any concerns about your father's health?
A. Yes.
Q. What was that?
A. He suffered from circulatory problems. At one time, kidney failure. And alcoholism.
Q. Have these been continuing problems?
I asked did anything happen within the last ten years. Have these been continuing problems, would you say, for the last five years?
A. Yes.
Q. Wasn't there a time when he had to have a leg amputated?
A. No.
Q. No?
Did he have to go to the hospital because of a circulatory problem?
A. Yes.
Q. When was that?
A. There have been several hospitalizations. I don't remember all of them.
Q. Did any of them occur while you were working under ___________?
A. Yes.
Q. When was the last one?

A. I don't recall.
Q. Was it more than five years ago?
A. No.
Q. Was it more than two years ago?
A. I'm not sure.
Q. You think it probably was within the last two years?
A. I—I don't know.
Q. When your father had to go to the hospital, did that place a burden on you?
A. Yes.
Q. And just what was that burden?
A. I was very concerned about his health.
Q. Did it also require you to do some—to take some—give some care to your mother or him or do something in addition to what you normally had to do in your life?
A. Yes.
Q. What did it require?
A. I did some caring for my mother, and I visited my father frequently.
Q. And these events happened through the period when you were working for ___________, is that right?
A. Yes. Some of them.
Q. There was a year when both your daughter and your stepdaughter had weddings; isn't that correct? Would that have been in 1987?
A. I need to think. That's not right. No.
Q. Did your daughter and stepdaughter have weddings?
A. Yes.
Q. And was that in the same year?
A. No.
Q. About how far apart were they in time?
A. They were over a year apart.
Q. Were you concerned about the monetary cost of these weddings?
A. Somewhat.
Q. Well, they both occurred while you were working under ___________, didn't they?
A. Yes. No, that's not true.
Q. Was there one that occurred while you were working under ___________?
A. Yes.
Q. Which one was that?
A. My stepdaughter's wedding.
Q. And when was your daughter's?
A. It was June—June of '88.
Q. So I believe you left ___________ in May of '88, right?
A. That's right.
MR. ______: Off the record.

(A discussion was held off the record.)

Q. **BY MR. LASKY:** At around the time of your dissolution of your first marriage, that was not a friendly dissolution, was it?
A. Not particularly.

Q. I believe, according to court records, that you contested—in around May of 1985, you were contesting your husband's claim to joint custody; is that correct?
A. I do not recall.
Q. Do you have any recollection of being concerned about who was going to have joint custody of your children?
A. No.
Q. You mean as far as you were concerned, that was fine for your husband—your first husband—
MR. ______: What was fine? I'm confused.
Q. BY MR. LASKY: —to have joint custody of the children.
MR. ______: Fine or acceptable?
MR. LASKY: I asked if it was fine.
MR. ______: Well, I don't know what "fine" means. That's why I'm asking you to be more clear.
THE WITNESS: I do not recall that being a concern.
Q. BY MR. LASKY: After your dissolution, which I believe was May 16th of 1985, did your first husband come to your home at any time?
A. I don't know.
Q. You mean not as far as you knew?
A. I don't remember.
Q. What were the terms of the joint custody agreement?
MR. ______: Well, now, you know, I think I've been very patient up until now, but the terms of her agreement are of no concern in this case whatsoever.
MR. LASKY: Well—
MR. ______: Let me finish. I'm going to instruct her not to answer unless you can show some relevancy to the terms of her divorce agreement. That is not of my affair and none of your affair. Unless you can show me some relevancy, I'm going to instruct her not to answer that question.
Q. BY MR. LASKY: Well, I will state to you that the court—that the court papers show that you opposed this request for joint custody on the ground that he had been drunk the last time he had custody of your child. Now, had that happened?
THE WITNESS: Do I answer?
MR. ______: Yes.
THE WITNESS: I do recall that now; and, yes, that is correct.
Q. BY MR. LASKY: Well, and I take it you did not like that; is that correct?
MR. ______: I'm sorry. I don't understand your question. The fact—
MR. LASKY: The fact—
MR. ______: —that he was asking for joint custody or the fact—
MR. LASKY: The fact that he was drunk when he had custody.
THE WITNESS: No, I did not like that.
Q. BY MR. LASKY: And weren't you concerned about him behaving that way in the future?
A. Yes, I was.
Q. And in the future—and this is the reason I ask about the terms of the agreement. I wanted to know how frequently he had custody of the children.
A. He has access to my son at—at—whenever he wishes. He has him one weekend a month.

Q. Well, going back to '85 and '86 and '87, did he have the same access that he does now?
A. Yes.
Q. And what about your daughter?
A. She was 18 at the time of the divorce.
Q. So the concern about custody only applied to the son; is that correct?
A. That's right.
Q. When he did have access to the boy, were you concerned about how he was going to behave?
MR. ______: You mean how the boy was going to behave or the husband?
MR. LASKY: How the boy was going to behave.
THE WITNESS: I don't remember.
Q. BY MR. LASKY: When he had access to the boy, were you concerned about how your former husband was going to behave?
A. I don't—I don't remember.
MR. ______: I assume you're talking about five years ago; is that correct?
MR. LASKY: I'm talking about on every occasion. On any occasion.
MR. ______: You mean today or five years ago or in between? I don't understand. I assume she answered your questions as of what I interpreted them to mean, and that's at the time of the divorce. Apparently there was some issue about custody.
Q. BY MR. LASKY: Well, you stated that you don't remember if you were concerned about your husband having—how your husband behaved when he had access to the boy. Now, does your statement that you don't remember apply to every occasion on which he had access to the boy?
A. I was concerned one time when it was brought to my attention that he had been drinking. I do recall that. I don't recall the specifics of the—any other time.
Q. And that time that you were concerned, was that a time when you were working under ____________?
A. Yes.
Q. Have you been concerned about the medical condition of your son at any time within the last five years?
A. Yes.
Q. And what was that concern?
A. The same day that I had the nervous breakdown at work, after I was sent home from my doctor's, my son was attacked by a dog and had his right thigh ripped apart.
Q. Did that have any permanent effect on your son?
A. Yes.
Q. Did he lose that eye?
A. His leg.
MR. ______: Thigh.
MR. LASKY: Oh, I thought you said his eye.
MR. ______: Thigh.
THE WITNESS: No. No. No. Thigh.
MR. LASKY: Thigh.
Q. Did he subsequently recover from that?

A. Yes.
Q. Did that have any emotional effect on him?
A. Not to any great degree.
Q. I believe you filed a lawsuit against the owner of the dog, did you not?
A. Yes, I did.
Q. Did that lawsuit allege that your son had sustained any emotional effects?
A. It may have. I don't recall.
Q. Has that case now been settled?
A. No.
Q. It's still pending?
A. That's right.
Q. Did anyone take your deposition in that case?
A. No.
Q. What time of day was your son attacked?
A. In the afternoon.
Q. Was he with you?
A. No.
Q. When did you find out about it?
A. Shortly after the attack.
Q. And where were you when you found out about it?
A. I was at home.
Q. Did they bring your son home after the attack or were you told about it—strike that.
Was he taken right directly home after the attack?
A. No.
Q. Was he taken to a hospital directly—
A. Yes.
Q. —after the attack?
Who informed you about the attack?
A. My husband.
Q. Was he at home?
A. Yes.
Q. And I mean, did he receive a phone call or—
A. Someone came to our door and told my husband what had happened.
Q. Was this a neighbor?
A. Yes.
Q. I mean, the owner of the dog?
A. Yes.
Q. And then did you both go to the hospital?
A. No.
Q. Did either of you go to the hospital?
A. My husband did.
Q. And then—well, did your son come back that day?
A. Yes.
Q. Then I assume he had a period of treatment after that?
A. Yes.
Q. Did you ever tell any doctor who treated you about this incident?
A. Yes.

Q. And who did you tell?
A. I recall telling Dr. ________.
And he began treating me immediately after the nervous breakdown.
MR. ______: For emotional problems?
THE WITNESS: Yes. As well as physical.

(Note that Dr. ________ was not her reporting psychiatrist. Her reporting psychiatrist was not aware of the dog attack when he stated his opinion of the cause of her condition because she didn't tell him about it. See **Chapter 16**.)

§ 14.6 Up in the World Case

The claimant was fired because of an argument with her new supervisor about taking sick leave instead of vacation time. The supervisor had been complaining about the amount and timing of her sick time off. The applicant said the new supervisor had unreasonably increased her work load.

The claimant's psychiatrist diagnosed a major depression with a slight to moderate disability. Her internist diagnosed a gastrointestinal disorder due to stress and prescribed avoidance of stress as a factor of disability.

The case had many elements of similarity to the one in **§ 14.3**. Thus, after the claimant lost her job, she immediately got a better one, paying more and with more responsibility.

In addition, the nervous stomach complaints were explained by a gall bladder problem, rather than industrial stress. There was no medical evidence that gall bladder problems are caused by stress.

The material at the end of the deposition concerning her early years and family relationships directly contradicted the interpretation of her Minnesota Multiphasic Personality Inventory (MMPI) by her reporting psychologist.

After the trial, at which the defendant won, the medical-legal charges were attacked on the ground of lack of probative value based on failure to consider evidence contrary to the applicant's position.

Q. When you left ________, did you quit, or did they fire you?
A. They fired me.
Q. What happened? How did that all happen? That was January 18?
A. Okay. When I came back from the sick leave that Dr. ________ had given me, I came back—what was it the 11th?—and I explained to ________ why I was out. In fact, she even had proof from the doctor saying I was going to be out that whole week because I had to go through several exams.
And when I came back, she told me that that week I was out I had to take it as a vacation week.
I said, "Why should I take it as a vacation week because I'm not going to take that as a sick leave from the doctor." I said, "I was sick and I have the doctor's proof to that and to the different exams I had."

And so she said, "Well, I want you to take it as a vacation week."

And I said, "I don't think that's fair, Cindy."

Then she said, "Are you going to take it or not?"

I said, "I don't think it's fair."

Then she said, "Well, we'll see what happens." And the following Friday she fired me.

Q. Had you looked for a job before that time?
A. No.
Q. You didn't have much trouble getting one?
A. No. Fortunately.

[The next part of the deposition reviews the claimant's more rewarding present employment.]

Q. As far as your present work is concerned, do you have any problems with that?
A. What do you mean "problems"?
Q. Well, do you have any?
A. In my job?
Q. Any difficulty in doing your job?
A. No. No.
Q. What is your job? What do you have to do?
A. Okay. I coordinate planning with production according to the customers' requirements.
Q. Planning with production?
A. Yes. And purchasing.
Q. Well, let's—do you have a supervisor?
A. Yes. Well, yes. The manager.
Q. And what is his name?
A. __________. __________.
Q. And you report to him?
A. Yes, I do.
Q. Is there anybody with the same kind of job as you who also reports to him?
A. There's nine of us.
Q. There are nine?
A. Nine of us.
Q. But is he the one direct, next above you, or is there someone else—
A. He's the manager. He's the only one we report to.
Q. Now, who else do you deal with in your work in that company? I mean, you indicated that I guess different departments or different types of work that you coordinate. So would you tell me?
A. Like I say, with purchasing I coordinate with __________.
Q. __________ and what do you just—
A. She's the purchasing manager.
Q. Who else do you have to coordinate with?
A. The production manager, __________, and production supervisors.
Q. Who is that?
A. Well, there's __________, and __________.

Q. All right. Who else do you have to coordinate with?
A. Well, that's with sales.
Q. Sales. And—
A. Yes.
Q. —who do you deal with in sales?
A. The sales manager, who is ___________, and ___________.
Q. Well, now, let's take a typical workday. Describe for me what you would be doing, say, when you arrive at work, how do you determine what your job is for that—what do you have to do for that day?
A. Okay. Well, I go to the plant to shop because they make parts there. And so I—
Q. Incidently, just what do they make there?
A. Ducts for airplanes.
Q. Ducts for airplanes?
A. Yes.
Q. So you go to the shop, and then what?
A. And then I—okay. I check to see in each department where my parts are because I'm already coordinating for the customers the parts that have to be shipped. So I check the parts to see where they're at and if they're there. If they're still sitting there, I'll talk to the supervisor and find out what the problem is. If not, just continue to each department, checking the parts; then I'll come back to my desk, and I'll start working with the computer, start planning for when the parts are going to ship, how many are going to ship, and see if there's any new requirements.
Q. How do you do that? How do you find out?
A. Normally we get reports every Monday, and that report tells us, you know, if there's any orders or there's—if there's been any changes in the customer requirements like due dates or quantities; so I have to check that report.
Q. Okay. After you've done that, how long would you say that takes you in a typical day?
A. It takes all day. It takes eight hours, sometimes ten.
Q. So you mean basically the job involves receiving the orders for what's to be done? Is that it?
A. Yes.
Q. You're the one when the customer orders something—
A. Okay. Goes to sales, and sales gives us a report.
Q. Is that the report you get on Monday?
A. Yes.
Q. So you mean the customer would say, "I want—." You make different kinds of ducts, I suppose?
A. Yes.
Q. Different sizes, different materials?
A. Right.
Q. Then when the order comes in, are you the one who decides what department is to be told to get to work?
A. No. I'm the one that decides if the parts can be made in a certain amount of time, like, in a month or two months or three months, depending if we have raw material in stock or if we have to order it.

Q. You mean when the order comes in, is it for delivery in a certain period of time?
A. Yes.
MR. LASKY: Off the record.

(A discussion was held off the record.)

MR. LASKY: Back on the record.
Q. So you decide whether it would be for delivering in a certain time. You have to decide whether you've got it on hand or how long it has to be ordered?
A. Right.
Q. You mean sometimes you might order it from elsewhere?
A. The raw material.
Q. Oh, okay. So you mean you might have it in stock. It might be something that can be made from the existing materials, or it might be something where you have to order the material?
A. Well, normally I have to order the material.
Q. And that job mainly, that's mainly what you do each day; so then when you go out—
A. Right.
Q. —to the plant, that's just sort of a general checkup?
A. Yes, a general checkup.
Q. Is this the same job you were doing when you first got that job as general coordinator?
A. Yes, it is.
Q. Did you have any kind of a training program?
A. Yes, I did.
Q. How long did that last?
A. Okay. I have to train and program before in 19—1981—1980, 1981, approximately.
Q. Where was that?
A. That was at ____________.
Q. That a different company you worked for?
A. That's a different company.
Q. When you went to general coordinator, did you have any particular training program—
A. No.
Q. You mean you just went there. You got the job—
A. Yes.
Q. —and started?
A. Yes.
Q. What was your pay when you started working for ____________?
A. 23,000.
Q. 23,000?
A. A year.
Q. Have you gotten any raises?
A. Not yet.
Q. Do they have any kind of performance review?

A. Yes, they do.
Q. How often do they have performance reviews?
A. It's going to be after a year.
Q. You mean you haven't had one, then?
A. No.
Q. Did you have any kind of probation period or anything like that?
A. No, not really.
Q. Did you have any kind of a meeting with a supervisor to talk over how your work was going?
A. Yes, I have.
Q. When was that? Or was it more than once?
A. That was around the sixth month.
Q. You mean that's a regular—
A. Well, it was a comment. It was, like, you know, we were talking about it, yes, but it's not like he had a form and—
Q. That's what I meant.
A. No. No.
Q. They don't have a customary practice of giving you a review after six months?
A. Not in this position.
Q. But you say you did happen to talk with your supervisor?
A. Yes.
Q. About when was that?
A. Around August—July. July. I'm sorry.
Q. Basically what was said in that talk?
A. That he was happy with my work.
Q. Did he tell you you were going to get a raise?
A. Yes.
Q. You mean like the end of the year?
A. Yes.
Q. How much were you making at ____________.
A. 21,000.
Q. When you started there, there must have been a certain period of time that you had to spend learning how things work, wasn't there?
A. Well, the system, yes—I mean, basically I know what a planner does, but the system at ____________—, all companies are different so, yes, the system at ____________—
Q. Did they have some type of manual for you to study?
A. No. The man whose place I was taking, he trained me.
Q. He trained you?
A. The person I substituted, yes. I—
Q. You mean you replaceed somebody?
A. I replaced somebody.
Q. How long did that training period last?
A. A week.
Q. So you had to learn how to understand their order forms?
A. Yes.

Q. You know what that meant in terms of what was being ordered, and then you had to know what parts went into those orders and how long it would take to get delivery if you had to order new materials, things like this? Is that about right?
A. Yes.
Q. Do you have any dealings with other people in the course of your work?
A. Well, in general, with all, you know, the workers we work from the plant, but—
Q. Well, do you do work with anybody when you are working? Do you have to explain things to anybody?
A. No.
Q. Do you have to tell anybody what to do?
A. No.
Q. Does anybody tell you what to do?
A. My boss, the manager.
Q. What sort of directions does he give you?
A. Well, we have meetings every week.
Q. Once a week?
A. Once a week.
Q. But I mean in terms of contacts on the job, is that just basically social?
A. Yes.
Q. In your orders, do you do that in writing or telephone?
A. In writing.
Q. Just by writing?
A. In writing, and I have two forms for purchasing.
Q. Do you like this work?
A. Yes.
Q. Do you get along all right with the people there?
A. I haven't had problems.

[The witness next discusses her gall bladder surgery.]

Q. **BY MR. LASKY:** Now, have you seen any other doctor for treatment—
A. No. Other than—
Q. Well, let me finish my question. Since the beginning of 1988?
A. Since the beginning of 1988?
Q. Yes. Since January.
A. Only Dr. ____________ and the ones I just mentioned.
Q. Your application also mentions "cardiovascular" on complaints. Now, is that covered by what you said about the chest pains?
A. About the chest pains and the pain on my—on my arm.
Q. ____________ were treating you for those conditions?
A. Yes. It was—I had surgery. In fact, ____________ performed surgery on me.
Q. When did Dr. ____________ perform surgery?
A. The 15th of August, 1988.
Q. What did he do?
A. He did the gallbladder. I had some stones in my gallbladder so—

Q. Do you feel that that may have improved your condition?
A. To a certain amount, yes, it has.
Q. In what way did it improve your condition?
A. I don't get the chest pains as often as I used to.
Q. You do, or you don't?
A. I don't. And I asked the doctor if it could have been—what causes gallbladder stones, and he said that a lot of things and among them could be stress because there's a liquid. He explainined the way, you know, the stone starts forming and—
Q. That's Dr. __________?

[The deposition continues with a discussion of the claimant's relationship with her current boyfriend.]

Q. Since the breakup with the man who you originally lived with, have you lived with anybody else?
A. I—I have a boy friend. I've been with him for nine years.
Q. Have you ever lived under the same roof?
A. No.
Q. How do you get along with him?
A. Well, very nice, in fact.
Q. Have you talked with him about being married?
A. Well, yes, we have talked about it and it could be in the near future.
Q. What is his name?
A. __________.
Q. What kind of work does he do?
A. He's a leadman in a paper company where they make boxes and—
Q. What company?
MR. ______: Objection.
MR. LASKY: Just curious. I have a friend and a client that owns a paper company, I mean, who makes boxes.
Q. Have you had any particular quarrels with Mr. __________?
A. No.
Q. —within the last two years?
A. No.
Q. In reviewing the notes of Dr. __________, she refers to a vaginal infection. You had made some reference to your boy friend?
A. I'm sorry. I didn't hear you.
Q. Dr. __________'s notes refer to a vaginal infection you had.
A. Yes.
Q. Did she discuss with you whether that could be connected to your boyfriend?

[The claimant goes on to discuss her childhood family relationships.]

I'm looking at the medical report, the initial psychiatric report filed by the doctor at __________ Clinic; so you'll understand where my questions are coming from.

A. Yes.
Q. Did you experience early hate, anger, or disgusted—
I'm looking at page nine, Counsel. I'll wait until you've located it.
MR. ______: Okay. Okay.
Q. **BY MR. LASKY:** Did you experience early hate, anger, or disgust from your mother?
A. No.
Q. Did you experience early hate, anger, or disgust from any other close relative when you were growing up?
A. No.
Q. Did you have any brothers and sisters when you were growing up?
A. I had a brother, yes.
Q. You had a brother. How old is your brother? Is your brother older or younger than you?
A. He was older.
Q. About how much older?
A. One year.
Q. Were you afraid of him?
A. No.
Q. Do you have strange and unusual thoughts and feelings such as unreality, concentration difficulties, memory problems?
A. Yes.
Q. Do they bother you in doing your work?
A. Occasionally, yes.
Q. Do you feel that the world is a threatening place where you're unlikely to be treated fairly and misunderstood?
A. Yes, occasionally.
Q. Do you feel you were treated fairly in your present job?
A. Yes.
Q. Do you think they misunderstood you?
A. No. Not in my present job.
MR. LASKY: I don't have any other questions.

CHAPTER 15

DEPOSITION OF PSYCHOTHERAPIST

Herbert Lasky

§ 15.1 Introduction

The general principles for taking the psychotherapist's deposition are no different than those for the taking of any expert's deposition. Thus, the attorney wants to know about the therapist's qualifications or lack thereof; any grounds for finding bias, such as a history of testifying primarily for one side or another; opinions formed; the basis for those opinions; and the extent of the witness's knowledge of relevant history or other facts in the case.

Matters unique to the psychiatric case include fundamental questions based on the American Psychiatric Association's *Diagnostic and Statistical Manual of Mental Disorders* (third edition, revised) (DSM-III-R): Is there a mental disorder as defined by DSM-III-R? What is the opinion as to the DSM-III-R diagnosis? If the therapist does not follow DSM-III-R, what, if anything, does the therapist follow? Has the therapist made the necessary factual findings to support the DSM-III-R diagnosis, and are those findings based on all of the evidence in the case? The last question encompasses the key area of the adequacy of the history on which the therapist's opinion is based.

To the extent that the doctor is basing an opinion on the applicability of medical principles to legal concepts, does the therapist correctly apply the legal concepts? Does the testimony have the requisite degree of certainty, expressed, for example, as the difference between "possibly" or "maybe" and reasonable medical certainty or probability? Another example would be a conclusion, in connection with the causation issue, that a preexisting schizophrenic condition or passive-aggressive disorder was triggered by the defendant's acts, rather than the defendant's acts setting the stage or convenient focus for the playing out of a preexisting mental condition. Or, is worry about financial loss due to termination an element of industrial causation or a matter personal to the claimant, not deemed to come within the scope of a workers' compensation law?

If the expert has found that disability exists or does not exist, does the doctor understand the legal definition of disability? For example, in a jurisdiction in which disability is defined as encompassing only an impairment for competition in the labor market, does the expert think of it as something broader?

One other approach to deposing a psychotherapist witness is a body of thought exemplified by the position of J. Ziskind, a psychologist with a legal background.[1] Briefly, this approach contends that all psychological diagnoses, in a litigation context, are invalid or unreliable. The rationale for this approach is that psychiatry or psychology are not sufficiently authenticated to merit the appellation *science,* and that therefore testimony of therapists is inherently unreliable. Proponents of this approach attack DSM-III-R as unscientific. They point out that studies have shown that psychiatrists often differ with one another on diagnoses; that studies have shown that it is possible for intentional falsifiers to deceive psychiatrists; and psychiatrists do not ordinarily follow up to test the accuracy of their diagnoses.

The author disagrees fundamentally with this approach. As an experienced forensic psychiatrist recently said at a workshop at which Dr. Ziskind spoke, "DSM-III-R is the friend of truth in the courtroom."[2] The use of psychiatrists and psychologists for treating mental health problems should be familiar enough to most Americans to dispel any notion of an "off-the-wall" discipline. This appears to be the current state of thinking in the judicial system. Thus, the American Bar Association's Torts and Insurance Practice Section's publication, *The Brief,* states: "The judicial system, however, has put the imprimatur of legitimacy on the ability of the psychotherapist to at least identify mental states and conditions. . . . Further, attacks on the ability of any psychotherapist to render opinions have been generally unsuccessful."[3]

It is sometimes suggested, as a ploy, that the testifying therapist be asked to admit that it is possible for her to be fooled, and that such an admission, which should be forthcoming, discredits the testimony. The author submits that it does not necessarily have this effect. The standard answer for the experienced expert is, "Anything is possible, but it's unlikely." The competent forensic therapist does

---

[1] *See* I, II, III J. Ziskind & D. Faust, Coping with Psychiatric and Psychology Testimony (1981).

[2] Dietz, *Defense and Evaluation of Psychological and Neuropsychological Injury Claims Seminar,* Defense Research Institute (1991).

[3] McCandless & Schickman, *Examining the Psychotherapist at Trial,* The Brief, Spring 1989, at 42.

not base an opinion simply on uncorroborated statements by the claimant. The history, investigative reports, and psychological testing are important factors. Second, a psychotherapist expert's function is not to be a judge of testimonial credibility, which is not within the doctor's training. The expert's role is to explain to the court or jury the significance of a particular set of facts, such as the diagnostic criteria, *if* established by the evidence.

Nevertheless, in a given case in which the psychiatric issue appears particularly spurious, the Ziskind approach might be advisable.

§ 15.2 Deposition of Dr. Concede It

In this case, the claimant filed a workers' compensation claim in a jurisdiction that allows recovery for mental-mental claims. See **Chapter 9**. She claimed that discriminatory and harassing treatment by a supervisor had caused a psychiatric injury which her psychiatric medical-legal consultant diagnosed as a major depression. The consultant found that the depression was caused by the supervisor's treatment and evaluated it as producing a "light to moderate disability," which in that jurisdiction meant a 35 percent disability award.

Investigation of the medical records showed significant stress-producing events that had not been revealed to the claimant's doctor. Her own testing psychologist's report showed Minnesota Multiphasic Personality Inventory (MMPI) validity scale scores that indicated either conscious exaggeration or a cry for help due to a serious emotional problem.

This deposition illustrates the importance of accurate history, the significance of MMPI validity scales, how to establish that an invalid MMPI is not a legitimate "cry for help," and how use of a doctor's preliminary questionnaire can establish the materiality of the omissions in the history.

The purpose of the cross-examination was to establish that the claimant had not disclosed a complete history, that the omission was material to her doctor's opinion, and to induce the doctor to withdraw his finding of industrial causation. It was also to gain an admission that, in the circumstances of this case, the MMPI validity scale scores indicated conscious exaggeration and ground for a diagnosis of malingering.

Q. **BY MR. LASKY:** Dr. ___________, you're licensed to practice medicine in the state of California, are you not?

A. I am.

Q. And that's the curriculum vitae?

A. Yes.

Q. That would be nice. Thank you for the curriculum. And I'll offer Defendant's Exhibit 1 to this deposition.

(The document referred to was marked by the Deposition Officer as Defendant's Exhibit 1 for identification and is hereto annexed.)

Q. BY MR. LASKY: And you have performed examinations and written reports on a patient ___________, is that correct?
A. To the best of my knowledge, yes.
Q. Well, either you did or you didn't?
A. I did.
Q. I have a report from you dated April 19th, 1988, and another one dated September 22nd, 1988.
MR. N: Those are your—
MR. LASKY: I'm trying to establish that we're talking to the right person. I just want to establish for the record that we are talking to the right person.
THE WITNESS: Yes.
Q. BY MR. LASKY: I note now in taking this report you interviewed the patient, you took a history, you did a mental status exam. Is there any other procedure that you would state that you followed?
A. As for my report on Page No. 9, last paragraph outlines the scope of the evaluation.
Q. What function do each of these procedures perform in allowing you to arrive at the basis for your conclusions?
A. You mean each subheading in the history?
Q. Yes, clinical interview. I assume mental status is something different than a clinical interview?
A. Each of these functions are—first of all, required functions according to the guidelines for writing—suggested guidelines for writing workers' compensation psychiatric report, as well as these, give good background about the patient and a chance to get some details of the antecedent's history and current history as well as observe the patient while conducting the mental status examination.
MR. N: I know you have misunderstood his question. You're talking about what's in the report.
MR. LASKY: I felt that he answered my question. I just want to make sure that we're talking about the same categories.
MR. N: Okay.
THE WITNESS: Which enable me to arrive at a working diagnosis and formulate further plan of action or care as dictated by the needs of the said patient.
Q. BY MR. LASKY: And then when you did a permanent stationary report, I assume that you also took into account the matters that you have covered in your initial report?
A. Yes.
Q. And all of those were given some weight in arriving at the conclusion you expressed in your permanent stationary report?
A. I would assume that's correct.
Q. Would you say that the history is important?
A. Yes, history is important.
Q. I take it that merely observing the patient as she sits in your office and talks to you would not be satisfactory?
A. Well, it depends on the issues we're dealing with at hand. If the patient were a worthy—disturbed or very insistent on repetitive statements, then one could observe everything just from the mental status examination.

Q. But that was not the situation in this case, was it?
A. I cannot recollect. However, most likely not.
Q. So then you would say that the history she gave you was an important factor in arriving at your conclusion?
A. I would say that the history was one of the factors in looking.
Q. Is it something that you take into account in arriving at your conclusions?

(Deposition was interrupted by a phone call.)

THE WITNESS: The history is, yes.
Q. BY MR. LASKY: In your initial—incidently, you have got the reports there. In your initial report of April 19th, you make reference to the fact on Page 2 that the patient was involved in an automobile accident, which you report that she stated it caused her to remain off the job.

And incidently, you don't necessarily have to answer "yes" or "no" to any of these things unless I'm trying to focus on the matters that I think have importance. This is my way of concentrating your attention. You don't have to answer.

The same report on Page 8 or Page 4, "Patient denies having any chronic illnesses." She again makes reference to the automobile injury, and on Page 4 she also says that no one in the family has ever had psychiatric treatment. And on Page 8 you state, "Patient appears to have an unremarkable past medical history. No previous for mental psychological. Appears to be within normal limit."

I assume that you made all those observations because you considered them a significant matter in the record?
A. In the history, yeah.
Q. Also, in addition, when you interview a patient or when you first see a patient, you have procedures or preliminary questionnaires being submitted to the patient, do you not?
A. Yes.
Q. And what is the purpose of those questionnaires?
A. Well, one is to focus on the patient's thoughts by putting down in writing to—is to have a record in their handwriting of what their understanding of the situation is. And also to maintain a record in the file. And three, is to help talk about these things; lest one might forget something.
Q. And now I'm—incidently, I'm going to ask some questions in relation to that questionnaire.
Q. BY MR. LASKY: I have it here. If you have any need to refer to it you can refer to it. I'm noting, among other things that she told you, you have a question before the address, "How was your life?"
MR. N: Can you give me the page when you make these?
MR. LASKY: Page SV 37.
MR. N: Thank you.
Q. BY MR. LASKY: And she gave certain answers in general. She said she was happy, content, had a better outlook. And then on Page—listed here is 49—well, as I say, I'm going to read you the question and the answer. "Prior to your set of job related problems . . . " And she answers "None." Next Page 48.

MR. N: Hold on because ours ends on Page 40 and the next thing I have in file—you can look at any of this you want—but I'm just going to talk about the paper clip pages.

MR. LASKY: I'm handing my records to you.

MR. N: The writing is my only concern.

MR. LASKY: I'm assuming if I'm wrong, you can correct me.

MR. N: I'm not trying to ascertain at this time. Is this for the patient—for example—

MR. LASKY: Assume that if he wrote it down that she said it to him.

MR. N: Is that hers?

THE WITNESS: Yeah, this is hers.

MR. N: All right. I believe you just have something slightly different.

MR. LASKY: Now, I'm going to 47.

"Have you ever experienced severe anxiety?" Answer, "No." And on Page 29 she says—there was a question, "If you have had emotional problems, mental health problems or stress reaction, have you had these three problems or the reaction or similar ones before?" And it's answered, "No."

On Page 27, there's a list of illnesses and then the question—or it says, it begins, "Have you had any chronic illnesses," and at the very bottom it lists some which are not involved here. It says "Others" and she answers that "No." That completes my enumeration of the aspects of the history which I want to focus my questioning on.

What I'm going to do is, I have a number of records which indicate, at least in my opinion, that she was very much less than candid with you.

MR. N: It wouldn't be the first time.

MR. LASKY: And I'm going to, rather than hand you this mass of records and say go through it, I'm going to read, let's say—my questions will be in the form of hypothetical questions assuming that the records show the following, and then I'll be questioning you whether that would change any of your opinions. Now, I'll begin enumerating, listing.

MR. N: We have no objection to that procedure at all.

Q. BY MR. LASKY: Well, she had told you that December 27th, 1987, she was in an automobile accident. In fact, the __________ Hospital records show that she was hit in the eye by a person and that that caused the injuries for which she was treated. And assuming that when I took her deposition on Page 23, that she was hit in the eye by her boyfriend while they were driving in the automobile. And this altercation, if such a one-sided event can be so described, was because she didn't want to have sex with him and as a result of that, she broke up the preceding relationship with him. To Page 25, she says she did not tell Dr. __________ about this.

A. While we're talking about her deposition, Page 40 says that she saw a therapist in 1983 at __________ because of problems she was having with her parents although there was just one visit.

MR. N: One visit you said?

MR. LASKY: That's right. She states on her deposition in response to the first question, similarly to her response to your questionnaire, that she had not been treated at a hospital for any condition prior to going to __________ (sic).

And I'll now go into what the hospital records disclose. ____________ Hospital record; spontaneous abortion, August 3rd, 1986.

Q. Doctor, could you enlighten me what is meant by the "spontaneous abortion?"

A. Generally, it means it was not induced either through an abortion clinic or by any medication or physical efforts. About roughly "X" number of percentage of pregnancies due to structural weakness either by the uterine walls or in the fetus, having deformities, et cetera, are rejected by the body. And those are spontaneously ejected through the uterine cavity outside the female body and those are called spontaneous. They have no help by any human or other source. They just—basically the body, it rejects the pregnancy.

MR. N: It would apply to a preexisting pregnancy, would it not?

THE WITNESS: That's difficult. It's not my field of expertise. It's difficult. Many women may not be aware that they have rejected very much earlier and suddenly, they have the bleeding and they go to the hospital and they are told that this could be a spontaneous abortion by conclusion or by finding the effects of pregnancy in the uterus.

Q. **BY MR. LASKY:** The reason I asked that question is because the records of ____________ Group refer to an induced abortion in May of 1986.

A. That's after or before this?

Q. That's before. The spontaneous one was in August, and then there is a report—one in May of '86.

A. That's awfully fast to be reimpregnated.

Q. That's why I'm asking.

A. Unless they have a pathology—spontaneous was passed. The fetus—there could be some left over. It's possible that there could be some left over that finally is ejected. Although some women do get pregnant. And probably, that's one of the reasons the body rejects it. It was so fast after the last pregnancy.

MR. N: You mean as near as you can tell, and you're not claiming to be an expert, it would? It's more likely that there was a—or whatever?

THE WITNESS: Especially since it shows, "active and did not use any birth control."

MR. LASKY: Well, I think I will ask you to glance through these records. It shouldn't take too long because then there are references following the abortion. I have a note that she had complained about abdominal problems in January of 1987, a date which is, I assume, important for our purposes because I believe she said she didn't start work. I'll ask you to look at some of these. That will be all I'll ask.

There were complaints of vaginitis for the preexisting period in January of '87 which was before she started working for ____________.

MR. N: I'm handing you these records now. It's kind of a beginning entry.

MR. LASKY: I'll go through it.

MR. N: I'm going to make a phone call. You can proceed without me.

Q. **BY MR. LASKY:** You were finished?

A. Yes. I read this page.

Q. Would you mind bringing us up to date, say through the beginning of 1987 since she had been—to have been reporting continuous problems?

A. Right. "April 30th, 1986, patient's mother called."

Q. You don't have to read it. I just want you to acquaint yourself with it.

A. Patient's mother called clinic and stated daughter pregnant and needs an abortion. And so she had an appointment on the same day at 2:00 p.m. for counseling. At 2:00 p.m. she had counseling. Various options were discussed with the patient and—
Q. Actually, I'm not even asking you that you just read it out loud. Since I will be—is it true to say that she had a lot of medical problems?
A. Right. Just this page alone—
MR. N: Bring it up to the beginning of 1987.
Q. **BY MR. LASKY:** Doctor, having reviewed the hospital record in question, would it be a fair characterization of applicant's medical history to say that she had some significant medical problems beginning in May of 1986?
A. Yes, it would.
Q. And that continued at least up until January of 1987 for one reason or another; is that correct?
A. Yes, indeed.
Q. Was vaginitis one of the problems?
A. Yes, it has been mentioned.
Q. What is the cause of vaginitis?
A. Vaginitis? Various causes. Usually infection or irritation by chemical substances, but usually it's from infection of the female genital system.
Q. Do you have any general knowledge as to the usual source of such an infection?
A. It could be from a fungal infection like yeast infection that could cause vaginitis which happens with various women, especially if they are having other medical problems, like diabetes or on birth control pills. It could be from sexual things. From transmitted diseases like gonorrhea, syphilis, but nongonococcal vaginitis, or it could be from physical infection after vigorous relation and getting—because the sexual partner is infected with some other organism or chemical vaginitis can be caused by using strong vinegar douches, contact-skin problem using chemicals that do not agree with internal lining of the vagina. Sometimes, if they have illnesses like diabetes, cancer, a radiation sickness, et cetera, they are more susceptible to vaginitis because the lubrication's dried up and hence, the white blood cells do not—are not able to do their job and kill off germs in those areas.
Q. Are you able to determine from the information that you have seen in these records what the cause of that vaginitis was?
A. There is one thing here that says Gardnerella vaginitis and they gave a vaginal for that by a suction that's the—that sends a smear of her vaginal secretion to the lab and came back negative for gonococcus and at that time there was a note saying she was not sexually active. She was allergic to penicillin and most likely, infection at that time was this Gardnerella—this is not clearly written, but it sounds like Gardnerella vaginal vaginitis. I think it's vaginitis that's susceptible to this medicine.
Q. Ordinarily, would one expect somebody who had the pregnancy problems that she had and the medical problems she had to have a degree of anxiety through that period?
A. Yes. In ordinary course of events, that would be a sense of concern.
Q. Would it be fair to say that she was not accurate to you with the portions of her history that I quoted to you?

A. Yes, indeed.

Q. Now, I also want to call your attention to a report from ___________, and I'm referring to the one in which she does her MMPI analysis. If you don't have that, I can hand you my copy.

MR. N: We have the bill.

THE WITNESS: You have her report dated February 5th, 1988.

MR. LASKY: I'm not sure that the information that it has is what I found in her order.

Q. If you'll look at the paragraph dealing with the validity analysis.

A. Okay. Yes.

Q. Now, would you hand that back to me now because I want to—

A. Sure.

Q. She states under "Validity Analysis" the soundness of this test profile is debatable—or before I go through the rest of that, I assume initially, that the psychological testing was part of the data on which you based your conclusion?

A. If it was present, this is February 5, 1988—and I saw an April 1988, I don't know. I cannot recall at this time.

Q. Generally speaking, the reason you have psychological tests is you regard it as useful in arriving at a conclusion?

A. If I have it—

Q. I'm going to read to you what she says in her validity analysis on the soundness of the test profile. "Is debatable and immature, attention seeking, unstable. Client may be attempting to emphasize the immediate"—"for exaggerating the symptoms or consciously malingering or it may be the accutely psychotic individual."

Independently, did you have any reason to believe that she was psychotic?

A. Not by my stated diagnosis. More complete evaluation is necessary to discriminate between these hypotheses. Thus, the test interpretation should be read as only provisional.

Q. Well, now we have more information for a more complete evaluation based on the status of the lack of candor which I told you about. Would that make it reasonable to believe she was a malingerer?

A. Well, it will raise a definite caution flag that one has to observe the rest of the history more carefully. Yes, malingering would be considered as a definite diagnosis.

Q. The incident of December 27th, 1986, when it appeared that she was hit by her boyfriend and therefore, it broke up a preexisting relationship, is—no, that's—I'm sorry. That was December 20, 1987. That's very close in time to the time that she left ___________.

MR. N: What's the breakup? Where does that come from?

THE WITNESS: She refused to have sex with the guy and he hit her in the eye.

Q. **BY MR. LASKY:** They then broke up their relationship. So that may have been an important factor affecting her emotional condition, may it not?

A. It's a factor that has been taken into account.

Q. And since it was not given, you would not have the opportunity to evaluate it?

A. That is true.

Q. Similarly, as to the whole history of 1986, when she had apparently two abortions, one induced, and then had persistent medical problems thereafter. Those were all matters that would reasonably be—

MR. N: Until—

Q. BY MR. LASKY: And into January of 1987 they would all be—weren't expected to affect her emotional condition?

MR. N: As of a year later, is that your question?

Q. BY MR. LASKY: Well, we're talking she started working for ___________ in April of '87. Well, that's my question. Couldn't those events have an effect on her emotional condition?

A. Yes. They certainly could have a bearing on her condition, yes.

MR. N: I think Dr. ___________ in response to one of your questions, he couldn't recall if he had reviewed Miss or Dr. ___________'s evaluation. And he says that he did make checkmarks on the February 5, 1988 report from Dr. ___________ and that it refreshes his recollection that he did in fact review it; is that correct?

THE WITNESS: True.

MR. LASKY: Now, the one that he reviewed did not contain the material that he—

MR. N: That's correct.

THE WITNESS: Yeah.

Q. BY MR. LASKY: Now, in her permanent stationary report of September 22nd, 1988, you arrive at a conclusion that she had a mental disorder, mainly major depression, and that her experience at ___________ was the cause. In light of the information which has now been brought to your attention which has not been previously brought to our attention, are you able to say at the present time with a reasonable medical probability that you would have the same opinion?

A. That she was depressed or what was the cause?

Q. What was the cause of her condition?

A. The opinion would be that, in light of the new material, that it would have a medical apportionment to point out to the preexisting nonindustrial factors that could have played a role, passive or active, in her mental state. But the diagnosis of depression stands unchanged because it's also corroborated by Dr. ___________'s psychological testing report that I have a reviewed, dated February 5, 1988, as well.

Q. Aside from the diagnosis and just focusing on the causation issue, wouldn't it be correct to state that at the present time, you don't have sufficient data to arrive at the conclusion that there was industrial causation?

A. Not when I did have the—didn't have the previous medical background that you have provided.

Q. That's a correct statement?

A. Yes, it is.

MR. LASKY: I have no further questions.

MR. N: No questions.

MR. LASKY: Off the record.

(A discussion was held off the record.)

We will stipulate that the court reporter may be relieved of her statutory responsibility under Section 2025 of the Code of Civil Procedure—off the record.

(A discussion was held off the record.)

§ 15.3 Deposition of Dr. Resistant

The claimant in this case was a bank manager who was terminated because his negligent oversight had permitted an employee to embezzle funds. He claimed that previously he had been unfairly criticized over a period of time by his supervisor and that this had caused him to have a nervous stomach, among other things. By the time the deposition was taken, the claimant had been employed by another bank in the same capacity, had good performance ratings, and said he liked his work. The deponent doctor had given the claimant a work limitation that included avoidance of stress and heavy work.

The purpose of the deposition was to show that the doctor had not elicited enough information about what was stressful for the claimant to give him such a work limitation, and that the prophylactic restriction against stress was not justified by the finding of psychophysiologic cardiovascular condition. The doctor also demonstrated the cursory nature of his investigation of the stress issue and the flimsy basis for his prophylactic restriction against stress.

Q. **BY MR. LASKY:** When the irritable bowel syndrome is lighted up, how does it manifest itself on a chronic basis?

A. The psychophysiological gastrointestinal reaction, the irritable bowel syndrome, is a functional condition of the large bowel without any underlying organic disease in which the normal activity of the large bowel is exaggerated or distorted so that the individual suffers typically from crampy abdominal pain, usually crampy lower abdominal pain, diarrhea, which may be bloody or mucousy, and/or constipation. Additional symptoms of abdominal bloating and excessive gas are somewhat common.

Now, the syndrome, once lighted up, tends to have the same chronic, same intermittent and same chronic symptoms on an intermittent basis; that is, crampy lower abdominal pain, diarrhea and constipation.

Q. In the case of Mr. ___________, when did you last see Mr. ___________?

A. I think I saw—I don't think I've seen Mr. ___________ since January of '87.

Q. In the last report I saw, it was dated January 7th.

A. That would be it.

Q. As to your prognosis, at that time what would you expect—what symptoms would you expect him to display?

A. In regard to his irritable bowel syndrome?

Q. Yes.

A. I would anticipate in the future, that is, added to that examination, he would have on an intermittent basis recurrent crampy lower abdominal pain which may be severe, alternating diarrhea and/or constipation as well as bloating, excessive gas and so on. The pain in these cases can be severe.

In 1976, which is the most recent year, I was able to find the figures. Mendeloff reported about 85 thousand hospital admissions with the first diagnosis of irritable bowel syndrome and about the same number with the second diagnosis so that clearly it—I mean, while the irritable bowel syndrome doesn't usually require hospitalization, it clearly may be associated with severe abdominal pain. So I would anticipate that he would have those symptoms—pain, diarrhea and/or constipation—on a recurrent basis.

Q. How frequently would you expect that to happen?

A. I would anticipate that the frequency would be related a great deal to his stress at that time. For example, at that particular time when I initially saw Mr. ________, he indicated he went to work for another company, ____________, and he missed a lot of days there and had poor health and he—I would anticipate that the frequency of the symptoms would be related to his level—his environment and his level of stress. I mean, I couldn't predict exactly how often, but based on the literature, the symptoms recur a significant amount of time and cause significant pain and disability to miss days from work, but I couldn't predict exactly.

Q. Well, do you predict that for the rest of his life?

A. Yes.

Q. So you expect that for the rest of his life, he would miss considerable number of days from work?

A. Yes. He would certainly for the rest of his life have that potential if exposed to significant stress.

Q. What do you call significant stress as far as Mr. ____________ is concerned?

A. As we discussed initially, it would be really what Mr. ____________ considers significant stress; that is, more stress than he can deal with. We don't have any good yardsticks for stress, any good quantitation (sic) for stress. It's really a very subjective matter. It's in the eye of the beholder, and it's simply more than he could deal with. Just enough to upset his balance.

Q. Well, now, you stated in your report something to the effect he should be working in an atmosphere completely free of emotional stress. When you use the term "emotional stress" there, is that incorporating what you just said in terms of significant stress?

To give you what I'm driving at, if we take that in its dictionary sense, I don't think you can do anything. Did you mean that—do you know of any occupations where there's no emotional stress?

A. No. But he must endeavor to work in an atmosphere as free as possible from stress insofar as that's possible.

Q. Well, your first report in which you took a history from him recounts the fact that his job responsibilities involve helping customers, counseling them about investments, dealing with irate customers. He had a supervisory staff of 25.

Do you think in your opinion, having lighted up his condition, do you think he can engage in such an occupation again?

A. I don't recall—

Q. Do you want to refresh your recollection?

A. I recall what his job duties were; I don't recall asking Mr. ____________ if he thought he could do that work in another company or not. I don't recall asking him or if I did what his reply was. But I would say in all probability that that sort of work probably has become too stressful for him.

Q. So you don't think he should return to the same occupation?

A. Well, again, I regret not having discussed that with him, but I would say probably not, that it would probably be more stress than he could handle.

Q. Are you able to describe what—well, you know what we're always concerned with is the earning capacity. The whole rating system reduces itself to that. While that's not your precise expertise, it's treatment-related to his physical capacities.

Are you able to list the types of occupations you think would be appropriate for him?

A. Well, you know, I only saw Mr. ___________ on two occasions and I reviewed a small amount of records from ___________, and it would really be speculation on my part. I would just have to really more or less leave that up to him insofar as what I would perceive as stressful or not.

Q. And you don't know what he perceives as stressful?

A. Other than—I believe that probably because of what happened to him, he would perceive doing what he did at ___________ as stressful. But in addition to that, I'm not really sure. I mean, I could guess, but that's all it would be. He could, for example, have problems in the future in dealing with the public in any capacity since he had problems with customers and so on, as you pointed out, at ___________, but I'm not sure.

Q. Now, turning to the psychophysiological cardiovascular condition for a minute. You gave Mr. ___________ a complete series of tests, did you not, to determine what the state of his cardiovascular system was?

A. Yes.

Q. And would it be fair to characterize the results of those as normal?

A. Yes.

Q. The few items that mean something to me are I notice pulse rate and blood pressure, both of which appear to be normal.

A. I put Mr. ___________ through a fairly complete cardiac workup. He, in addition to the EKG and chest x-ray and exercise test here, he had a maximum exercise treadmill test and an electrocardiogram, which were all normal, which is of course typical of the syndrome. It's an interesting problem.

Q. So did you in effect arrive at your diagnosis on an exclusionary basis? I mean having ruled out—

A. Well, the psychophysiological cardiovascular reaction by definition is a syndrome which involves primarily respiratory symptoms, shortness of breath, chest pain and nervous symptoms, anxiety in the absence of other explainable pathology and is thought to be mediated again through the autonomic nervous system. So before we can make that diagnosis, we must exclude other organic pathology of the heart.

It's an interesting problem. Califf, who we referred to earlier, Califf's work really duplicated work which was done much earlier by Wheeler. This syndrome has been known by a number of names over the years, "Soldier's Heart" and other names, which aren't really important, but it's been really extensively studied, and Wheeler in the fifties I think published a study with about 80 references and he studied several hundred individuals with this syndrome and found really similar results to Califf; that is, in Wheeler's study about half—I'm sorry. In Wheeler's study about a sixth of those with the syndrome, despite a lack of any apparent objective problems, never went back to work. I mean, they were permanently and totally disabled.

One of Califf's points is how disappointing it was for the doctors in his study to do these angiograms which of course are not benign studies. They carry a certain risk and certain expense and so on to do the angiograms. And then to try to reassure the patients, "Now, look. Everything seems okay. Your heart seems okay. You're not probably going to have a heart attack or a stroke and you're probably going to be fine," well, while this seemed to clear the air in the physician's mind, it didn't help the patients or it didn't help the significant number of patients. And despite the lack of significant objective problems that we can find at this point in time, these people don't do well. They have a poor prognosis. It may be surprising, but it seems to be borne out by the literature.

Q. I had one detailed question. Under the symptoms or signs of it, you mentioned difficulty breathing, chest pain and what else?

A. Anxiety.

Q. Well, in this case dealing with Mr. ____________, your whole basis for arriving at that diagnosis, then, was history, wasn't it?

A. Well, of course the history is a very important part of any internal medicine examination. The history combined with the examination and all of the additional studies which were negative.

Q. What I'm getting at is this: Why didn't you conclude that he had no heart problem?

A. Well, his chest pain wouldn't go away. If I did that—I mean, he tried to deal with the problems before us and his symptoms, his constellation of symptoms—chest pain, anxiety, and shortness of breath—really were very typical of this syndrome, but before we make the diagnosis, I mean, we certainly don't want to exclude—we certainly don't want to miss some organic heart problem; so these patients need to be worked—

Q. He didn't have anxiety when he was talking to you, did he?

A. No, but he didn't have chest pain either at the time.

Q. So my question was: Therefore, you based your entire diagnosis on the way he told you he had felt in the past?

A. Well, I based it on my diagnosis.

Q. You ruled out an organic basis for what he described?

A. I ruled out organic basis and I reviewed the medical file, which in this case was remarkably consistent with the patient's history, his ____________ records.

Q. How do you differentiate chest pains? I mean, with the information given to you with this patient, how do you differentiate chest pains from pains due to the irritable bowel syndrome? I mean, how do you know it wasn't gas?

A. Well, typically the pain associated with the irritable bowel syndrome is in the lower abdomen and Mr. ____________ described substernal chest pain.

Now, how do I know it wasn't related to his gastroesophageal reflex?

Q. That's the next question.

A. That's the next question. That's an interesting question. I don't. As I mentioned before, one area of speculation in Califf's report is that in fact maybe some of these people have angiographically normal amounts of chest pain from gastrointestinal problems, specifically esophageal problems, and, in fact, there seems to be accumulating a body of literature which indicates that in fact individuals may develop chest pain associated with the gastroesophageal reflex.

This pain can be severe and disabling and usually lifelong and so far is amenable to treatment.

There's a recent report in the literature in the Lancet by Van Trampen and he describes a series of individuals with chest pain with normal cardiac exams and pain probably secondary to spasm of the esophagus and/or gastroesophageal reflex. Most of these individuals, once the syndrome was lighted up, had chronic intermittent problems which were severe and really unresponsive to therapy. So I don't see that it changes his prognosis.

It's really, I figure, a question of etiology. I mean, it's interesting to speculate, but it doesn't really—I mean, if we could prove it's from his esophagus, it's really not—it doesn't seem to be associated with less disabling pain and at this point in time, there's not anything we can do about it to treat it. There is, though, effective medication or treatment, so it's—we may—which may say in certain cases that chest pain is esophageal in origin, but these patients still have chronic relapses of chest pain with not much benefit from any medication or other treatment. It doesn't improve their prognosis any.

Q. Well, now, you put certain restrictions on him because of the psychophysiological cardiovascular condition, didn't you?

A. Yes.

Q. And for the purpose of my inquiry, I'm trying to do it systematically so that we—I don't want to talk about the esophageal aspect of it unless it can't be differentiated, but I mean, just thinking in terms of the psychophysiological cardiovascular condition, what were your restrictions?

My question—I'll go ahead of that. My question is: Why restrict him at all? What's going to happen if he goes ahead and does whatever you said he shouldn't do?

A. Well, as far as the psychophysiological cardiovascular reaction, I restricted him to no stress and no very heavy work.

Q. Well, seeing that it's all in his head, what's going to happen if he doesn't?

A. Well, pain. If his chest pain is cardiac, the main problem is pain which of course can be disabling. Most studies, studies that I've quoted, Wheeler and Califf, indicate that the most commonly aggravating factors in this condition are stress and heavy physical work.

Now, interestingly in the fourth edition of Hurst, which is H-u-r-s-t, which is a standard textbook of cardiology—I think now we're up to the 6th edition—but in the fourth edition in the discussion of this problem, the author also noted, who might have even been Wheeler, but the author of the textbook chapter also noted that stress and heavy physical work activities aggravate this problem and the problem results in severe disabling chest pain.

Q. Well, wouldn't it be preferable from Mr. ___________'s standpoint for him to try to engage in whatever kind of an occupation he thought desirable? I mean, because if he gets severe pain, that's all that's going to happen to him, but then he can quit. But you don't know what's going to give him some severe pain.

He doesn't risk a heart attack, does he?

A. There is in this population, there is a slight but not really significant increase in sudden cardiac event. But pain, you know, it's not a rational—it's not a problem that usually is amenable to a rational approach. If you have severe pain, it's hard to work.

As far as his occupation, I think that he should do, you know, what appeals to him, and certainly that would seem to me that he wouldn't pick something out that he would think he would have a hard time in and the risk is that of stress on the job. If he has stress, he's going to have pain.

Q. I'm just now thinking about that—

A. And whether I know or not and you know or not that he's probably not going to have a heart attack, it's just like in Califf's study: For whatever reason, people with this syndrome, they don't do well. Half those people couldn't get through the daily activities of living, just brushing their teeth—you know exactly what I'm talking about—without chest pain. They're functionally incapacitated.

Q. Suppose he was doing very heavy work that he liked doing that wasn't stressful?

A. Well, I would advise him he could do it, but I would advise him against it because heavy work activities are known to aggravate this syndrome.

Now, he may be out there digging ditches, or I don't know what he's doing today, but he shouldn't be.

Q. You mean even if he was happy with it?

A. Well, he's running a risk. I mean, he can do what he wants and patients frequently do.

§ 15.4 Deposition of Dr. Flexible

This case primarily involved issues of apportionment between successive carriers, causation, the role of history in a psychiatrist's opinion, and an interesting distinction between the psychological effect of termination and the effect of the loss of income due to being unemployed.

Some years before, the claimant had sustained a myocardial infarction and had returned to work for the same employer. The author represented the carrier on the risk in the last year of employment. The claimant was terminated, according to the employer, for insubordination. The medical records showed he had serious marital problems that had not been disclosed to his medical-legal consultants. Disclosure of the marital problems at the deposition caused a change in the apportionment.

The doctor also opined that the termination was less important in affecting disability than the income loss and that the termination probably merely had a temporary effect. The distinctions were important because the jurisdiction held that mere termination could be a sufficient basis for finding industrial causation of a disability.

The doctor also stated that the dysthymic disorder was not work disabling, illustrating the importance for the examiner of knowing the DSM-III-R categories. Summary of first part of deposition:

1. Reasons why not major depression but merely dysthymic disorder
2. The former heart condition and its contribution to the disability

3. Effect of new supervisor
4. Difference between concern about out of work and concern about being fired.

Q. Are you saying that you found that he had the required elements of a major depression before 1981?
A. No. I'm saying that he never had the criteria for a Dysthymic Disorder.
Q. We're beginning to understand it. Okay. What you mean is that he commenced this condition of Dysthymic Disorder in about 1981 as far as you could determine?
A. That's correct.
Q. Now, what was it about his condition at that time that made you decide he had a Dysthymic Disorder as distinguished from major depression?
A. Dysthymic Disorder is less severe. It's partly—it's a matter of judgment, but on clinical presentation as well as maybe the psychological testing, he was not as slowed down as a major depression would usually indicate or alternately as agitated as might be the case, and the second significant thing is that he was not suicidal. If he had been suicidal, it may have made me think more of major depression.
Q. Do you think that it affected his work performance from 1981 on?
A. Not that I could determine.
Q. When would you say was the onset of the disabling condition?
A. After the myocardial infarction in May of 1983.
Q. At that point is it your opinion that there were elements of disability in a work sense—
A. Yes.
Q. —even though he was continuing to work? I'm not saying that this is not necessarily inconsistent. I just want to know what you mean. In other words, was his work performance impaired after the infarct of 1983?
A. Yes, it was.
Q. Okay. So you feel that was the result of the infarct?
A. Well, I don't want to comment on his cardiovascular exam since I've not examined him for that, but psychiatrically, it's my opinion he began his emotional disability coinciding with his myocardial infarct.
Q. In your opinion, was that a reaction to his myocardial infarct?
A. Partly, yes.
Q. What were the other parts? You said "partly," so what was the remaining part?
A. He returned to work fairly early. He felt he was put under pressure right again. He indicated to me that he returned to work after approximately four weeks after his heart problems, and if he didn't, he felt or perceived at least that he was going to be fired. When he returned to work, he was under a lot of pressure at work again. He was afraid that he'd have another heart problem, and there was no way for him to escape this. In addition to that, there was increasing pressure from a coworker who was promoted over him. A fellow that I believe is called ____________ who was putting pressure on him, and Mr. ____________ felt he was trying to get him fired, and finally Mr. ____________ felt he did get him fired.

Q. Do you know where the pressure with ___________ started?
A. When he was promoted, and I—the dates are a little bit difficult to determine exactly, but the main pressure with that was following the myocardial infarct. As far as ___________ was concerned, he may have been promoted as early as '85.
Q. Was it your understanding that ___________ was promoted so that he was above, that he was in a supervisory relationship to the Applicant?
A. He was over Mr. ___________, yes. Prior to that he was a coworker.
Q. So—
A. At the same level.
Q. So you feel that the psychological pressure became a factor when ___________ became his boss?
A. That was one of the things, yes.
Q. What else?
A. I mentioned his fear of having another heart attack.
Q. Yes.
A. The hours and so on he was working. The responsibilities of his work. I think all those things were determined.
MR. LASKY: Off the record.

(A discussion was held off the record.)

MR. LASKY: Let's go back on the record.
Q. You stated, Doctor, while we were off the record, that ___________ became his supervisor sometime early in 1986; is that correct?
A. That's what Mr. ___________ indicated to me.
Q. That's what the Applicant told you?
A. Yes. As a stress, also, I don't know if I mentioned, I should have mentioned the fact that he was fired in July of '86 and out of work following that. There were certainly pressures upon that.
Q. Now, going back to the period preceding becoming his boss—I'll have one division to make this less mystifying to you as to what I'm getting at is between ___________ and me there's a dispute since our clients have different interests. We have the latter period, and he has the earlier period; so it's important for us to try to identify as much as possible an allocation of such things as apportionment and that sort of thing.

Going back to the period preceding ___________ becoming a supervisor, I believe you previously stated that sometime in that period after the infarct the Applicant was actually disabled, had a degree of disability for psychological reasons; is that correct?
A. That's correct.
Q. Could you give us an estimate for purposes of apportionment?
A. I'm sorry. Of what period of time are you referring to?
Q. Well, in part that depends on what you think, but as of when the time he returned to work after the infarct in 1983, is it your opinion that he at that time had a degree of disability for psychological reasons?
A. Yes.
Q. Could you give us an estimate of what that would amount to for apportionment purposes?

A. Yeah. And let me indicate to you this is based upon current evidence that I have at hand.

Q. Right.

A. It would be my opinion.

Q. If you want to specify the evidence, please do.

A. Well, the evidence is from his history only. I want to point out to you that I have not reviewed other medical records, okay? So it's based upon the psychological testing and the history that he gave me.

Q. So incidentally it might be helpful to you—well, we'll see that I can maybe be able to make the relevant records available. I have some records. I don't know if there's everything you consider relevant, but what is your opinion at the present time based on what he told you?

A. My opinion would be that at the time he returned to work after the incident of May 1983, he had approximately 30 to 40 percent of his current emotional disability, and then following that next period of time, from June of '83 to July 14 of '86, the rest of the disability was produced.

Q. You've mentioned that he was concerned about keeping up with the demands of the job, and that he had problems with the new supervisor. Now, you also, of course, mentioned the previous concern of returning to work after the infarct.

A. Yes.

Q. You've already given us your estimate on the infarct so are other remaining—and I haven't gotten to the firing yet—or only stress factors are his concerns about keeping up with the demands of the jobs and problems with the supervisor. Now, since we can pin down the new supervisor's arrival, would you say there was any additional disability that developed after this 30 to 40 percent development but before the new supervisor arrived? Do you understand my question?

A. Yes, I understand what you mean. I don't know how to divide that up accurately. I have reasons for making the other division that I mentioned, but it's difficult—

Q. Okay.

A. —for me to know that exactly. I can explain some of the factors that are involved in the conversation.

Q. All right.

A. He returned to work sooner than he wanted to, number one. He had the usual pressures of the job which are more difficult for him to handle, not only because of his heart conditions, but also because of his back problems. He was concerned about holding onto his job as much as possible, and stresses that he worked under before became much harder for him to bear even before ____________ came along and became a supervisor. But when ____________ became a supervisor, that became much worse. I don't know how to divide those two things up accurately. Those are the factors.

Q. And then you considered the fact of the firing itself to be a substantial additional factor?

A. An additional factor, yes.

Q. Can you attribute a percentage, approximately, to the additional factor of the firing, just the firing, assuming he hadn't been fired and was still there?

A. When you're talking about him being fired, do you include that as being out of work as well? Because it's a separate factor.
Q. Being fired and being—I think that, again, they have to go together because, if I said he was fired and then got a job a week later, would you think he would have had any additional disability?
A. The reason I bring that up because I've been involved as an A.M.E. here. That is the issue separated from being out of work as from being fired.
Q. Can you make such a separation?
A. Yes. Sometimes you can.
Q. Then we want you to tell us.
A. This man was temporarily upset about being fired. It was a shock to him. He was trying to hold onto his job. He felt that he was threatened to be fired by ____________ when he became a supervisor. He was trying to work the best he could. He was simply shocked and upset by it. When I saw him the several times that I did, he was not continuing to be angry and upset at ____________ specifically, nor did he have major defects in his ability to deal with people.
If somebody has an incident like that where you're involved in a work situation and someone fires you, you're not only angry at that person. You can be angry at other people as well. That was in the continuing fear. It's not so much of a concern about his being fired which was a temporarily upset. What was more of a concern to him was the longer term being out of work because this is a man who very much valued his long work relationship with ____________ and his ability to work and support himself. So being fired was a temporarily upset and concern. Being out of work was more of a concern.
Q. Taking the two events together, what can you give us as an estimated proportion of his disability that you would attribute to that?
A. You mean his overall disability related to his being fired?
Q. Yes. Let's see. What did you find?
A. Well, let's say an overall degree of disability from slight to moderate, and you've already taken 30 to 40 percent and attributed it there.
Q. What is the percentage of the remainder? Let's not get mixed up with percentages, but what portion of the remainder would you attribute to the combination of being fired and being out of a job?
A. I would say of the total overall disability here approximately 25 to 30 percent I would give to his combination of his being fired and being out of work.

Summary of second part of deposition:

1. Role of history in diagnosing causation, mental disorder
2. Lesser significance of claimant's complaints
3. Timing significant for causation
4. New information about marital problems—effect.

Q. Okay.
A. So the history is important, very important in making the diagnosis of mental disorder. As far as causation is concerned, that's somewhat different because I think we're vectoring now on more medical-legal terms rather than strictly

medical terms. It's very important, I think, to have as accurate history as possible because you can be easily misled from what a patient tells you if you base just your conclusions upon the history. The timing of events, for example, is important in determining the causation. As an example, if somebody claims to be under emotional stress while at work and they have problems with their supervisor and they say they're nervously depressed as far as they are aware beginning before they left work, that's different than somebody that was not nervous and depressed while they were at work but only after they are fired because they were caught stealing. You're dealing with a different matter as far as causation is concerned as far as medical purposes.

As far as the rating of emotional disability, it is somewhat important. One of several factors that are important. Subjective complaints are important because in my opinion are probably less reliable for example than mental status observations, psychological testing. As far as apportionment is concerned again, I think, although I believe I understand to some degree the difference between causation and apportionment of emotional disability, the history is quite important in the issues of apportionment as well.

Q. Did the Applicant give you any information about how he got along with his supervisor preceding (new supervisor)?

A. He didn't specifically mention that.

Q. Now, assume that the evidence would show that the supervisor was a friend of his, his former supervisor was a friend of his, and gave him very good performance ratings. This was a company where there were yearly performance ratings. Would that be consistent with your picture of the Applicant's work experience from let's say, from 1983 to 1986?

A. Yes.

Q. Why do you say that?

A. Because he didn't complain specifically to me or indicate to me the history that his difficulties with management were really significant until (new supervisor).

Q. Would you consider it important, assuming he was getting consideration, that he was getting regular medical checkups for his cardiovascular condition, if during the period from the time he returned to work after the infarct up to the time, let's say, that ____________ came in, the frequency of the visits lessened and there weren't any complaints, well, if for about two years prior to that he was only seeing his doctor once every six months—

A. Significant as far as what is concerned?

Q. To whether he was undergoing stress.

A. Perhaps that would be one consideration.

Q. Did you discuss with him whether there were any non-industrial factors that affected his emotional health during this period, let's say, from 1983 to 1986?

A. I took a detailed history, yes.

Q. Well, specifically directing your attention to his relationship, his marital status.

A. Yes.

Q. I gather you concluded that his marital status had no effect on his emotional condition at the time you examined him?

A. According to the history he gave me and his emotional reaction while he was talking about this, there was little other than a temporary effect, no long-lasting ones.

Q. I think you would agree that his relations with the spouse could be extremely important from an emotional standpoint?
A. I think to anybody they could, sure.
Q. This is not a remarkable new discovery?
A. I'm afraid not.
Q. Before I go on with that, did you get any picture from him as to whether he liked his job before the new supervisor came on?
A. Basically he did. And he wanted to continue working there. His like of the job—his like for the job changed to some degree, however, when in about 1980 or '81 they forced him to be a manager in his perception as opposed to his subleasing a lot. I believe the current history that he gave me he was more kind of like an owner subleasor, and he forced him out of that.
Q. They made him in effect an employee?
A. Employee-manager. Put him under pressure, and that's where the problems began.
Q. You say that was less pressure than being an owner?
A. It was more pressure.
Q. I mean, it was more pressure than being an owner?
A. Yeah.
Q. Physically or mentally or both?
A. I can only talk about mentally here, certainly there was.
Q. Now, I'm looking at your September 5, 1987 report.
A. Okay.
Q. Which I'm looking at at page 4. I'm looking at the very bottom of the page:

> "He was married for the first time about ten years and separated and divorced when he was age 35 apparently because his wife stayed in ____________. He has no children from that first marriage. He has no children from the second marriage which lasted two years, and he was separated and divorced from that marriage in 1982 about one year before his heart attack. He is not sure of the reasons for the breakup of that marriage."

Was it your understanding that he had a second marriage to a different woman?
A. Yes. That was implied.
Q. All right. Well, I have there is information—you haven't seen any other medical records; is that right?
A. No, I haven't except for the psychological testing.
Q. Yes. Right.

So apparently according to these, I'm going to give you the records, and I've got Dr. ____________'s report here which is, in effect, what I'm getting at is according to other medical records, he remarried his first wife, and they lived together in this country, and in June of 1986 he reported to his treating doctor that she had left him a second time, and he was extremely depressed and wanted to die. I'm going to show you those records.

MR. ______: Okay.
THE WITNESS: Okay.

(Remarks off the record.)

Q. **BY MR. LASKY:** You're going to find that Dr. __________ was the treating doctor, and I have paper-clipped the particular reference there. That's the area that those progress notes were what I thought particularly relevant, okay?

A. Okay.

Q. All right. Does that affect your opinion with regard to any of the matters, you know, that you previously discussed?

A. Yes. It does suggest that his marital problems were more significant than he had indicated to me in part of history.

Q. Considering in June, whatever that date is, he's making that statement to Dr. __________, and in July of '86, he's fired, wouldn't you say that combination of being fired and his wife having left him would be the reason for thinking that, attributing a much greater percentage proportion of his disability to those events than you previously estimated, not knowing about what he had said?

A. Yes, I would agree with that.

Q. In the light of that, could you give me an estimate—I don't know if it's possible—could you differentiate the effect of his wife leaving him from the effect of the firing, if you can give me your opinion?

A. It would be pretty difficult to do because some of the history that's suggested here is somewhat different than what he gave to me.

Taking this history as being accurate and true, I have no reason to believe that he was not—he was separated from his wife of 20 years that is different from the ten years that he indicated to me, and being divorced from somebody he'd been married to for a couple years and that having occurred a year before the heart attack, is a lot different than being separated from a wife, a separation of two years of marriage with your wife as to the situation of being separated from a wife of 20 years and then one month later fired would raise the significance of marital problems quite substantially. And he was obviously clinically depressed according to the physician's note of June '86 of him hoping to die. So I think that's pretty significant depression at that point.

Q. If you want to take a little time, it may not be fair to give me an answer in three seconds.

A. You want me to base this just upon the records that I have here?

Q. Well, that's just, you know, if you're attempting—incidentally __________, you can look at his report which in effect confirms the statement about having his wife leaving him. I think he says it here in February of 1986. You can look at it.

A. Okay. Let me see if there's a reference which might help us. Do you want me to read the whole report or some specific part?

Q. Whatever you want. I'll just share this, cooperating. He essentially said, Dr. __________, what Dr. __________ says he said to him. Yeah. Well, on page 4 here, at the top?

A. Okay. Thank you.

Well, these notes are somewhat helpful in that they're slightly different than the other notes in the fact that they add that this stress had been going on for some time. Well, these particular notes indicate that his wife ran away which he says occurred in February of '86. He had been married for 20 years. Prior to the heart attack in 1983, he tried to apparently go back to __________. So the problems from preceding as well as stemming over a period of time 20 years maybe.

I would think that would be really quite significant. I would think of the overall disability based upon the additional records you've presented to me, that approximately 30 to 40 percent of his overall disability would be attributed to that.

MR. ______: To the marital discord?

THE WITNESS: To the marital discord, yes. That's quite significant. It's quite different than the history I had previously.

Q. BY MR. LASKY: Obviously. You note Dr. ____________ said that he said that she ran away in February; then he told Dr. ____________ that he had gone back to ____________. His wife had left, and he had gone back to ____________, which kind of suggests that he went back to try to get her.

A. Yes, that's what is implied in the notes of Dr. ____________. The first note that you presented to me actually just indicated he was depressed in June of '86. This note—I'm glad you indicated that to me—has this going on over a period of time; so I think that's more significant.

MR. LASKY: I don't have any other questions.

§ 15.5 Deposition of Dr. Didn't Think We Knew It

This deposition demonstrates in particular the value of understanding the general principles of psychological testing, what the tests test, and what the scores mean. It again shows the utility of knowing DSM-III-R classifications and how the diagnostic criteria can be used as a standard for testing the doctor's diagnosis against the evidence in the case.

Plaintiff had an admitted serious knee injury due to a defectively manufactured product. His treatment for the knee had not yet been completed because he was planning to undergo further surgery. At the time of the deposition, he had already been diagnosed by the deponent psychiatrist as having a slight to moderate permanent disability due to major depression.

In the questioning, the doctor conceded that the psychological testing did not support her diagnosis. She also exhibited a very sketchy basis for her disability evaluation. This was shown by her failure to distinguish the effects of pain during the convalescent period from the allegedly permanent injury to the psyche and by her failure to inquire fully into the nature of plaintiff's new employment.

Q. Dr. ____________, I'm Herbert Lasky, and I am an attorney representing the intervenor, which—consider this a piece of a three-cornered litigation. So that I have some interest in common with the plaintiff and other interests not in common with the plaintiff. And I have some interests in common with the defense and other interests not in common with the defense.

Now, I assume that there has been no impairment of your memory for recent events, so I won't repeat all of the instructions about what the rules for a deposition are like. I assume that you remember those?

A. I do.
Q. Why did you perform psychological testing?
A. I performed psychological testing as an additional means of collecting data and information about a client so that there are—it's part of the information that I gather in terms of being able to assess someone and render opinions regarding their condition.
Q. Then would it be correct to say it played a role in forming your opinion?
A. That's correct.
Q. Now, isn't it correct to say that essentially the psychological testing revealed that he had a normal psychological condition?
A. The psychological testing indicated that he had a common concern about somatic complaints and a report of a large number of complaints, so there was a—that was something that bothered him a great deal. The testing for anxiety that—the IPAT anxiety scores were essentially within normal limits on both occasions. The Beck depression inventory score at first was in the normal range and upon second testing indicated a mild degree of depression.
Q. When you use the term "mild," can you explain that further? What does it mean in terms of how the person behaves?
A. Well, depression would be made up of a number of different symptoms. Patients can be experiencing fewer or greater number of these symptoms; for example, sleep disturbance, feelings of worthlessness, depressed mood, loss of pleasure in various activities. They can be experiencing them with different frequency. And so a mild level of depression would indicate fewer of these symptoms on a not-as-frequent basis as somebody who had a severe depression.
Q. Well, would you say that the average member of the population does not have mild depression from time to time?
A. Following deaths and—and other life circumstances, I think it's normal to—to feel depressed. In general, according to test criteria, if you were administering the—this particular test to a population, most people would be scoring within the normal range.
Q. You're saying this is slightly above the normal range?
A. Slightly above normal.
Q. Now, turning your attention to the MMPI, the score on the depression scale, there is an inconsistency with the Beck, isn't there?
A. That would be correct.
Q. And what is the difference in the nature of the questions on the MMPI which are used to determine the existence of clinical levels of depression as compared with the Beck questions?
A. The MMPI is a test that's empirically derived, so it was based on—the test questions are based on responses from a group of patients from a psychiatric population, patients who had a diagnosis of depression. And the test scale for depression is—takes the questions that that population answered in a—in a particular fashion so—
Q. The MMPI questions are designed, are they not, to be used in such a manner that they don't suggest the effect of the answer to the person who's taking the test?
A. That's correct. The—the Beck questions are more obvious.

Q. Now, you had different Axis I diagnoses after the latest examination, did you not?
A. That's correct.
Q. What is the difference between the criteria for an anxiety disorder not otherwise specified and the DSM-III major depression?
A. Excuse me. The question is what's the difference in criteria—
Q. Yes.
A. —between anxiety disorders and major depression?
Q. No, no. You have—
A. Between depressive disorders?
Q. Between depressive disorder not otherwise specified and major depression?
A. The criteria for major depression would be what the patients are experiencing, the depressive symptoms on a more frequent basis, on a more intense basis. The—and the depressive symptoms, again, would be things like depressed mood, loss of pleasure in various activities, sleep disturbance, concentration problems, feelings of worthlessness, and that kind of thing. The criteria for depressive disorder not otherwise specified would be prominent depressive symptoms that did not meet the criteria for any other mood disturbance, including depress—including, rather, major depression.
Q. So what was missing with regard to Mr. ___________ in terms of the major depression diagnosis?
A. Mr. ___________—the—was not—was not feeling a lot of subjective distress from—from the depression. He did not—he reported some symptoms indicating depressed mood, including symptoms of emptiness, agitation, a sense of loss. But these—and he reported feelings of worthlessness, difficulty concentrating, and sleep disturbances. Some of the other criteria he would not display on a frequent ongoing basis.
Q. Now, actually, the only score on the MMPI above the normal level is the hypochondriasis scores; isn't that correct?
A. That's correct.
Q. Incidentally, how did you—when you say you used the computer to score it, did you use the computer that had a program so that it gave you a computer-generated score?
A. It gave me a computer-generated score. I don't use the computer for interpretation.
Q. Well, now, the original population—or the population that's the basis for the MMPI scoring is not one that includes people who have had serious knee problems, is it?
A. It would be—the original population would include—it's a different scale. It's—and the MMPI were derived from different population groups. And so there were a number of—of patients for the depression scale. They would include depressive patients. Whether or not they had other health problems, I don't know. The main criteria for including them in the—in the group was on the basis of depression or on the basis of meeting a diagnosis for some of the other scales.
Q. Well, isn't it a general caveat in the terms of the MMPI that the context of the person's life has to be taken into account in assessing its significance?

A. Oh, absolutely. I think that you have to do that with—with the MMPI and with other test results. You have to consider all the information.

Q. The idea being if—you're saying that somebody's very worried about the condition of his knee and the fact that he can't do things he used to be able to do, that would be significant if there was nothing particularly wrong with his knee, correct?

A. Excuse me. Can you repeat the question?

MR. LASKY: Would you repeat the question, please.

(The last question was read back by the reporter.)

THE WITNESS: That would be clinically significant if he were worried about a condition that—that wasn't there.

Q. **BY MR. LASKY:** Now, in this instance the patient in question has very rational grounds for being worried about the condition of his knee, doesn't he?

A. It would seem so from the orthopedic records and his report of injury that there are substantial back, neck, and knee problems.

Q. So that under those circumstances it would not be correct to use the hypochondriasis score as an indication of psychic abnormality; isn't that correct?

A. I think you have to be careful in using the score. Mostly, it's referred to as Scale 1. So we've really gotten away from using the term hypochondriasis because I think that that implies in lay terms something that—a physical condition that has no organic base. So that it's not—it's not unusual that somebody with Mr. ___________'s physical problems is displaying prominent concern about his body functioning.

Q. Would you say that the fact that Mr. ___________ is engaged in ongoing litigation has an effect on his mental condition?

A. I think that ongoing litigation is a stressor for people.

Q. Would you expect the level of his symptoms to diminish when the litigation is concluded?

A. I think it would depend on whether the physical condition gets worse or has stabilized. So that if the—if his physical condition continues to deteriorate, I think that his emotional condition's going to get worse regardless of whether the legal problems have resolved.

Q. And, conversely, if his physical conditions stabilize, you would expect his psychic symptoms to alleviate, would you not?

A. Or to be stabilized at this level.

Q. Well, would you say that at the present, as of the time that you drew your conclusions, you thought he had a degree of impairment from a psychological standpoint?

A. I do.

Q. And are you saying that assuming that his physical condition stabilizes, you expect him to have that same degree of impairment the rest of his life?

A. That's correct.

Q. Did you inquire of Mr. ___________ to what he does in his present job?

A. Yes. He schedules appearances for radio shows and does some—some degree of radio engineering work, such as turning off and on microphones.

Q. You said appearances for radio shows. What does that mean?

A. I believe that he's working for a radio station that has talk shows. And so there are various guests, such as authors, and Mr. ____________ schedules these appearances.
Q. You mean schedules the appearances—he's not involved in the talk show itself?
A. That's correct.
Q. And what does scheduling the appearance involve?
A. I would expect that it would involve calling the office of the—the guest and trying to coordinate schedules in terms of whether the guest would agree to appear on the show or not and schedule a mutually convenient time for the guest to appear on the show.
Q. Do you know whether his duties have anything to do with him deciding what guests should be used?
A. I don't know.
Q. Do you know whether his duties have anything to do with his determining the scripting for these programs?
A. I don't know.
Q. And with respect to the radio engineering, what is the full extent of his duties in that respect, as far as you know?
A. When I asked him about that, he said it was things like turning off and on the microphone. Beyond that, I'm not sure what—what else would be involved.
Q. You mean he is working while the show in question is being put on, and part of his duties are in connection with seeing that the appropriate microphones are on or off, as the case may be?
A. I am not sure. He said that he had to turn on the microphone. Whether he is there on an ongoing basis during the shows or not, I'm not sure whether this is—my impression was that this is an occasional kind of task that he does and perhaps every once in a while is told to go over and turn on a particular microphone or to turn it off.
Q. Did he say whether he liked this work?
A. He said that he was happy to be working. I think that he had some mixed feelings about the—about the job, particularly about the salary that he was receiving. But he seemed very pleased that he was back at work.
Q. Did you talk to him about how he got along with the people that he worked with?
A. He seemed—he said that he was getting along fine with—with coworkers.
Q. Now, would it be fair to say that there's no impairment in his present vocational functioning?
A. Impairment can—can mean a lot of different things. I think that there is impairment in terms of his overall vocational functioning, his ability to perhaps move on from this job to find other jobs. There are the obvious orthopedic restrictions upon him. He experiences a lot of fatigue from this job. I'm not sure how he's going to do on an ongoing basis with the—with the level of fatigue, particularly with the neck and back problems that he is currently reporting.

I think that there can be—we can expect to see more difficulty with concentration, perhaps some more attendance problems. As of right now, the job duties appear to be fairly light and the job is fairly flexible. With a different kind of situation, I think that you would definitely see impairment in his occupational functioning.

Q. Now, just what type of events would you expect to cause this impairment?

A. I think the ongoing stress of working eight hours a day. Were any overtime required of him, I think that there would be problems in fulfilling those requirements. I think that if he is put into a supervisory kind of position requiring mental efficiency, flexibility, he's going to be having some problems with that, given the emotional problems and the ongoing pain problems. I think there are some workplace problems in terms of fear of reinjury and perhaps being slower and more reluctant to pitch in and get things done, so that we can expect to—to see some impairment—ongoing impairment in him.

Q. Well, then, you are relating the impairment as being a secondary effect of the physical problems; is that correct?

A. The physical problems and the emotional problems that have been an outgrowth of the physical problems.

Q. So if his physical situation improved, you would expect the emotional situation to improve, would you not?

MR. ______: You're asking for her opinion, right?

MR. LASKY: Yes.

THE WITNESS: Yeah, I would expect that if the back and neck and knee problems resolve, that he would feel a lot better emotionally.

Q. **BY MR. LASKY:** I guess as of the time that you had last examined him, he was still drinking a rather high degree of alcoholic—

A. He was drinking a lot.

Q. —beverages?

Would you characterize that as a problem?

A. I—I think that it's representative of a problem in terms of needing a criteria for—to be included in diagnosis, it doesn't do that. But that degree of alcohol use to me indicates an attempt to self-medicate in terms of—of the emotional pain problems.

Q. Did you question him at all concerning the individual answers on the Beck inventory?

A. No, I did not.

Q. Have you seen the individual answers on the Beck inventory?

A. Yes, I have.

Q. I note the answer to Question 1, he said, "I do not feel sad."

A. Yes.

Q. What significance do you attribute to that?

A. I think, in general, Mr. ____________ is a person who tends to deny emotional problems. He presents the appearance of somebody who is doing fine. There are no problems until you start to question him. More so, he—in general, his overall response stance would be to be more of a defensive position in terms of denying problems.

Q. You mean you think he has problems he doesn't admit to having?

A. I think that he's having problems with depression and anxiety that he doesn't fully recognize.

Q. What is your basis for that conclusion?

A. Based on his report of his behavior and my mental status examination.

Q. Now, the MMPI is supposed to be kind of an overall assessment of aspects of his character, isn't it?

A. It's a test of personality functioning.
Q. And, as we said before, it's not very easy for somebody to fake answers to?
A. That's correct.
Q. And, according to that, he's essentially normal if you take out the answers to Scale 1; isn't that correct?
A. That's correct. The depression scale was within normal limits on the MMPI.
Q. So you're saying that your basis for the conclusion that he has these emotional problems is really based solely on terms of what he's told you himself?
A. That's correct, about his behavior, things like the difficulty sleeping, and his remarks about himself indicating worthlessness, the trouble concentrating, that kind of thing.
Q. On your original testing you did WAIS-R, didn't you?
A. No. I gave one of the subtests, a similarity subtest on—one of the subtests out of eleven.
Q. One of the subtests?
A. Right.
Q. Which one did you give?
A. The similarity subtest, which is a measure of abstract thinking, its inability to relate classes of objects, and whether somebody is going to be doing that in more concrete terms or more abstract terms.
Q. That's closely related to a general concept of intelligence, isn't it?
A. Well, intelligence has many aspects to it. So that would be your ability to think in abstract terms and to conceptualize would be one aspect of it.
Q. And that involves pattern recognition, for example?
A. It involves being presented with two names of a dog and a lion, for example, and—how are these similar? How are these related? And to look at the pattern of responses that a person gives to questions like that to see whether it's indicative of being able to conceptualize classes of objects in more abstract terms.
Q. And it would require an ability to concentrate in order to determine what the thrust of the questions was, would it not?
A. It would involve some ability to concentrate. For the most part, it involves the ability to think conceptual—to think in abstract terms.
Q. And you said that the patient's response indicated good abstraction ability?
A. That's correct.
Q. So that he wouldn't have—you wouldn't expect him to have any difficulties from an intellectual standpoint in handling any foreseeable vocations?
A. He is a man I consider to be of average to above-average intellectual ability. And so purely from an intellectual point of view, I think that he is quite capable.
Q. You elicited certain information from him concerning his educational background, did you not?
A. I did.
Q. And could you tell me just what have his educational activities been since leaving high school?
A. He's attended Glendale College and completed three semesters of classes.
Q. I didn't hear.
A. He's completed three semesters at Glendale College.
Q. Is that a junior college?

A. No. I believe that that's a four-year college.
Q. Did he complete the three semesters consecutively?
A. He has been attending school, and I would have expected that he would have completed more—more units and more classes. So I'm surmising that he's not—that his work or his class load is lighter or that he's not attending school consecutively. Because since his injury he's been attending Glendale College. And he was injured three and a half years ago. And it would seem in that amount of time he should have completed more than three semesters, had he been attending on a full-time, regular basis.
Q. Well, you say you're surmising. I gather that he didn't say that to you?
A. I didn't ask him. I asked him how many semesters he had completed, and he said he completed three semesters.
Q. Did you ask him what courses he took?
A. He was taking classes in broadcasting.
Q. And what did he have to learn in order to be taking a class in broadcasting?
A. I'm not sure what classes in broadcasting consist of.
Q. Do you know how many classes per semester he had?
A. I don't know.
Q. Do you know what kind of grades he got?
A. He said that he—his grades were A's and B's.
Q. His performance in that area would be an important indicator of his intelligence, would it not?
A. His—it would be an indicator of several things, one factor being intelligence.
Q. What else would it be an indicator of?
A. It would be an indicator of motivation, of how a person's applying themselves and that kind of thing.
Q. Well, it certainly is an indication, since he got A's and B's, that he was able to concentrate sufficiently to perform at an above-average academic level. Isn't that true?
A. I think that would be true if you—he were talking a full workload—or full load of classes, rather. And if he's taking one class a semester, I think that that's also a factor to be considered in what that's telling us about his ability to concentrate and perform.
Q. Well, just confining our attention to what he does, what he's taking the class and studies for, it would indicate that he did not have problems with concentrating. Isn't that true?
A. That under some circumstances he is able to concentrate and perform well.
Q. So that Mr. __________ is a person who sustained a serious injury back in 1987, I believe, and since that time has gone through convalescence, has maintained a continuation of his academic activities, and is now getting a job and now has a job at a higher level of responsibility than he had before. Isn't that true?
A. I believe that the level of responsibility is less than previously, in that before he was supervising and overseeing security operations for large events. I don't believe his present job involves that kind of supervisorial demand.
Q. Would it be fair to say that he is on a probably more rewarding career track than he was before?
A. He really enjoyed his job at __________ Corporation. And, to him, he was very happy with that job.

Q. Well, didn't he indicate to you that the reason he was continuing his college study was that he wanted to find a different profession or vocation?
A. I believe what he said to me is that he had—he was taking classes because he wasn't doing anything else during the time that he was not—not working.
Q. Did you discuss with him what his career goals were before his injury?
A. No, I did not.
Q. Don't you consider that important?
A. I was being asked questions, and that wasn't relevant to the questions that I was addressing in terms of my report.
Q. What questions were you addressing?
A. Well, I was addressing what—whether there was permanent disability or temporary disability and what the extent in nature of that disability and impairment and vocational functioning would be. I was being asked about the nature of the injury and—and—you know, specifically to render opinions in terms of disability impairment.
Q. Then you don't think that what his career goals were had any relationship to an assessment of disability?
A. I believe that I gathered the information that I needed in terms of making an accurate determination for the opinions which were being used.
Q. Well, can you answer my question "yes" or "no"?
Could you repeat it?
MR. ______: She's attempted to answer your question.
MR. LASKY: What's that?
MR. ______: I think she's attempted to answer your question.
MR. LASKY: Well, I asked her if she can—
MR. ______: Would you read the question back?
MR. LASKY: Would you read the question back?

(The record was read as follows:

"Q. Then you don't think that what his career goals were had any relationship to an assessment of disability?")

THE WITNESS: No.

§ 15.6 Checklist for Examining Psychotherapist Witness

____ I. General Background

Name and address, prior practice locations, partners or employees, registered name of practice, involvement in any other business.

____ II. Education

Description of all formal education with schools, dates, degrees, and honors, undergraduate major, postgraduate field or residency.

____ III. Clinical Training and Experience

Place, type, and period of training. How much "hands on"? How much classroom lecture? Types of disorders treated. How many patients treated? Numbers and types of psychological tests administered, scored, and/or interpreted. Types of clients, whether child, adult, or forensic, type of therapy, whether individual, family, or marital. How long were the patients in therapy? Was there any other clinical experience or training and what type?

____ IV. Memberships in Professional Organizations and Requirements for Membership

Has any membership ever been suspended or terminated, and if so, why?

____ V. Licensure

What licensure? Where? What type of licensure? Requirements for obtaining licensure. Specialize in any area of psychiatry or psychology? Qualifications for that specialization? Board certified, and, if so, in what?

____ VI. Area of Certification

When certified? What is name of certifying board? Ever fail board examination? How many times?

License or certification ever been suspended or terminated?

____ VII. Publications and Lectures

____ VIII. Nature of Current Practice

Job title? Length of current practice? Responsibilities? Numbers and types of offices in which service is rendered. Allocation of time per week between individual psychotherapy, group psychotherapy, psychological testing, administering medication, consulting (type of consulting), lecturing or teaching, expert witness work.

Characteristics of current clientele.

What types of therapy used, whether individual group, psychopharmacological, or other?

Number of patients usually seen each week, average duration of therapy, sources of referrals. Any other aspects of current professional practice.

Names of hospitals at which therapist practices and has practiced, treatment fee rates, forensic fee rates.

____ IX. Treatment Approach

Does therapist use DSM-III-R? Is it used by most psychiatrists and psychologists in formulating diagnosis? Use in this case? Were DSM-III-R diagnostic codes used on health insurance forms?

Desirability of review of medical records before making diagnosis. What is generally accepted procedure in performing a psychiatric or psychological evaluation? Clinical history of psychological testing, general medical history, interviews with other persons, mental status exam.

Who does history taking in the witness's office and how is the history taken?

____ X. Referral Sources for Patients, Any Previous Referrals from Claimants or Defendants' Attorneys

____ XI. Professional Discipline

Ever been investigated by any type of professional organization or public law enforcement facility? Been involved in any lawsuits? Subject to disciplinary action by hospital or medical group or denied hospital privileges? Has any client committed suicide?

____ XII. Forensic Experience

Percentage of income from forensic work? Ratio of plaintiff as against defense cases? Standard retainer form. How many times testified in court and type of case, side for which appeared, name of case, names of attorneys, what was diagnosis?

Deposition experience: where, case name, attorneys, diagnosis.

Any relationship with referral service for attorneys. If so, does the service charge client's attorney referral fee or percentage of award or settlement? Name and address of service. Number of cases handled for service.

____ XIII. Personal Information

Currently undergoing treatment by any mental health care provider? Use of controlled substances? Ever indicted or arrested? Ever received bonuses from drug companies?

____ XIV. Role in Particular Case

Consultant, treater, and/or expert, outstanding balance for treatment, who's paying, if anyone, how much paid to date for forensic work? How much for this deposition?

____ XV. Examination and Treatment of Claimant

A. Source of referral

B. Reason claimant came in? Was litigation mentioned in first session?

C. Dates, periods, and frequency of treatment. How many sessions has plaintiff missed?

____ XVI. Mode of Treatment Used

By type of psychological theory or approach, such as psychodynamic, behavioral, cognitive, and so forth.

Reason for choosing type of treatment. How was treatment plan followed? What was claimant's response? Any alternative approach?

Content of sessions: What were plaintiff's symptoms, and how were they determined? Were any alternative diagnoses considered, and if so, were they ruled out?

Was claimant informed of diagnosis? Claimant's response?

Is the diagnosis a DSM-III-R diagnosis, and if not, what was it?

Was clinical history taken? Any past records obtained? Was there psychiatric or neuropsychological or psychological assessment?

Were any medications prescribed, and if so, what were they? Patient's reaction. Knowledge of any medications prescribed by other health care providers.

Description of therapy progress. Other sources of information; interviews with others and plaintiff; records from other treaters.

Treatment notes. What notes were taken, where kept, and production of copies.

Extent of discussion by claimant of legal case during treatment.

____ XVII. Adequacy of Examination

A. Personal data, person's present employment status, place of address, whether living alone or with others, date of birth, use of other names at any time

B. Insurance information. Has therapist filled out any type of insurance forms, whether social security, disability, state, health service, state unemployment service?

C. Information obtained about educational background

D. Past employment history, such as types, places, promotions, terminations, length of employment.

____ XVIII. Military Service

Assignments, performance, achievement, records, including promotions or honors, physical or mental illness problems.

____ XIX. Medical History

Childhood and adult including illnesses, injuries, hospitalizations, courses of treatment.

____ XX. Substance Abuse History

____ XXI. Family Medical History

A. Family of origin: parents' age, education, occupational history; siblings likewise. Composition of family in childhood and youth, mental health history and relevant health history of family members, family response to illness, relevant social history of family members, quality of family relations

B. Family of procreation; present marital status, age, education, occupational history, number of offspring and similar information for adult offspring, mental health history and relevant medical history of family members, relevant social history of family members, quality of family relations, history of previous marriages

C. Developmental history; first age of school attendance; rate of progression in education, sexual development

D. Social and recreational activities. Present and postinjury activities should be taken up first, and the same question should be addressed as to activities before the injury

Sports and physical exercise

Outdoor activities

Hobbies

People, type, activities, religious, community, social club, volunteer activities

Repeat for past activities

E. Recent traumatic events or worries. Other health problems with spouse or significant other, problems with children, financial worries, social relationships, educational difficulties

____ XXII. Mental status exam

Level of consciousness

Mood, such as depressed, labile, elevated, anxiety, inappropriateness

Cognition/thinking; orientation, estimated intelligence, memory short term and remote

Perceptual and communication disorders

Thought content

Thought disorders, such as ideas of reference, looseness of associations, delusions, perceptual disorders, including hallucinations, intrusive thoughts, or obsessive thinking

Deficits in learning, problem solving, or judgment

Insight, including perception of relationship between injury and psychological condition

Behavior; retardation or hyperactivity, appropriateness in interview

Evidence of physiologic disturbance, if any

____ XXIII. Signs and Symptoms That Are Basis for Mental Disorder

Note that in medical terminology *signs* are observations by the clinician and *symptoms* are statements by the patient.

First ask, "Did you find any signs indicative of a mental disorder?" and if so, what were they and what information about its duration, causes of onset, and so on?

What symptoms did therapist find? As to each symptom, how often does it occur? How long does it last? How serious is it? Ever occur in the past? Patient's version of reason for symptoms. Has the therapist considered other causes of symptoms?

____ XXIV. Diagnosis

Axis I disorders? Reasons for conclusion. Axis II disorders? Reasons for conclusion.

Axis IV finding (psychosocial stressors)

Axis V finding: current and past year highest level of functioning

____ XXV. Considerations Applicable to Specific Claims of Mental Disorder

DSM-III-R has specific diagnostic criteria for each of the mental disorders described. Somewhere in the course of the deposition the questioner will want to know whether the doctor's diagnosis is in accordance with these criteria. It is recommended that the questioner have at hand copies of the relevant DSM-III-R criteria. If the questioner represents the defendant, the questioner would wish to avoid the leading question type of examination, such as listing the criteria and asking about their existence. If representing the claimant, the situation could of course be in the reverse, and the questioner would want to know if each of the elements of the diagnosis had been considered and the reason for rejecting it. The examiner might well wish to pose hypotheticals at this point, suggesting the existence of certain factual allegations with the purpose of getting the deponent to agree that if the factual allegations were established, they would in fact constitute the basis for a diagnosis of a particular mental disorder. Following are examples of types of questions that could be posed for each of the major disorders.

A. Post-traumatic Stress Disorder

One requirement is persistent symptoms of increased arousal (not present before the trauma), as indicated by at least two of the following: difficulty falling or staying asleep, irritability or outbursts of anger, difficulty concentrating, hypervilic vigilance, exaggerated startled response, physiologic reactivity upon exposure to events that symbolize or resemble an aspect of the traumatic event (a woman who was raped in an elevator breaks out in a sweat when entering an elevator).

Do you find at least two different symptoms of increased arousal?

If the answer is yes:

Q. What were the symptoms?
A. I found difficulty in concentrating and increased arousal response.
Q. What is your basis for the finding of difficulties in concentration?
A. Patient told me she had trouble concentrating on anything.

If one were examining on behalf of the defendant and evidence was contradictory—for example, the claimant had been attending night school courses requiring substantial reading homework and had received good grades—one would wish to follow up by getting more specific examples of what it was that the claimant said she could not do. The attorney would ask how much time the claimant spent in activities requiring concentration and for how long the claimant could concentrate. The next question could be along the lines of:

Q. Were you aware that claimant recently completed a course in basic computer programming?

If the answer is no, the deponent could be given an "out" by being asked to agree that her findings can be no better than the accuracy of the history on which she bases them, and that she gave the claimant every opportunity to give her the full facts.

If the examination is from the claimant's standpoint and the defense therapist has denied the existence of any basis for finding post-traumatic stress disorder, the elements of the diagnosis could be presented with hypothetical questions. Obviously, the questioner had better be prepared to back up the hypotheses with actual testimony.

B. General Anxiety Disorder

This requires a finding of at least 6 out of 18 listed symptoms. It also includes increased arousal and difficulty in concentrating. Another symptom that manifests itself in observable behavior is easy fatigability. Examining from a defense standpoint, one would again begin by finding out whether this criterion had been met by the doctor without suggesting answers by way of leading questions. Assuming that the doctor listed specific symptoms, the next question for any listed symptom is, what is its duration? What brings it on? How often does it occur?

Again, if examining from a defense standpoint, the questioner would proceed from strength, if the questioner has it. Thus, if there was evidence that the claimant played tennis, this would contradict a finding of easy fatigability. If the claimant claims palpitations or accelerated heart rate, there could be contradictory evidence from physical examinations that were done during the period in which claimant was claiming these symptoms. Generally, any type of activities in which the claimant engages that require a degree of sustained attention, such as playing bridge, taking educational courses, even sitting through a three-hour play, could contradict some of the claimed symptoms listed among the diagnostic criteria.

If examining from the claimant's standpoint, the procedure would parallel that of the defense.

C. Major Depression

Again, begin with noting the symptom list. Note that five symptoms are required to have been present during the same two-week period, and one of the symptoms is required to be either depressed mood or loss of interest or pleasure.

Obviously, engaging in any type of pleasurable activity, whether going to theater, athletic events, or normal social recreation, is inconsistent with these criteria. The questioning would be along the lines similar to those previously suggested.

D. Personality Disorders

Chapter 2 discussed the significance of personality disorders. As lifelong patterns of behavior, they are more likely to be matters of interest to the defense than the claimant's side in litigation because, by definition, they cannot be caused by a trauma in adult life. However, there are situations in which a particular personality disorder creates a preexisting vulnerability to the onset of an Axis I disorder. For example, dependent personality disorder is predisposing to major depression. In a jurisdiction in which subjective perceptions are considered to be sufficient basis for establishing an industrial injury, such evidence could be significant in showing that the employer's behavior, though not objectively distressing to most people, had that effect in the given case. In one case, a young lady who had an excellent job history because of her desire to please was finally promoted to a supervisory position for which she was ill suited. Attempts to give her helpful suggestions about how to improve her dealing with subordinates were interpreted by her as criticism. She eventually wound up in a psychiatric hospital.

As indicated in **Chapter 2**, each of the personality disorders may have its disabling features. Thus, in most cases, a defense examiner would wish to establish the existence of a preexisting personality disorder should there be evidence for the same.

The passive-aggressive personality is a very common type of claimant because such an individual has a basic underlying resentment against the world. These claimants are likely to have a poor employment history and frequent complications, including depression and alcohol abuse or dependence. These people are often dependent, lack self-confidence, and are pessimistic about the future.

The passive-aggressive disorder should be considered in defending claims for wrongful termination, sexual harassment, infliction of emotional distress, and the like. Defense claims for hedonic damages also would require consideration of this disorder.

From a defense standpoint, it would be a matter for direct examination of a defense psychotherapist. The basis for such a diagnosis would have to be established by detailed testimony about plaintiff's previous employment history and, more specifically, plaintiff's work habits, such as frequent complaints or being written up, history of resistance to efficient work or meeting deadlines, or resenting suggestions for improvement. In addition, psychological testing can further furnish a basis for these conclusions.

When examining a claimant therapist on the subject of preexisting personality disorders, the approach should begin with a question such as, "Have you considered the existence of any personality disorders?" The usual answer is, "I saw nothing in the history to indicate the existence of such a disorder." Ordinarily, the claimant's therapists do not obtain psychological testing interpretations that indicate the existence of such disorders. In examining a claimant's therapist, one would indicate the existence of symptoms that would be a basis for such a diagnosis by using hypothetical questions and then proceed in an effort to have the deponent admit that if such symptoms were established, they would constitute a basis for such a disorder. The following type of questioning is suggested:

Q. Assume, doctor, that the claimant's performance rating over the past three years indicates a pattern of procrastination so that she frequently fails to meet deadlines, has been described as irritable and argumentative when given assignments, unreasonably protests about reasonable demands by others, is not receptive to suggestions about how to improve performance, and has been admonished for rudeness to persons in position of authority (this would meet the DSM-III-R requirement for the diagnostic criteria).

Assume the deponent admits that if such evidence is established, it would constitute a basis for making the diagnosis. Follow-up questions would establish responsibility for the claimant's anhedonia (lack of pleasure) as being the effect of the personality disorder, as distinguished from the claimed job events. ("Isn't it true, doctor, that frequent complications of this disorder include a depressed attitude?") One would follow up with remaining DSM-III-R-associated features and impairment, such as alcohol dependency (if appropriate), pessimistic attitude about the future, and irritability.

Such an approach can be considered with each of the personality disorders, depending on the type of evidence available.

E. Physiological Conditions That Mimic Mental Disorders

The following physiological conditions can have some of the symptoms of mental disorders. Ordinarily, these will not be conditions related to the asserted basis for litigation.

For these reasons, the following information should be obtained in each case:

1. What medications is the claimant taking? Many medications produce effects associated with various other mental disorders.
2. Any evidence of drug abuse, which also can produce most of the symptoms of mental disorders.

Each of the following may produce one or more of the symptoms of mental disorders: Addison's disease, anemia, arterial venous malformations, brain tumors, chronic obstructive pulmonary disease, combined system disease, coronary artery disease, Cushing's syndrome, epilepsy, hepatic encephalopathy, hepatitis B, hypertension, hyperthyroidism, hypoglycemia, hypotension, hypothyroidism, infectious mononucleosis, meningitis, menopausal distress, mitral valve prolapse, multiple sclerosis, myocardial infarction, pancreatic carcinoma, Parkinson's disease, pernicious anemia, pheochromocytoma, polycythemia, porphyria, postpartum disorder, rheumatoid arthritis, syphilis, systemic lupus erythematous, uremic encephalopathy, Wilson's disease, Creutzfeldt-Jakob disease, Huntington's disease, and subacute sclerosing panencephalitis.[4]

---

[4] P.B. Silvain, Defense Deposition Atlas 5-367 (1990).

CHAPTER 16

EVIDENTIARY REQUIREMENTS FOR PSYCHIATRIC MEDICAL TESTIMONY

Herbert Lasky

§ 16.1 Introduction

Although it is very common in many proceedings to submit psychiatric testimony in the form of a written report, the principles of what constitutes substantial evidence apply both to the testimony of a psychotherapist appearing in court and to testimony in writing.

A psychotherapist preparing a report should understand that it has a specific function in a specific medical-legal framework. When using words that have particular and important meaning in the law, such as *causation, disability,* and *apportionment,* they must be employed in the legal sense, not in the medical sense. See **Chapters 4, 5, 9**, and **10**.

The source requesting the report is important because a certain format may be required. If the psychotherapist is reporting to an attorney for either the claimant or the defense, he must be certain to answer any specific questions directed to him. He must remember that any written materials he sends to the referring attorney may be filed as a matter of public record. Therefore, the material will be open to the other side. It is sometimes possible under the law, by request of the parties to the trial judge, to close the report or records to public inspection, although they cannot be withheld from the other side. If the psychiatrist is reporting as an agreed or assigned medical examiner, the report is subject to the same filing and publicity requirements. He must also answer any specific questions presented to him in addition to the general material. He must remember that any questions or requests he has should be directed to both parties when acting as an assigned neutral examiner.

From the standpoint of the claimant, the report of his psychiatric consultant will serve not only as an evaluation and important supporting evidence of disability, but also, for practical purposes, as a marshalling of evidence comparable to a trial brief. From the standpoint of the defense attorney, the psychiatrist's report should be an important investigative tool as well as corresponding defense evidence.

This chapter alternates between the viewpoints and concerns of the person who prepares the psychiatric medical-legal report, the medical-legal consultant, and the person who uses it, the attorney or claims evaluator. Often, the typical medical-legal report has only a very hazy relationship to the basic issues in a case. The doctors do not really understand the function of the report. The lawyers understand the function of the report, but they do not know how to elicit the needed information from the doctors. Moreover, many, if not most, therapists—incredibly—do not realize that the claimant may not be telling the truth. One must remember that the statements of the claimant are not conclusive statements of fact but are evidence that, if credible, should be considered in arriving at conclusions.

A second, fundamental problem is that doctors, and some lawyers, do not understand the difference between legal conclusions and medical conclusions and factual findings and medical conclusions.

Although these distinctions may seem academic, their importance is demonstrated in some of the cases discussed.

§ 16.2 Basic Legal Framework

To understand the legal framework upon which a medical-legal report must be constructed, one must separate the legal approach and the medical approach.

Though the law and medicine have overlapping concerns, their purposes are very different. Medicine is trying to heal; it uses science to give it the tools. A legal proceeding has been called a substitute for combat; the purpose is to resolve disputes in a socially acceptable manner. Social acceptance requires a sense that the proceeding has been fair and as accurate as possible. Thus, *proof* in medicine is in the scientific sense. One has assembled all the available data and has excluded all other possible causes of an event. Legal proof is a lesser standard. A person has proven his case if the judge or jury finds it more likely than not that he should win, *even though* the fact finder is aware he might be wrong. All that is required is *probability.*

The Anglo-American legal system provides the device of a trial to determine contested factual issues. Both sides are entitled to present evidence. Only evidence presented in a proceeding in which parties have the opportunity to participate can be considered by the judge or jury. Evidence must meet certain requirements to insure its reliability. If it does, it is accepted as a basis for decision and can be *substantial evidence.* In a case involving psychiatric issues, medical testimony is essential to proof of the case. If it violates the evidentiary rules, it cannot be substantial evidence, and the referring source has lost.

§ 16.3 Relevance and Competence

The function of a medical-legal report is as evidence in a contested case. To be evidence, information must be *relevant* and *competent.* It is *relevant* if it relates to legal issues and has a logical tendency to prove a relevant proposition.[1] It is *competent* if it does not violate a rule of admissibility. If the report meets these requirements, it is *substantial evidence* and may be a basis for a decision by a trial judge. If it is not substantial evidence, it cannot be a basis for a decision by a trial judge.[2]

The recommended guidelines of the California Subcommittee on Permanent Partial Psychiatric Disability go at length into the recommended subject matter of the report of a psychiatric examination made for purposes of medical-legal consultation. Its recommendations represent standard principles of good practice in preparing forensic psychiatric reports from a medical standpoint. See **Appendix A.**[3]

The relevant legal issues with which the report must deal are those presented in earlier chapters:

---

[1] Fordyce v. Workers' Compensation Appeals Bd., 197 Cal. Rptr. 626 (Ct. App. 1983); *see* 29 Am. Jur. 2d *Evidence* § 252 (1989).

[2] Insurance Co. of N. Am. v. Workers' Compensation Appeals Bd. (Kemp), 176 Cal. Rptr. 365 (1981).

[3] *See also* Comprehensive Textbook of Psychiatry-III, ch. 10 (H. Kaplan & B.J. Sadock eds., 1981).

1. Is there a mental disorder?
2. Is the mental disorder disabling?
3. Is the condition work related?
4. Is there apportionment to nonindustrial factors?
5. Has the claimant reached a permanent and stationary condition and, if so, when did it become permanent and stationary?
6. Is further treatment indicated, and if treatment has been rendered, was it appropriate, considering type, duration, and frequency?

As the California guidelines say:

> The expert's duty is to describe findings and to provide and document an expert opinion on the above issues that meets the reasonable medical-legal standard ("reasonably medically probable"). Furthermore, the clinical procedures and assessment measures utilized in forming the expert opinion must be generally accepted in the expert's scientific community. Frye v. U.S., 293 F. 1013 (D.C. Cir. 1923).[4]

It is also important for doctors to understand their limitations. It is not their function to decide who should win the case or whether there is legal causation. It is their function to present a professional opinion on the specific issues detailed on the basis of the information presented to them. For example, a psychiatrist said:

> I was reporting on a case in which the man says he was fired from his job unjustly because his supervisor had it in for him but says that he was in fact a good worker. Now he appears to be depressed. I don't know of anything else about the job that could have depressed him. Nothing he said to me indicated that he had any serious problems up until the time he was told he was being fired. On the other hand, I heard from his attorney that at the deposition it appeared that the employer would contend that he had been "written up" for absenteeism and his firing was with cause. I don't know which of these is true, and furthermore I've heard that legally mere firing isn't a basis for an industrial injury. I don't know whether to say it's industrial or not. What should I do?

The answer given was that it is not the responsibility of the psychiatrist to decide the outcome of the case. He cannot give answers to legal questions such as, "Is it industrial?" or, "Is mere termination a basis for finding industrial causation of an injury?" Regarding the actual fact of the firing and the reasons for it, because the psychiatrist at the time of preparing the report does not know which is true (this can only be finally determined by the judge), all he can say is

[4] Medical Advisory Comm. of the Cal. Div. of Indus. Accidents, The Evaluation of Permanent Psychiatric Disability (citing Frye v. United States, 293 F. 1013 (D.C. Cir. 1923)). See **App. A**.

what his training as a professional qualifies him to say, which is whether the termination was the medical cause of the depression he found. The legal relevance of that statement is for the judge to decide. As to the question of whether the firing was justified, this is relevant to the physician's opinion only to the extent that it is significant as a medical matter. For example, if the doctor thought that the information of a major depression in the claimant might be influenced by whether the claimant perceived the firing as unjust, he should say so; otherwise, it would be a purely legal question.

§ 16.4 Expert Qualifications

Because medical-legal reports in workers' compensation proceedings are the written testimony of an expert witness, they are subject to the general rules for admissibility of the testimony of such witnesses. The general rule is that expert testimony may be offered only on a subject that involves matter beyond the understanding of the ordinary lay witness. This, of course, presents no problem regarding the admissibility of medical testimony in workers' compensation cases or other cases involving disability issues. Most courts require that a decision by a judge as to industrial causation must be supported by the testimony of an expert witness in the field of psychiatry.[5]

A corollary of this principle, however, has more significance. That is, the person offering the expert opinion must have the special knowledge, skill, experience, training, or education necessary to qualify as an expert in the subject area of his testimony.[6] For example, a marriage and family child counselor is not qualified to testify to the standard of practice for a psychologist in California.[7] A physician who was an expert in the fabrication and use of a catheter, but who did not know the product's chemical composition, strength, or material construction, was not qualified to give an opinion as to whether the catheter kinked because of a defect in its walls.[8]

Thus, it would appear that a psychotherapist could not give an opinion as to an orthopedic injury. Therefore, if a psychiatrist states that between the orthopedic and psychiatric injuries, a claimant is unable to do any kind of work, not being an expert as to the disability evaluation of orthopedic injuries or of their combination in connection with a psychiatric injury, a psychiatrist is incompetent to formulate such an opinion.

---

[5] Insurance Co. of N. Am. v. Workers' Compensation Appeals Bd. (Kemp), 176 Cal. Rptr. 365 (1981).

[6] 31 Am. Jur. 2d *Expert and Opinion Evidence* §§ 55, 56 (1989).

[7] Cooper v. Board of Medical Examiners, 123 Cal. Rptr. 563, 573 (1975).

[8] Putensen v. Clay Adams, Inc., 91 Cal. Rptr. 319, 331 (1970).

§ 16.5 Sources of Information

The more important issue in determining the acceptability of expert testimony is the adequacy of its basis. An opinion of an expert witness must be based either upon facts ascertained through his personal observation or on the type of material, though not ascertained on personal knowledge, upon which it is reasonable for an expert of his type to rely. In the case of physicians, this clearly includes the history related by the patient,[9] the reports and opinions of other doctors,[10] and studies of medical works.[11]

The appropriateness of information is not always easy to determine. In *In re Cheryl H.,*[12] a psychiatrist had testified in connection with the conviction of a person for rape that in her opinion there had been a rape of the three-year-old child of the defendant in question and that the defendant was the perpetrator. The court of appeal reversed and stated that although it was proper for the psychiatrist to testify that in her opinion a rape had occurred, she could not base her testimony that the father was the perpetrator on the minor's hearsay statement because that opinion depended on the minor's credibility rather than the psychiatrist's expertise in her own field.[13] Thus, conclusions on legal issues are the exclusive province of the trial judge. Moreover, a psychiatrist may be an expert on the symptoms that indicate a three-year-old child has been raped, but a psychiatrist is not an expert on the credibility of the child as a witness.

§ 16.6 Matters Precluded by Law

Some matters may be precluded by law from constituting a basis for expert opinion. A pertinent example is the judicial exclusion expressed in the leading case of *Frye v. United States.*[14] The court held that evidence of the results of scientific testing is not admissible unless the principle contended is sufficiently established to have gained general acceptance in the particular scientific community in which it belongs. Thus, although there is no question about the fact that the results of tests such as the Minnesota Multiphasic Personality Inventory (MMPI) are accepted and their scores are admissible in evidence, this would not be the case if a therapist sought to offer in evidence the results of a test devised by himself that had not yet been subjected to the consideration of the scientific community to which he belongs. (Note that this is not the same as saying that the expert cannot use his tests as one of the bases for his opinion. It is merely that

[9] People v. Wilson, 25 Cal. 2d 341, 348, 153 P.2d 720, 724 (1944).

[10] Kelly v. Bailey, 11 Cal. Rptr. 448, 454 (1961).

[11] Healy v. Visalia & Tulare R.R., 36 P. 125 (1894).

[12] 200 Cal. Rptr. 789 (1984).

[13] *In re* Cheryl H., 153 Cal. App. 3d 1116, 200 Cal. Rptr. 799 (1984).

[14] 293 F. 1013, 1014 (D.C. Cir. 1923).

a non-generally accepted test score may not stand on its own feet as evidence of a fact in issue.)

§ 16.7 Degree of Certainty Required for Expert Opinion

Expert opinion must be expressed in the form of probability. It is not relevant when merely expressed as a possibility or conjecture.[15] Although *probability* cannot be defined with mathematical precision, the cases make very clear that the courts do not want to rely on mere "possibilities" as a basis for decision. However, the courts will look at the entire context of medical testimony to determine if the requisite degree of certainty is present.[16] It is not a "magic word" situation.

In *Twentieth Century Fox v. Workers' Compensation Appeals Board (Conway),*[17] one of the bases for reversing was the acknowledgment of the claimant's reporting psychiatrist that he had some uncertainty as to the truth of the events that claimant described as the cause of his condition.

§ 16.8 Inadequate or Mistaken History

Probably the single most significant principle involved in expert testimony is that the medical-legal opinion cannot be based on either an inadequate history or a mistaken assumption as to the facts.[18] In *Georgia Pacific Corp. v. Workers' Compensation Appeals Board (Byrne),*[19] the appellate court reversed because, among other things, a medical-legal report had found industrial causation on the assumption that the claimant had been threatened with termination, whereas the claimant in fact testified at the hearing that he had been offered a choice between demotion and termination.

§ 16.9 Conjecture or Speculation

The medical-legal report may not be based on conjecture or speculation.[20] In *Twentieth Century Fox v. Workers' Compensation Appeals Board (Conway),*[21] the

---

[15] 31 Am. Jur. 2d *Expert and Opinion Evidence* § 86 (1989).

[16] *Id.*

[17] 190 Cal. Rptr. 68 (1983).

[18] 31 Am. Jur. 2d *Expert and Opinion Evidence* § 246 (1989). *See* Place v. Workers' Compensation Appeals Bd., 90 Cal. Rptr. 424 (1970); Zemke v. Workers' Compensation Appeals Bd., 69 Cal. Rptr. 88 (1968).

[19] 144 Cal. App. 3d 72, 192 Cal. Rptr. 643 (1983).

[20] 31 Am. Jur. 2d *Expert and Opinion Evidence* § 87 (1989).

[21] 190 Cal. Rptr. 68 (1983).

reporting psychiatrist had stated that he was not altogether certain as to the underlying facts and could not be sure how much of the facts as reported by the claimant were reliable. In reversing, the reviewing court said it could not tell from the evidence presented and the opinion of the doctor whether the opinion was based on an assumption that claimant's alleged psychiatric injury was due to the conduct of an employer (to which the reporting psychiatrist had referred in stating he was not sure as to the exact accuracy of these facts) or to the effect of a nonindustrial event, namely, the rejection of claimant's screenplay, or to a combination of both. In view of these factual ambiguities, the appellate court was compelled to reverse.

Thus, the opinion of the reporting psychiatrist is no better than the facts upon which it is based. However, that does not mean the psychiatrist is necessarily at an impasse in framing an opinion. This again illustrates that it is not the psychiatrist's job to determine the result of the case. Often the medical-legal reporter will not know the definitive factual situation with which he is dealing because he cannot be certain of this until the judge has actually arrived at a decision. That does not preclude the doctor from basing his opinion on assumed facts, when to do so is reasonable, as long as he states what assumptions he is making and makes clear under what circumstances his opinion would change if the factual assumptions were inaccurate.

§ 16.10 Inferences from Evidence

Inferences drawn by the reporting doctor should be reasonably drawn from the evidence. Otherwise, the court will reject them. In *National Convenience Stores v. Workers' Compensation Appeals Board (Kesser),*[22] claimant was a store manager who allegedly suffered an industrial injury to his back, shoulder, arm, leg, and psyche when he fell off a box. He testified that he could not pick up even a glass of liquid, that he could not grasp anything, and that he had pain in the knees when he walked or stood. Surveillance motion pictures showed him playing a round of golf and not even using a golf cart to carry his clubs, but carrying them over his shoulder. He played 18 holes with considerable effectiveness.

The claimant's psychiatrist, in his report, diagnosed the condition as a posttraumatic neurosis. He concluded that because the claimant had been working free of psychiatric disability before the injury and there had been no outside nonindustrial causes of stress to account for his emotional deterioration, the industrial injury must therefore be the cause of all of his symptoms, including his lack of candor. He also referred to his manner of speech as markedly hypochondriacal in tone. The trial judge and the Workers' Compensation Appeals Board, on petition for reconsideration, found that the claimant was an

[22] 175 Cal. Rptr. 378 (1981).

"unconscious malingerer" and therefore suffered from a compensable condition because of his hypochondria.

In reversing, the court of appeals said that it did not accept the claimant's psychiatrist's conclusion that because there was no previous psychiatric or physical disability, claimant's present behavior was the product of a mental disorder. It found instead that his present behavior was a simple conscious attempt to increase his recovery. The court said that the Workers' Compensation Appeals Board may not blindly accept a medical opinion that lacks a solid underlying basis, and that substantial evidence does not exist when conclusions are not reasonably drawn from evidence.[23]

§ 16.11 Contrary Evidence

A principle related to that discussed in **§ 16.10** is important also. An expert witness is not allowed to disregard facts or other evidence inconsistent with his opinions, or to disregard countervailing factors, unless he gives a reasonable justification for doing so.

For example, in *Richard v. Scott,*[24] the court excluded the testimony of an accident reconstruction expert when he estimated the speed of the defendant's vehicle at the point of impact by using "average acceleration" and "average turning radius" for total length of skid marks. He used the traffic officer's measurement of the north skid marks but used his own estimate of the deviated easterly skid marks. He purported to fix the point of impact by using unmeasured deviated skid marks without precise evidence of their precise angle of deviation or location with respect to the intersection, and he assumed, without explanation, a particular coefficient of friction of tires on pavement.

This case illustrates that the factual basis for an expert witness's opinion must be accurate and precise[25] *and* must not knowingly disregard inconsistent evidence. In one case, the doctor reporting for the claimant found that she had a serious disability due to a major depression. However, the doctor made no reference to the fact that the claimant had a much higher level job than she had left and was handling it successfully and happily.

Note the importance of the fact that these rules relate to the requirements of substantial evidence. Because of the majority rule that expert testimony is required to prove a psychiatric injury,[26] failure to meet the substantial evidence requirement can require a reversal on appeal.

---

[23] *See* 31 Am. Jur. 2d *Expert and Opinion Evidence* §§ 247, 251 (1989).

[24] 144 Cal. Rptr. 672, 674 (1978).

[25] 31 Am. Jur. 2d *Expert and Opinion Evidence* § 251 (1989).

[26] A. Larson, Law of Workmen's Compensation § 79.54(h) (1989).

§ 16.12 Unrealistic Assumptions

Expert testimony may be disregarded if the assumptions made by the expert are unrealistic in the light of general knowledge. The testimony of an economist has been excluded when he made certain assumptions regarding various economic factors that influenced an estimate of the value of lost wages, and those assumptions had no basis in reality. In *Shatkin v. McDonnell Douglas Corp.,*[27] a wrongful death action, the plaintiff offered the testimony of an economist to prove the value of a mother's lost expectation of support from her son, who had died in the accident. The economist had assumed for the purpose of proposing a lump-sum award that the son would have devoted 20 percent of his disposable income to his mother's support; the only related evidence showed that he had given her sums amounting to 6 percent. The expert had assumed that the decedent's earnings would have increased at a 7.89 percent rate from 1979 to 1998, based on the price inflation rate since 1971. The court pointed out that the appropriate standard would have been the wage inflation rate and also that it was not reasonable to assume that the inflation rate would continue at the rate of 7.89 percent. The court stated:

> The Court is aware that Federal Rule of Evidence 703 allows an expert to base his/her opinion on data of a type reasonably relied upon by experts in his/her particular field even where the underlying data is not admissible in evidence.
>
> Rule 703 does not, however, allow an expert to base his/her opinion on assumptions and data that are so contrary to the evidence in the record or on assumptions that are so speculative that they amount to gross conjecture and nothing more.
>
> [2] The Court also has a duty to inquire into the trustworthiness of the underlying data and can exclude testimony where an expert has not reasonably based his/her opinion on trustworthy underpinnings.
>
> See Zenith Radio Corp. v. Matsushita Electric Industries Company, 505 F. Supp. 1313, 1325 (E.D. Pa. 1981).
>
> [3] Indeed, the Court's determination whether an expert is truly qualified for the circumstances of the particular case can take into account the fact that his/her opinion is based on self-evident untrustworthy underpinnings. id. at 1325 and n. 11. (id. p. 95).[28]

The court's reasoning and the facts of the case have some similarities to Kesser (**§ 16.10**). They emphasize that the expert witness cannot disregard the credibility of his factual assumptions.

---

[27] 565 F. Supp. 93 (S.D.N.Y. 1983).

[28] *Id.* at 95.

§ 16.13 Conclusions That Are Really Legal Opinions

A physician may not offer what amounts to a conclusion of law as distinguished from a finding of medical fact on a matter within his professional competence. In *Insurance Company of North America v. Workers' Compensation Appeals Board (Kemp),*[29] the appellate court held that the claimant's medical-legal report was not substantial evidence because the report had found that "claimant was suffering emotional trauma as the direct result of work related tensions, pressures and constant harassment which forced her termination from employment," but it did not specify any of the events that constituted "tensions, pressures and harassment."[30] The appellate court held this was a mere conclusionary statement that was no more than the equivalent of a conclusion as to whether or not the case was "compensable." This intruded upon a matter that was not a medical question, but one for ultimate determination by a workers' compensation judge.[31]

§ 16.14 Incorrect Legal Theories

The doctor's conclusions must not be based on incorrect legal theories. There are several classic examples of this error in psychiatric cases in which the evaluating psychiatrist was unwilling to accept the implications of the legal principle that pathology cannot be a basis for apportionment.

In *Gay v. Workers' Compensation Appeals Board,*[32] the agreed medical examiner in psychiatry found disability related to Gay's employment, but concluded that apportionment was appropriate. He stated that 50 percent of the symptomatology was attributable to a preexisting personality disorder; 25 percent to stress of previous employment, and possibly the truancy of the claimant's daughter for three months; and 25 percent to the recent employment, which was the main issue in this case.

The basis for these conclusions was that the claimant had a schizoid personality with passive-aggressive features of long standing. The doctor found that the claimant probably had symptomatology therefrom, although he said, "Whether any of the symptoms pre-existed his/her current employment is speculative since the patient denies it."[33]

The claimant had been employed as a bill collector for a period of years, going beyond the time of his employment by his present employer. Also, there had been

---

[29] 176 Cal. Rptr. 365 (1981).

[30] *Id.* at 376.

[31] *Id.* at 373.

[32] 158 Cal. Rptr. 137 (1979).

[33] *Id.* at 139.

a period in which the truancy of the claimant's daughter gave him considerable difficulty. On the basis of these facts, the agreed medical examiner made the apportionment in question, which, as he saw it, amounted to allowing 50 percent for the preexisting personality disorder; a combination of 25 percent for both preceding employment and the truancy of the daughter; and 25 percent to the most recent employment. On cross-examination, the doctor admitted that the apportionment was based on the extent of contributing factors to the disability. Both the trial judge and the Workers' Compensation Appeals Board applied an apportionment of 50 percent to nonindustrial factors.

On appeal, the decision was reversed. The court of appeals' reasoning and its language are instructive because they illustrate the difficulties courts have in arriving at decisions in cases in which they do not have an adequate record in terms of appropriate medically relevant facts to support the legal conclusions required. The court referred to the familiar principle that apportionment of pathology is not appropriate, only apportionment of disability. The apportionment in question to "contributing factors to the disability" was inappropriate. It also noted that the doctor was not aware that under California Labor Code § 5500.5, which limits how far back the courts will go in apportioning disability to prior employments, the attempted apportionment to a prior employment was legally impermissible.

The court pointed out that during his cross-examination the doctor was not sufficiently questioned with regard to the basic apportionment inquiries of what portion of the present disability was related to the natural progression of the preexisting, nonindustrial condition (California Labor Code § 4663) and what portion was preexisting, nonindustrial disability (§ 4750). The court was clearly concerned with the problems facing the reporting psychiatrist in cases such as these and devoted a good bit of its opinion to an attempt to formulate some guidelines:

> In order for the Board to rely upon a physician's evaluation as to apportionment under Section 4750 (the pre-existing disability standard) . . . the physician must describe in detail the exact nature of the pre-existing disability and the basis for such opinion in order for the Court to be able to determine whether the physician appropriately apportioned under correct legal principles. Thus, in order to apportion Gay's permanent disability to a pre-existing disability or impairment under Section 4750, Dr. Naftulin should have translated how his apportionment figure fits into the nature of alleged pre-existing psychiatric condition.[34]

This could have been done if the approach outlined in **Chapter 2** had been followed. Thus, the appropriate personality disorder could have been described, its effect on each of the temperament capacities could have been estimated in terms of degree of impairment, and the final sum could have been subtracted from the present disability found. Continuing with its guidelines, the court said:

---

[34] Gay v. Workers' Compensation Appeals Bd., 96 Cal. App. 3d 564, 117 Cal. Rptr. 137 (1979).

> We do not comprehend how the parties can expect any physician to properly report in workers' compensation matters unless he is advised of the controlling legal principles. Physicians are trained to discover the etiology of an illness. Finding the causes is important in preventive medicine and curing illness once developed. (Duthie, supra, 86 Cal. App. 3d at pp. 728–729.)[35]
>
> * * *
>
> Legal apportionment is not identical to theories of medical causation. Physicians in workers' compensation matters must accordingly be educated by the parties on the correct legal standards of apportionment. (Transcripts of 1979 Developments Tapes (Cont. Ed. Bar. 1979) Developments in Workers' Compensation Practice—1979, § 10.3, p. 231.) Thus, here, the failure of Dr. Naftulin to discuss apportionment in terms of the proper legal standard is not actually his fault but that of the parties. (id. p. 563)@1.[36]

Another portion of the court's opinion is instructive. The claimant argued that the agreed medical examiner's opinion was inadequate as a matter of law because of his statement that whether the symptoms preexisted the current employment was speculative, because the patient denied it. The court answered this by saying:

> Gay argues that Dr. Naftulin's opinion will not under any circumstances support apportionment as Dr. Naftulin in his report states: "Whether any of the symptoms preexisted his current employment is speculative since the patient denies it." Gay urges that Dr. Naftulin thus acknowledges there is no legal basis for apportionment because there is a lack of evidence of preexisting disability and that Dr. Naftulin is improperly "speculating" about apportionment. We do not entirely agree.
>
> In evaluating a medical report, isolated statements may be misleading. Intellectual candor of a physician may lead to single statements which, when isolated, may be misunderstood. In evaluating the evidentiary value of medical evidence, a physician's report and testimony must be considered as a whole rather than in segregated parts. (See Lamb v. Workmen's Comp. Appeals Bd. (1974) 11 Cal. 3d 274, 281 [39 Cal. Comp. Cases 310, 113 Cal. Rptr. 162, 520 P.2d 978]; McAllister v. Workmen's Comp. App. Bd. (1969) 69 Cal. 2d 408, 416–417; Travelers Ins. Co. v. Ind. Acc. Com. (Odello) (1949) 33 Cal. 2d 685, 687 [14 Cal. Comp. Cases 54, 203 P.2d 747]; Mann v. Workmen's Comp. App. Bd. (1968) 265 Cal. App. 2d 333, 339 [33 Cal. Comp. Cases 531, 71 Cal. Rptr. 237]; Foremost Dairies v. Industrial Acc. Com. (1965) 237 Cal. App. 2d 560, 572 [30 Cal. Comp. Cases 320, 47 Cal. Rptr. 173].) Thus, the physician's entire report and testimony when considered as a whole, must demonstrate that, based upon reasonable medical probability, there is a legal basis for apportionment. (See McAllister, supra, 69 Cal. 2d at pp. 416–417; Travelers Ins. Co., supra, 33 Cal. 2d at p. 687.)[37]

---

[35] 158 Cal. Rptr. 137, 141 (1979).

[36] 96 Cal. App. 3d 563.

[37] 158 Cal. Rptr. 137, 141 (1979).

Finally, the court suggested an overall guideline—the "reasonably medically probable range":

> We are cognizant that it may at times be a formidable task for a physician to state precise figures on apportionment. The physician often must make conclusions when faced with matters difficult to measure and with conflicting factual contentions made by the parties. (See Liberty Mut. Ins. Co. v. Industrial Acc. Com. (Serafin) (1948) 33 Cal. 2d 89 [13 Cal. Comp. Cases 267, 199 Pac. 302].) Accordingly, it is permissible for the physician to state his opinion on apportionment in terms of the reasonably medically probable range (see U.S. Auto Stores v. Workmens' Comp. App. Bd. (Brenner) (1971) 4 Cal. 3d 469 [36 Cal. Comp. Cases 173, 93 Cal. Rptr. 575, 482 P.2d 199]); provided, however, that the physician states in his report the basis and variable facts determining the range of apportionment. The appeals board may then, after determining the true facts based upon the conflicting evidence, determine the issue of apportionment based upon the range of evidence in the record. (De La Tova v. Industrial Acc. Com. (1955) 137 Cal. App. 2d 516, 523 [20 Cal. Comp. Cases 296, 219 P.2d 377].)[38]

This language applies with equal force to disability issues or any other issue in which quantitative estimates are required.

Perhaps the best statement of the court's requirements for expert evidence in cases of this type is in *People v. Bassett.*[39] There, the California Supreme Court said:

> In evaluating expert evidence in this light, our duty is again twofold. "Mental illnesses are of many sorts and have many characteristics. They, like physical illnesses, are the subject matter of medical science. They differ widely in origin, in characteristics, and in their effects on a person's mental processes, his abilities, and his behavior. To make a reasonable inference concerning the relationship between a disease and a certain act, the trier of the facts must be informed with some particularity. This must be done by testimony. Unexplained medical labels—schizophrenia, paranoia, psychosis, neurosis, psychopathy—are not enough. Description and explanation of the origin, development and manifestations of the alleged disease are the chief functions of the expert witness. The chief value of an expert's testimony in this field, as in all other fields, rests upon the *material* from which his opinion is fashioned and the *reasoning* by which he progresses from his material to his conclusion; in the explanation of the disease and its dynamics, that is, how it occurred, developed, and affected the mental and emotional processes of the defendant; it does not lie in his mere expression of conclusion." (Italics added.) (Carter v. United States (D.C. Cir. 1957) 252 F.2d 608, 617 [102 App. D.C. 227].) [8a] In short, "Expert evidence is really an argument of an expert to the court, and is valuable only in regard to the proof of the facts and the validity of the reasons advanced for the conclusions." (Italics

[38] 96 Cal. App. 3d 563, 565, 158 Cal. Rptr. 137, 142, 44 Cal. Comp. Cases 823 (1979).

[39] 70 Cal. Rptr. 193, 205 (1968).

added.) (People v. Martin (1948) 87 Cal. App. 2d 581, 584 (197 P.2d 379, 380); accord, People v. Jones (1964) 225 Cal. App. 2d 598, 611 [37 Cal. Rptr. 454].)

§ 16.15 Prototypical Medical Report

Following is an example of a prototypical medical report that leaves much to be desired. It is a composite profile suggested by various cases and is in no sense an exaggerated example.

PSYCHIATRIC DIAGNOSTIC EVALUATION REPORT

I performed, on February 9, 1985, a comprehensive psychiatric evaluation augmented by historical data obtained by Ph.D. intern. Psychological test results, as well as the entire testing section, were provided by ____________, Ph.D.

Identifying Information

____________ is a single Puerto Rican female referred for psychiatric psychodiagnostic examination regarding a possible psychopathological condition secondary to her industrial cumulative stress and strain and continuing disabilities from same. The patient was evaluated through a psychiatric evaluation and a diagnostic test battery.

Presenting Complaints

1. *Physical:* Headaches, dizziness, blackouts, upset stomach, alternating diarrhea and constipation, difficulty breathing, rapid heartbeat, tremors.
2. *Psychological:* Anxiety, depression, irritability, homicidal ideation, appetite disturbance, sleep disturbance with nightmares, impaired sensorium, loss of libido, and social withdrawal.

HISTORY OF PRESENT DIFFICULTIES: BY PATIENT

Claimant has been employed approximately one year with her employer as a stockroom manager. She was terminated about two months before date of examination on accusation of stealing merchandise. She denies that she had, but she accepted her termination. She says her supervisor was biased against her. One example was a time when she claims to have found $5,000 in cash on the premises and returned it to the employer. She was given a $50 reward, but was refused a written acknowledgement of the incident for her files. On another occasion, she was told that another woman employee accused her of verbally and sexually harassing her. She denied this to her boss. They investigated and issued her a formal warning and two-week suspension. She says this was not justified.

Thereafter she returned to work. Other employees were hostile to her. On another occasion, she did not witness against a co-employee who was accused of smoking marijuana in a bathroom. She says she saw no evidence of it. She feels that management harassed her after that. They made her do unnecessary reports and didn't give her enough help.

REVIEW OF MEDICAL RECORDS (Unremarkable)

PERSONAL HISTORY

She was born in New York. She has one older sister, 48; and one younger brother, 27. Her father owned a store in the Bronx. Her mother was a housewife. She describes her father as a person who enjoyed life and was "a hard worker." She has a close relationship with her father. She describes her mother as simple and very religious.

When she was 12 years old, she realized she was homosexual. When she was 16 years old, she began working for her father at the store. She graduated from high school. She left home when she was 18 years old. While in her 20s, she began living with a female lover in a relationship that has recently ended. She is very happy with her lifestyle.

Employment History

She was employed as a salesperson from January 1981 until January 1982. From January 1982 until August 1982, she worked for a freelance security office. From September 1982 until August 1983, she was employed as a salesperson. In August 1983, she began working for the present employer and continued until she was terminated in November 1984.

REVIEW OF PSYCHOLOGICAL SYSTEMS

1. *Anxiety:* The patient reports experiencing anxiety, including nervousness, worry, and tension.
2. *Depression:* The patient reports experiencing depression, including feelings of hopelessness and pent-up anger, irritability, insecurity, and homicidal thoughts. She states that she is afraid she may kill someone. Subsequently, she purposely does not keep guns at home. She would not state who she had homicidal thoughts about.
3. *Psychophysiological Symptomatology:* The patient reports experiencing severe headaches. She has been experiencing these headaches since March. She states that when she is very angry, she experiences blackouts. She also reports experiencing heavy perspiration and nosebleeds. She suffers from "stomach trouble" and vomits after eating. She relates that anything she eats hurts her stomach. She further reports experiencing alternating diarrhea and constipation. At times she feels as if she is suffocating due to

trouble breathing. She experiences rapid heartbeat and chest pain, usually when she is angry. She suffers from a skin disorder on her stomach.

4. *Sleep:* The patient reports experiencing sleep disturbances, including insomnia, problems remaining asleep, and early awakening. She also experiences violent nightmares.
5. *Appetite:* After each meal the patient vomits and reports having "no desire to eat healthy foods any more."
6. *Sensorium:* The patient reports impairment of her remote and recent memory, immediate recall, and concentration.
7. *Sexual Behavior:* The patient states that she no longer engages in sex.
8. *Social Behavior:* The patient states that she has become socially withdrawn.
9. *Activities:* The patient noted that she no longer engages in otherwise previously enjoyable activities.

DIAGNOSTIC EVALUATION

The patient was administered a diagnostic test battery.

Clinical Observations During Testing

Patient was cooperative during the testing. She followed directions and did not ask unnecessary questions, indicating some emotional independence. It was not difficult to establish a positive relationship with this person.

Tests Administered

Wechsler Adult Intelligence Scale-Revised (subtests)
Bender Gestalt Visual Motor Test
Beck Depression Inventory
House Tree Person Test

Intellectual Functioning

On the Wechsler Adult Intelligence Scale-R, a standard intelligence test, she was administered a number of subtests. Her current overall intellectual functioning is estimated to be within the lower limits of the normal range. Her social judgment appeared poor to fair at this time, and her visual-motor coordination was also impaired. This may be due to the serious psychopathological state she is experiencing.

Cognitive Functioning

On the Bender Gestalt Visual Motor Test, a common screening test for organicity, her performance was within normal limits. There were no signs of organic impairment. There were signs of clinically significant anxiety, however.

Personality Functioning

On the Beck Depression Inventory, the patient showed evidence of sadness, pessimism, a sense of failure, dissatisfaction, guilt, expectation of punishment, self-dislike, self-accusations, suicidal ideation, crying, irritability, social withdrawal, indecisiveness, changes in body image, psychomotor retardation, insomnia, fatiguability, anorexia, weight loss, somatic preoccupation, and loss of libido. Her overall score on the Depression Inventory shows severe depression.

On the House Tree Person Test, prominent features are anxiety, depression, and a lack of bodily integrity. Her human figure drawing only contains the head and there is considerable identity confusion. Her tree drawing indicates that her ego strength is very low.

MENTAL STATUS EXAMINATION

1. *Appearance:* The patient is an averagely groomed, Latino female who appeared fatigued. She appeared slightly overweight.
2. *Behavior:* She appeared angry in responding to questions during the interview.
3. *Speech:* Patient spoke in a low, slow voice.
4. *Affect:* The prevailing affect was somewhat flat, although appropriate to content.
5. *Mood:* The patient seemed to be depressed, anxious, and angry.
6. *Orientation:* The patient was oriented to person, time, and place. However, reality contact was somewhat impaired.
7. *Thought Content:* There were no loose associations, autistic thinking, or suicidal ideation. Ideas of reference were indicated. She has experienced auditory hallucinations since April 1984. She relates that no one is there when she hears the voices and believes they are coming from her unconscious. She believes she has special perceptual abilities. She often hears someone calling her name. Homicidal ideation is also indicated, and she fears she may kill someone, but she would not state who. Attention and concentration were fair. Psychological insight was fair. Judgment and abstract thinking were fair. Fund of information was adequate.

DIAGNOSIS

Axis I	296.24	Major Depressive Episode with Psychotic Features
	316	Psychological Factors Affecting Physical Condition: Gastrointestinal difficulties, headaches, nosebleeds
Axis II	Mixed Personality Disorder Characterized by Schizoid and Borderline Features	
Axis III	Nosebleeds, headaches, and gastrointestinal problems	

Axis IV Extent of psychosocial stressor: severe

Axis V Highest level of adaptive functioning past year: good

DISCUSSION

The prognosis in this case is guarded due to the patient's level of depression and anxiety. The patient is unable to deal with many of the events of her daily life. The level of anxiety and depression is severe.

Psychiatric Disability

This patient's condition is now permanent and stationary. Patient's disability is total from a psychiatric point of view. This patient will not be able to function in the same area of the open labor market as she did previous to the work-related stress and strain. Careful examination of background history prior to the work-related stress and strain does not indicate mental or emotional problems constituting a disability. That is, this patient would have been able to continue working but for the work-related stress and strain.

Factors of Disability

1. *Anxiety:* Patient has clinically significant levels of anxiety due to her concern about her future ability to earn a living and the effects of this on her life situation.
2. *Depression:* Patient is severely depressed. This contributes to feelings of listlessness and lack of energy. In addition, she has the following:
3. *Sleep Disturbance:* Patient suffers from nightmares and sleeps less than before. This diminishes her energy.
4. *Psychophysiological Symptoms:* Patient complains of headaches, appetite disturbance, dry mouth, excessive sweating, difficulty concentrating, memory disfunction, and excessive nervousness. These symptoms are likely brought about by anxiety and depression.

Apportionment

There is no indication patient had mental or emotional problems that interfered with work function before this work trauma. Therefore, apportionment is not indicated.

Recommendations

Patient should continue to receive treatment on an as-needed basis, including medications as needed, hospitalization as needed, and possible chemotherapy.

Vocational rehabilitation is not recommended.

Thank you for referring this interesting patient.

Very truly yours,

John Doe, M.D.
Diplomate, American Board of Psychiatry and Neurology

Facts Not Contained in History

Approximately six months subsequent to this examination and report, the defense obtained a medical legal examination by its own consulting psychiatrist. He found that claimant had procured other employment as a stockroom clerk in a large wholesale establishment. She had been working at this for approximately three months at the time of his examination. She mentioned that she had seen about 15 different employers before finding this job. He also ascertained that she had previously had about 20 counseling sessions with a psychologist over a period of six months, ending about a month before her termination from the employment involved in this case. Review of these records indicated that the principal topic under discussion had been her emotional problems related to the fact that she had broken up with her live-in lover during this period.

This medical report also indicated that there had been a thorough investigation prior to her termination for stealing; that it had been originally initiated by inventory shortages and, ultimately, she had "been caught redhanded" passing goods to a confederate who had a waiting pickup truck in the alley behind her workplace.

Also, he described her as identifying herself as an Italian girl from New York City, not as a Puerto Rican, as stated by the claimant's medical report. This would raise some question as to the accuracy of the history taken, and even a possibility as to confusion of identity in the reporting office as to the patient about whom the report was made.

His diagnosis was preexisting mixed personality disorder with borderline, paranoid, passive-aggressive, and other features. Psychological testing consisting of the Minnesota Multiphasic Personality Inventory indicated neither a clinically significant depression level nor a valid profile.

§ 16.16 —Critique

Following is a critique of the profile in § **16.15**:

Adequacy of history. Most important here is the fact that the history contains no reference to the previous psychotherapy that was occurring during the period of claimant's employment and that appeared to be principally concerned with her emotional upset about her breakup with her live-in lover. If the examining physician was simply unaware of this, either because he had not asked about it or claimant had been an inaccurate historian, the report would, nevertheless, be questionable with respect to the causation issue. How could the doctor have weighted the significance of this personal problem as against the significance of the alleged work stress if he was not aware of the prior psychiatric problem? Also, there was at least an assertedly strong basis for the termination of the claimant having been justified and not spurious as claimed by the claimant. Some reference should be made by the reporting doctor to the significance of whether the termination was justified. This could have a bearing, not only on the accuracy of the claimant as an historian, but also on inferences to be drawn from the effect of the firing on her. An honest perception of an unjust dismissal may be one kind of a stress, and a concealed knowledge that the dismissal was, in fact, proper and just, is something entirely different. Finally, note the discrepancy between the report describing the claimant as Puerto Rican and the claimant identifying herself to the defense psychiatrist as Italian. There could be considerable differences in cultural outlook, and, therefore, the effect of various stressors on the individual. A question is also raised as to the reliability of the reporter's fact gathering if this kind of a mistake could be made.

Reliability of information sources. The claimant, as a source of the history, is an appropriate source for the basis of an opinion. However, there is a question as to the adequacy of the Beck Depression Inventory, referred to by this report under "Diagnostic Evaluation." The Beck Depression Inventory is a self-reporting type of test in which the intent of the questions is obvious. They are in the nature of leading questions, which, in effect, ask the claimant if she is depressed and how depressed she thinks she is. In this regard, it is not like the Minnesota Multiphasic Personality Inventory, in which the intent of the questions is not necessarily obvious to the examinee. It is significant that in the section, "Personality Functioning," it states that on the Beck Depression Inventory, the patient showed evidence of a sense of failure, guilt, expectation of punishment, self-dislike, self-accusations, and weight loss, whereas none of these symptoms are mentioned in any other portion of the examination. Thus, under "Mental Status Examination," it is noted that she appeared slightly overweight and had no suicidal ideation, a direct contradiction of the Beck report. In "Review of Psychological Systems," it reports the patient as experiencing depression and feelings of hopelessness with anger, irritability, and insecurity, but it makes no reference to suicidal ideation or any feelings of lack of self-worth.

Appropriateness of conclusions. There is a serious deficiency here, in that it cannot be determined whether the examiner is drawing an improper legal conclusion in assuming that the "stresses and strains of employment" were the cause of the claimant's disability. This is because the report lumps together both the described stress and strain of employment and feelings of harassment and claimant's reaction to being terminated. If the cause of the disabling condition was the reaction to being terminated, then from a legal standpoint it might not be industrial causation. Recalling the rejection in the Kemp case of mere general complaints of harassment without specifics as a basis for a conclusion of medical causation,[40] note that all claimant has actually described here, out of a period of about one year's employment, is that she was once disciplined for sexually harassing another woman; she was refused a written acknowledgement of an incident where she found a large cash sum and returned it to the employer; and she was asked to be a witness against a co-employee who was accused of smoking marijuana and refused to. These three incidents are the only specifics other than the fact of the termination.

Similarly, as to the issue of disability, there is no discussion of the effect of the alleged mental disorder on the claimant's ability to perform the 11 basic job functions or temperament capacities described in **Chapter 7**. The only statements made under "Factors of Permanent Disability" are that she has a level of nervousness, irritability, and fearfulness regarding her future ability to earn a living; she has feelings of listlessness and lack of energy and sleep disturbances that contribute to lack of energy. There is a rather summary statement to the effect that the patient's disability is total from a psychiatric point of view and she will not be able to function in the same area of the open labor market as she did previous to the work-related stress and strain. This is, at best, ambiguous. No specific findings are made with respect to actual factors of disability. The statement that she will "not be able to function in the same area of the open labor market" would leave a vast area of the open labor market in which she could function. Disability is not measured by the inability to return to the job in which one was employed; it is the impairment for competition in the whole range of work embraced by the open labor market. This indicates a conclusion based on an improper legal theory rather than on medical knowledge. It also represents an opinion that goes beyond the area of the doctor's expertise.

Finally, the diagnosis of major depression, single episode, is not explicitly stated in terms of the diagnostic criteria of DSM-III-R, which requires at least four of the following symptoms to have been present every day for a period of at least two weeks:

1. Significant mood loss
2. Insomnia
3. Psychomotor agitation
4. Loss of interest in usual activities
5. Loss of energy
6. Feelings of worthlessness and self-reproach

---

[40] Insurance Co. of N. Am. v. Workers' Compensation Appeals Bd. (Kemp), 176 Cal. Rptr. 365 (1981).

7. Evidence of diminished ability to think or concentrate
8. Recurrent thoughts of suicide.

Taking account of all information necessary for formation of opinion. Related to the possible inadequacy of the diagnostic criteria, there is another question here in connection with whether what was diagnosed as a work-traumatic major depression was, in fact, the symptoms of a borderline personality, which is not a work-induced condition. The doctor's report indicates that there are borderline personality traits. DSM-III-R lists, as one of the complications of a borderline personality, major depression. It also lists, as characteristic of the borderline personality, marked shifts of normal mood to depression, irritability, or anxiety, as well as identity disturbance manifested by uncertainty about such issues as gender, identity, friendship patterns, values, and loyalties. Constant anger is another aspect listed with respect to borderline personality. These symptoms are present here, but the report does not consider a differential diagnosis.

Another issue that should have been considered in arriving at a conclusion as to industrial causation is the significance of whether claimant's statement that she was unjustly terminated for stealing is correct. If the report's conclusions are conditioned on whose version of the truth is correct in this issue, it should say so.

Reasonableness of inferences drawn by report. The report makes the statement that, if it were not for the stresses and strains of her job, the claimant could have gone on working, but the fact is she did go on working until she was fired. That indicates that the "stresses and strains" did not prevent her from working. The report refers to her statement about vomiting after each meal and complaints of weight loss, but does not reconcile these statements with the observation under "Mental Status" that she appeared slightly obese. It would appear that this is an appropriate matter to consider, both with respect to the correctness of the diagnosis of major depression and with regard to the accuracy of the claimant as an historian.

Reliance on the Beck Depression Inventory does not appear reasonable, in view of the discrepancies between claimant's answers on that and the information she gave in other portions of the examination. The fact that it is quite obvious from the nature of the questions in the Beck Inventory as to what the significance of answers would be suggests that claimant was willing to exaggerate her symptoms. This would be borne in mind by the trier of fact.

§ 16.17 Appropriate Medical-Legal Report

The appropriate medical-legal report takes heed of the admonitions of *People v. Basset.*[41] See **§ 16.14**. Whether for oral or written testimony, the doctor should

[41] 70 Cal. Rptr. 193 (1968).

remember that after he has (1) acquired all the available data, (2) considered it in the light of the legal requirements, and (3) arrived at his answers to the referral questions, *then* comes the critical part of the assignment. He must persuade the judge or jury that he is right *and* the opposition is wrong. To do that, he must give reasons that will be judged by the legal rules.

Following is an appropriate report prepared by an experienced forensic therapist. Note that copies of all DSM-III-R diagnostic criteria referred to are appended to the report. This is recommended for two reasons: judges are used to seeing authorities cited in support of arguments, and the diagnostic criteria will be in the record and thus available for appellate argument, should that be necessary.

____________ M.D.
______ WILSHIRE BOULEVARD, ________
BEVERLY HILLS, CALIFORNIA 90212
TELEPHONE (313) ____________

August 2, 1989

Samuelsen, Coalwell & Gonzalez
350 West Fifth Street, Suite 105
San Pedro, California 90731-2737
Attention: Herbert Lasky, Esq.

Re: ____________
WCAB Case No.: ____________
Claim No.: ____________

Dear Mr. Lasky:

In response to your request, this is a report of my findings with regard to Mr. ____________:

IDENTIFYING INFORMATION

Mr. ____________ was seen by me at my office on July 25, 1989, for a psychiatric evaluation and report regarding an alleged injury to his ear, nose and throat, neurological and orthopedic systems and psyche on July 14, 1986. The examination lasted for two and one-half hours.

He is a 36-year old divorced Hispanic male who worked as a Safety Coordinator for ____________ until ____________. His present source of income is rehabilitation payments of $394 every two weeks.

He was the only source of information except for the records reviewed in this report.

DESCRIPTION OF APPLICANT

Mr. ____________ was casually but neatly dressed and groomed. He had short dark hair, a mustache and wore glasses. He related to me in an open and pleasant manner. His affective state was normal and appropriate until I asked him about the depression he had spoken about, and then he *acted* depressed for a few moments. His stream of speech was normal and appropriate. He had a cooperative attitude toward the interview.

CURRENT COMPLAINTS

Loss of balance
Ringing in the ears
Pain in neck and behind left ear
Nightmares
Depression
Fear of forklifts

HISTORY OF PRESENT ILLNESS

Mr. ____________ stated that he liked his job very much and had no problems of any kind with regard to it. He was not only doing his job but going to California State College ____________ at the same time.

On July 14, 1986, he was driving a forklift and put a load up high. He was getting into position to go forward and leaned forward to see if he had a clear path. He stated that something hit his head near his left ear. He has no idea of what it was or where it came from. Although he did not lose consciousness, he fell to the ground on all fours and stated that he began to talk nonsensically.

He bled from his ear and face. Another worker helped him to the office. He was taken to Humana Hospital.

He was an inpatient at Humana for three days. He stated that he had a fracture of his temporal bone and that a surgeon reconstructed his auditory canal. A CAT scan was negative. He states that he was followed primarily by Dr. ____________, an ear, nose and throat doctor, and by Dr. ____________, a plastic surgeon, Dr. ____________, a neurologist, Dr. ____________, a psychiatrist who saw him for one or two evaluations only and then was allegedly disapproved by the insurance company, and Dr. ____________, a neurologist, who gave him physical therapy and biofeedback at St. Jude Clinic.

He was out of work for six months and then returned to light duty. He stated that the symptoms he was experiencing were loss of balance, nightly nightmares, difficulty expressing himself (using the wrong words), as well as difficulty with numbers and difficulty in concentrating; this continued for several months. He stated that he was disturbed about his condition but not truly depressed.

He returned to work in February 1987 and was very happy about being able to do so. The light duty consisted of running errands at first and not working on a forklift, which he feared very much. He stated that they then created the job of Safety Coordinator in approximately July 1987. He was very happy with that job and did it very well.

He also resumed his schooling as a handicapped student (because he had difficulty concentrating) and received a BA in Sociology in June 1987.

He still continued to see Dr. ____________, but he did not see any other doctors.

In January 1988, Mr. ____________ stated that he called Dr. ____________ office (he believes he is an ear, nose and throat doctor) to reschedule an appointment. He was told that the doctor was out but that they would call him with regard to scheduling another appointment.

In February 1988, the head of the company called him into the office and told him that he was not keeping his doctor's appointments. Mr. ____________ stated that he explained his position but was told that "you're lying." His job as Safety Coordinator was terminated and he was told he had to return to the yard. This took place on a Friday. Mr. ____________ stated that he did not sleep well over the weekend and could not return to work on Monday. He stated that on Tuesday he returned to work and was told by the superintendent that he would have to have a full release from his doctor and "don't return without it."

He was allegedly told by Dr. ____________ that he would not have the results for two weeks so that he was not able to give him a full release, but that he had been superceded by Dr. ____________. According to Mr. ____________, Dr. ____________ told him that he should go back to light duty, and the company in turn stated that he had resigned. Mr. ____________ strongly denied this.

He also indicated that he has been drinking excessively for the past year and a half. He consumes a six pack a day and also stated that he has been utilizing cocaine for the last six months. When I asked him where he got the money to pay for the cocaine and how often he used it and in what quantities, he became very vague and evasive.

Mr. ____________ stated that he had never sought the help of an attorney until after he was terminated. He was very angry about his termination and then saw an attorney who sent him to an ear, nose and throat doctor whose name he could not remember and to a psychiatrist whom he saw one time. The psychiatrist sent him to Dr. ____________, a psychologist, who gave him tests and psychotherapy for four sessions. Mr. ____________ feels that it helped him. His last session was two or three months ago.

His attorney also sent him to rehabilitation two months ago. He does not receive any training but has been given job leads and has had six or seven interviews.

Mr. ____________ states that he wants to go back to work and feels that his only impairment has to do with his physical condition. He stated that he is now looking for an entry level job as a counselor and does not feel that he has any impairment on an emotional basis.

OCCUPATIONAL HISTORY

Mr. ____________ worked as a salesman for ____________ in El Paso, Texas, from August 1972 to April 1976. He left for more money.

He worked for ____________ State Center monitoring clients from April 1976 to June 1978. He moved to Los Angeles.

He worked for ____________ from August 1978 to June 1982 as a forklift operator. The company closed.

He worked for ____________ from December 1982 to February 1984, as has been described until he was "forced to resign."

He states that he has never been fired from any previous jobs or disciplined.

PAST MENTAL HEALTH AND MEDICAL HISTORY

He denies any prior mental illness, emotional problems or psychiatric treatment.

He denies any significant medical illnesses.

He denies any significant accidents or injuries or hospitalization or surgery.

FAMILY HISTORY

Family of Origin

He was born in Texas and moved to Los Angeles in 1978. His father died of a stroke in 1956. He does not know his age. He was only three years old. His father was a foreman in a meat packing company. His mother is a 74-year-old housewife who is in good health. He states that they had an excellent marriage until his father died.

He is the youngest, having three sisters and five brothers, all of whom are in good health. He states that the family was a close-knit one.

Marital

He married a woman six years his junior in 1978. They divorced in 1987. They had no children.

He now sees a medical technician and has for the past year and a half. She is ten years his junior. They have a good relationship and he says that sex is "great"; they do not live together.

DEVELOPMENTAL HISTORY

The only unusual aspect of his childhood was his father's death when he was three years old. He states that other than that there was nothing unusual and he was relatively happy.

He enjoyed football, bike riding and swimming. His first sexual experience was at age 21. He states he has never had any sexual difficulties.

SOCIAL HISTORY

He gets along well with other people and has many friends.

He has a BA from Cal State __________ in Sociology. He had a 3.4 average before his accident, he states. He has never been in the military.

He denies any prior workers' compensation claims or any other lawsuits. He has never been in trouble with the law.

He does not smoke. He states that he never drank heavily before a year and a half ago and states that he had never taken any illicit drugs other than cocaine in the past six months, as has been described.

On a typical day he goes for rehabilitation evaluations and he goes out on job interviews. He watches television and allegedly sleeps a lot.

MENTAL STATUS EXAMINATION

Mr. __________ was alert. He had no difficulty understanding any of my questions.

There was no evidence of anxiety. He, as has been described, occasionally had a very slight depressed affect in that his voice would choke a little bit when he discussed either feeling depressed or what had happened to him at __________. At those times his momentary depression would change to a mild anger. Otherwise his emotions were not inappropriate.

He was oriented as to time, place and person. His intelligence appeared to be high average. His memory was fairly good. There was no pressure of speech and he expressed his thoughts clearly.

The content of his thought was normal and appropriate. He was able to think logically. There was no evidence of obsessive thinking. He concentrated well and he was able to think abstractly.

There was no evidence of ideas of reference, loose associations, delusions, hallucinations or any other psychotic thought disorder.

His judgment and insight appeared to be fair.

His behavior was appropriate.

There was no evidence of any physiologic disturbance.

REVIEW OF RECORDS

Cal State __________ records.

__________, M.D., September 13, 1988.

__________, M.D., March 31, 1988.

__________, M.D., November 4 and November 14, 1988.

Humana Hospital records.

____________, Ph.D., November 26, 1988.

____________, Ph.D., no date.

____________, M.D., October 17, 1986, November 3, 1986, November 12, 1986, January 6, 1987, February 10, 1987, May 27, 1987, February 25, 1988.

____________, M.D., October 27, 1986.

____________, M.D., November 19, 1986, February 11, 1987, February 27, 1987, April 22, 1987, May 19, 1987, May 27, 1987, September 25, 1987, October 28, 1987, February 29, 1988, September 29, 1988.

____________, M.D., September 5, 1986.

____________, M.D., no date.

DSM-III-R DIAGNOSIS

(Based on the *Diagnostic and Statistical Manual of Mental Disorders,* third edition, revised, of the American Psychiatric Association. DSM-III-R is regarded as the most authoritative and reliable classification of psychiatric diagnostic categories.)

Axis I *Clinical Syndromes.*
300.00 Anxiety Disorder Not Otherwise Specified, stabilized.
305.00 Alcohol Abuse.
305.60 Cocaine Abuse.

Axis II *Personality Disorders.*
Dependent Personality Traits.

Axis III *Physical Disorders and Conditions.*
To be diagnosed by appropriate specialists.

SUMMARY AND CONCLUSIONS

History and Findings

Mr. ____________ was perfectly fine until July 14, 1986. On that date, he was driving a forklift and after putting a load up high was leaning forward to see if he had a clear path to go forward. Something suddenly hit his head near his left ear. He has no idea of what it was or where it came from. He did not lose consciousness, but fell to the ground on all fours and allegedly began to talk nonsense. He was bleeding from his ear and face. Another worker helped him to the office.

He was taken to Humana Hospital, where he was told that a temporal bone had been fractured, and he had reconstructive surgery on his auditory canal. A CAT scan was negative. He was an inpatient for three days and then followed by Dr. __________, an ear, nose and throat doctor. He was also sent to Dr. __________, a neurologist, and Dr. __________, a psychiatrist, whom he saw one or two times until the insurance company allegedly disapproved.

His symptomatology at the time consisted of a loss of balance, nightly nightmares, difficulty expressing himself (using the wrong words at times), difficulty with numbers for several months and difficulty in concentrating. He stated that he had only normally disturbed feelings about what had happened to him.

He returned to work in February 1987 and was given light duty. This was at the recommendation of Dr. __________, a neurologist, who had given him physical therapy and biofeedback at St. Jude Clinic. He was not to use a forklift, but rather ran errands. He feared forklifts a good deal and they created a new position of Safety Coordinator in approximately July 1987. He liked doing the work very much and he stated that he did it well. He also returned to school, where he had been studying while he had been working before (Cal State __________); he received a BA in Sociology in June 1987. He was attending as a handicapped student after his accident.

He continued to see Dr. __________, but no other doctors.

In February 1988, he was accused by the head of the company of not keeping doctor's appointments. He explained that that was not true but was told that he was lying and that the Safety Coordinator job would be terminated and that he would have to return to the yard. This happened on a Friday. He stated that he did not sleep well over the weekend and could not return to work on Monday. However, he did return to work on Tuesday. On that day the superintendent demanded that he get a doctor's full release and not to return without it.

He was told by Dr. __________ that he would not be able to get test results for two weeks, but Dr. __________ gave him a slip stating that he should return to light duty.

Mr. __________ indicated that the company stated that he resigned. He denies that he did so.

Mr. __________ did not see an attorney until after his termination. He was quite angry about what happened. His attorney sent him to an ear, nose and throat doctor and to a psychiatrist, who in turn sent him to Dr. __________, a psychologist, who gave him tests and psychotherapy. His last visit was two or three months ago. He was also sent to vocational rehabilitation two months ago and was not given any training but was given job leads and he has gone on six or seven interviews. He is now looking for an entry-level counseling job.

He states that he wants to return to work, and feels that his only impairment is based on his physical condition.

He indicated that he began to drink excessively in the past year and a half. He drinks a six pack a day and has utilized cocaine for the last six months. He was very vague about any details with regard to the latter.

Mental status examination revealed no evidence of any true psychopathology. There was no evidence of anxiety. With regard to depression, Mr. ________ spoke in a choked-up voice and showed momentary indication of some very slight depressive affect when he talked about his depression; this quickly changed to a feeling of anger at what had happened to him. It is my medical opinion that he does not have true depression at this time. There was no evidence of any lack of alertness or difficulty in concentrating or impairment of his ability to relate effectively to the examiner.

Mr. __________ himself stated that the only emotional symptomatology that he has at the present time are nightmares on a very occasional basis, depressed feelings *very* occasionally, and a fear of forklifts. The nightmares usually consist of something hitting him in the head; he is frequently not awakened by them. When he does not have the nightmares, he sleeps well.

On the basis of the above findings, it is my medical opinion that Mr. ________ had an Anxiety Disorder Not Otherwise Specified which has now stabilized. As per DSM-III-R, this consists of "Disorders with prominent anxiety or phobic avoidance that are not classifiable as a specific Anxiety Disorder or as an Adjustment Disorder with Anxious Mood, which has now resolved. Although he meets some of the criteria for the diagnosis of Post-traumatic Stress Disorder, it is my medical opinion that he does not have sufficient of the criteria required by DSM-III-R to justify that diagnosis (see attached form). Although he had reexperienced the traumatic event with recurring distressing dreams, there was no indication of three elements of persistent avoidance of stimuli, as would be required; in fact, although Mr. __________ could not return to driving a forklift, he was able to return to his place of work as a Safety Coordinator and be in contact with all parts of the company, including forklifts. His history indicates dependent traits, which are not sufficient to warrant a diagnosis of Dependent Personality Disorder.

Causation

It is my medical opinion that as a result of the accident on July 14, 1986, the only emotional symptoms Mr. __________ experienced were nightly nightmares and fear of forklifts; his other symptoms, such as loss of balance, difficulty expressing himself, ringing in the ears and difficulty concentrating, were on a neurological, rather than a psychiatric basis.

However, it can be stated with reasonable medical probability that his abuse of alcohol and cocaine were the direct result of the natural progression of preexisting personality traits, namely his underlying Dependent Personality Traits with feelings of devastation and helplessness when close relationships end (see attached form) and was triggered by his being terminated from his job. Personality traits are, by definition, a lifelong set of characteristics and are not industrially caused. (Although he indicated to me that he had never been a heavy drinker before his termination, Dr. ____________'s report of November 4, 1988, indicates that Mr. ____________ began to drink alcohol at 16 or 17 and although he did not abuse it "began to drink more regularly on the weekends at about 18.")

Disability

On a psychiatric basis, there was a period of temporary total disability from the date of his accident, July 14, 1986, until he returned to work in February 1987.

Mr. ____________'s condition is now permanent and stationary and has been since he returned to work in February 1987, when his only psychiatric disability was not being able to operate a forklift.

At this time, he has only very occasional nightmares and feelings of depression and a constant fear of forklifts.

In accordance with the Guidelines of the Division of Industrial Accidents, see the attached form for the levels of psychiatric impairment found. The overall impairment is Very Slight.

Apportionment (see attached form)

Absent the alleged workplace injury, it is reasonably medically probable that the overall level of impairment would be none.

Treatment; Rehabilitation

From an industrial standpoint, there are no indications for psychotherapy in view of the fact that Mr. ____________ has no work-disabling emotional symptomatology at the present time except for his fear of forklifts, and he is already receiving vocational rehabilitation in view of the fact that he cannot resume his usual and customary occupation as a forklift driver.

Referral Reports

Dr. ____________ made diagnoses of Organic Mental Syndrome Not Otherwise Specified, residual Post-traumatic Stress Disorder and Major Depressive Episode on Axis I as well as Dependent Personality Traits on Axis II. It is my medical opinion that the symptomatology that Dr. ____________ described to support his diagnosis of Organic Mental Syndrome Not Otherwise Specified are neurological rather than psychiatric phenomena. With regard to the diagnosis of Post-traumatic Stress Disorder, I have already indicated that Mr. ____________ did not meet the requisite criteria for this diagnosis, although he did manifest some of them. It was for that reason that I felt that my diagnosis of Anxiety Disorder Not Otherwise Specified was more appropriate. With regard to the diagnosis of Major Depressive Episode, Dr. ____________ felt that this was a reactivation of unresolved grief over the death of his father when he was three years old, and Dr. ____________ described the patient becoming almost uncontrollably disturbed when he described his father's death. In contrast, in my office Mr. ____________ showed no such emotional upheaval when he mentioned his father's demise. Further, as has already been stated, neither the history nor the mental status examination revealed evidence of sufficient criteria to warrant this diagnosis (see attached form); that is, there was not the markedly diminished interest or pleasure in all or nearly all activities most of the day nearly every day or depressed mood to that degree; as has been stated, Mr. ____________ himself indicated that he was only "normally" disturbed by what had happened to him, and when he returned to work and was given light duty felt very good about what he was doing.

In spite of Dr. ____________'s comments about Mr. ____________ having higher cognitive levels of impairment, Dr. ____________ stated on February 25, 1988, "Clinically he is stable and has no neurological residuals with regard to any organic memory impairment." On May 27, 1987, Dr. ____________ had indicated that, "He does not complain in any intellectual function and his previous difficulties with memory and concentration and speech have all improved and have basically resolved."

The entire history, psychiatric examination, review of records, and preparation and dictation of this report were performed solely by the undersigned.

Thank you for referring Mr. ____________ to me.

Sincerely yours.

Diplomate, American Board of
Psychiatry and Neurology

Diagnostic criteria for 309.89 Post-traumatic Stress Disorder*

A. The person has experienced an event that is outside the range of usual human experience and that would be markedly distressing to almost anyone, e.g., serious threat to one's life or physical integrity; serious threat or harm to one's children, spouse, or other close relatives and friends; sudden destruction of one's home or community; or seeing another person who has recently been, or is being, seriously injured or killed as the result of an accident or physical violence.

B. The traumatic event is persistently reexperienced in at least one of the following ways:

---

*American Psychiatric Association, *Diagnostic and Statistical Manual of Mental Disorders, Third Edition, Revised,* Washington, D.C., American Psychiatric Association, 1987. Used with permission.

Work Function Impairment Form

Work Function	Level of Impairment	Supporting Data (Cite Findings)
1. Ability to comprehend and follow instructions	None	Nature and severity of emotional symptomatology not work disabling as per history and mental status examination; patient agrees.
2. Ability to perform simple and repetitive tasks	None	Nature and severity of emotional symptomatology not work disabling as per history and mental status examination; patient agrees.
3. Ability to maintain a work pace appropriate to a given work load	None	Nature and severity of emotional symptomatology not work disabling as per history and mental status examination; patient agrees.
4. Ability to perform complex or varied tasks	Slight	Patient unable to work with forklifts.
5. Ability to relate to other people beyond giving and receiving instructions	None	Nature and severity of emotional symptomatology not work disabling as per history and mental status examination; patient agrees.
6. Ability to influence people	None	Nature and severity of emotional symptomatology not work disabling as per history and mental status examination; patient agrees.
7. Ability to make generalizations, evaluations, or decisions without immediate supervision	None	Nature and severity of emotional symptomatology not work disabling as per history and mental status examination; patient agrees.
8. Ability to accept and carry out responsibility for direction, control, and planning	None	Nature and severity of emotional symptomatology not work disabling as per history and mental status examination; patient agrees.

LEVELS OF IMPAIRMENT

Minimal —discomfort, but not disabling
Very Slight—detectable impairment
Slight —noticeable impairment
Moderate —marked impairment
Severe —unable to perform work function

Overall impairment: Very slight

Apportionment Work Function Impairment Form

Work Function	Level of Impairment	Supporting Data (Cite Findings)
1. Ability to comprehend and follow instructions	None	As per history
2. Ability to perform simple and repetitive tasks	None	As per history
3. Ability to maintain a work pace appropriate to a given work load	None	As per history
4. Ability to perform complex or varied tasks	None	As per history
5. Ability to relate to other people beyond giving and receiving instructions	None	As per history
6. Ability to influence people	None	As per history
7. Ability to make generalizations, evaluations, or decisions without immediate supervision	None	As per history
8. Ability to accept and carry out responsibility for direction, control, and planning	None	As per history

LEVELS OF IMPAIRMENT

Minimal —discomfort, but not disabling
Very Slight—detectable impairment
Slight —noticeable impairment
Moderate —marked impairment
Severe —unable to perform work function

Overall level of impairment: None

(1) recurrent and intrusive distressing recollections of the event (in young children, repetitive play in which themes or aspects of the trauma are expressed)

(2) recurrent distressing dreams of the event

(3) sudden acting or feeling as if the traumatic event were recurring (includes a sense of reliving the experience, illusions, hallucinations, and dissociative [flashback] episodes, even those that occur upon awakening or when intoxicated)

(4) intense psychological distress at exposure to events that symbolize or resemble an aspect of the traumatic event, including anniversaries of the trauma

C. Persistent avoidance of stimuli associated with the trauma or numbing of general responsiveness (not present before the trauma), as indicated by at least three of the following:

 (1) efforts to avoid thoughts or feelings associated with the trauma

 (2) efforts to avoid activities or situations that arouse recollections of the trauma

 (3) inability to recall an important aspect of the trauma (psychogenic amnesia)

 (4) markedly diminished interest in significant activities (in young children, loss of recently acquired developmental skills such as toilet training or language skills)

 (5) feeling of detachment or estrangement from others

 (6) restricted range of affect, e.g., unable to have loving feelings

 (7) sense of a foreshortened future, e.g., does not expect to have a career, marriage, or children, or a long life

D. Persistent symptoms of increased arousal (not present before the trauma), as indicated by at least two of the following:

 (1) difficulty falling or staying asleep

 (2) irritability or outbursts of anger

 (3) difficulty concentrating

 (4) hypervigilance

 (5) exaggerated startle response

 (6) physiologic reactivity upon exposure to events that symbolize or resemble an aspect of the traumatic event (e.g., a woman who was raped in an elevator breaks out in a sweat when entering any elevator)

E. Duration of the disturbance (symptoms in B, C, and D) of at least one month.

Specify delayed onset if the onset of symptoms was at least six months after the trauma.*

Diagnostic criteria for 301.60 Dependent Personality Disorder*

A pervasive pattern of dependent and submissive behavior, beginning by early adulthood and present in a variety of contexts, as indicated by at least five of the following:

---

*American Psychiatric Association, *Diagnostic and Statistical Manual of Mental Disorders, Third Edition, Revised,* Washington, D.C., American Psychiatric Association, 1987. Used with permission.

(1) is unable to make everyday decisions without an excessive amount of advice or reassurance from others
(2) allows others to make most of his or her important decisions, e.g., where to live, what job to take
(3) agrees with people even when he or she believes they are wrong, because of fear of being rejected
(4) has difficulty initiating projects or doing things on his or her own
(5) volunteers to do things that are unpleasant or demeaning in order to get other people to like him or her
(6) feels uncomfortable or helpless when alone, or goes to great lengths to avoid being alone
(7) feels devastated or helpless when close relationships end
(8) is frequently preoccupied with fears of being abandoned
(9) is easily hurt by criticism or disapproval

Diagnostic criteria for Major Depressive Episode*

Note: A "Major Depressive Syndrome" is defined as criterion A below.

A. At least five of the following symptoms have been present during the same two-week period and represent a change from previous functioning; at least one of the symptoms is either (1) depressed mood, or (2) loss of interest or pleasure. (Do not include symptoms that are clearly due to a physical condition, mood-incongruent delusions or hallucinations, incoherence, or marked loosening of associations.)

(1) depressed mood (or can be irritable mood in children and adolescents) most of the day, nearly every day, as indicated either by subjective account or observation by others
(2) markedly diminished interest or pleasure in all, or almost all, activities most of the day, nearly every day (as indicated either by subjective account or observation by others of apathy most of the time)
(3) significant weight loss or weight gain when not dieting (e.g., more than 5% of body weight in a month), or decrease or increase in appetite nearly every day (in children, consider failure to make expected weight gains)
(4) insomnia or hypersomnia nearly every day

*American Psychiatric Association, *Diagnostic and Statistical Manual of Mental Disorders, Third Edition, Revised,* Washington, D.C., American Psychiatric Association, 1987. Used with permission.

(5) psychomotor agitation or retardation nearly every day (observable by others, not merely subjective feelings of restlessness or being slowed down)

(6) fatigue or loss of energy nearly every day

(7) feelings of worthlessness or excessive or inappropriate guilt (which may be delusional) nearly every day (not merely self-reproach or guilt about being sick)

(8) diminished ability to think or concentrate, or indecisiveness, nearly every day (either by subjective account or as observed by others)

(9) recurrent thoughts of death (not just fear of dying), recurrent suicidal ideation without a specific plan, or a suicide attempt or a specific plan for committing suicide*

---

*American Psychiatric Association, *Diagnostic and Statistical Manual of Mental Disorders, Third Edition, Revised,* Washington, D.C., American Psychiatric Association, 1987. Used with permission.

CHAPTER 17

SPECIFIC TYPES OF PROCEEDINGS AND CIVIL ACTIONS

Herbert Lasky

§ 17.1 Introduction

As stated earlier, the basic principles in this book are applicable to any types of legal proceedings that involve issues of the existence and causation of mental disorders and resultant disability. This chapter demonstrates the application of these principles to specific types of actions and proceedings. It is not intended to cover the substantive elements of the particular legal doctrines involved, but merely to deal with the issues that arise when mental injury of some type is claimed or becomes an issue in the application of these doctrines. Discussed are the Americans with Disabilities Act, sexual harassment or abuse, infliction of emotional distress, wrongful termination, and related issues.

§ 17.2 Americans with Disabilities Act

In broad summary, the Americans with Disabilities Act (ADA)[1] prohibits employers from discriminating on the basis of an individual's disabilities regarding

[1] 42 U.S.C. §§ 12101–12213 (Supp. III 1991).

application for employment and terms of employment. In determining rights under the Act, the relevant issues with respect to the concerns of this chapter are:

1. **Is an individual disabled?** *Disability* is defined as (a) a physical or mental impairment that substantially limits one or more of the major life activities of such individual, (b) a record of such an impairment, or (c) being regarded as having such an impairment.[2]
2. **Is the individual a "qualified individual with a disability?"** This means an individual with a disability who, with or without reasonable accommodation, can perform the essential functions of the employment position that such individual holds or desires. The Act states that for the purposes of this question, consideration shall be given to the employer's judgment as to what functions of a job are essential, and if an employer has prepared a written description before advertising or interviewing applicants for the job, this description shall be considered evidence of the essential functions of the job.[3]
3. The duty not to discriminate includes the duty to reasonably accommodate a person who is otherwise qualified.[4]
4. Defenses include undue hardship, business necessity, or direct threat to health or safety of the individual or others in the workplace.[5]

The overall purpose of the Act is to remove barriers that prevent qualified individuals with disabilities from enjoying the same employment opportunities that are available to nondisabled individuals.

The author believes the principal value of the Act is that it will cause many employers to take a second look at an individual they might otherwise have rejected out of hand as being "disabled" and not worthy of consideration. Many types of disabilities have narrowly limited impact on an individual's ability to perform the essential functions of a job, and many disabilities can be reasonably accommodated. In this connection, the experience of the Job Accommodation Network, a service of the President's Committee on Employment of People With Disabilities, is hopeful. The Job Accommodation Network is an information network and consulting resource that, at no cost to the caller, provides information on methods and available equipment that have proven effective for a wide range of accommodations. The network discusses with appropriately concerned persons their problems and information needs and makes immediate suggestions on solutions to accommodation problems.[6] Its experience to date shows that 31 percent of

---

[2] *Id.* § 12102(2).

[3] *Id.* § 12111(8).

[4] *Id.* §§ 12111(a), 12112(b)(5).

[5] *Id.* §§ 12111(10)(A)(B), 12113(a), 12113(b).

[6] The Job Accommodation Network is at West Virginia University, 809 Allen Hall, Morgantown, West Virginia 26506-6123. Telephone 1-800-526-7234 in the United States, 1-800-526-2262 in Canada, 1-800-526-4698 in West Virginia (all lines voice/TDD).

accommodations suggested are no cost, 19 percent between $1 and $50, 19 percent between $50 and $500, 19 percent between $500 and $1,000, 11 percent between $1,000 and $5,000, and only 1 percent more than $5,000.[7]

The Act explicitly applies its definition of a covered disability to a "mental impairment." Under 29 Code of Federal Regulations § 1630.2(h)(1) and (2), this includes any "mental or psychological disorder."

Thus, the approach to dealing with problems arising under the ADA is consistent with the principles outlined in the preceding chapters. The first question is whether the individual in question has a mental illness. The answer is found by referring to the definitions set out by the American Psychiatric Association's *Diagnostic and Statistical Manual of Mental Disorders* (DSM-III-R). See **Chapters 1** and **2.** Assuming that the claimed mental disorder is found to be consistent with the DSM-III-R criteria, the next question is, what are the "essential functions" of the job for which the employee seeks consideration, and what effect does the impairment constituted by the mental disorder have on the ability to perform those essential functions? See **Chapters 7** and **8. Chapter 7** is particularly on point because it describes the effect of particular elements of the diagnostic criteria for given DSM-III-R or mental disorders on the *temperaments,* as described by the Department of Labor's *Revised Handbook for Analyzing Jobs.* These are:

D—Directing, controlling, or planning activities of others.
R—Performing repetitive or short-cycle work.
I —Influencing people in their opinions, attitudes, and judgments.
V—Performing a variety of duties.
E—Expressing personal feelings.
A—Working alone or apart in physical isolation from others.
S—Performing effectively under stress.
T—Attaining precise set limits, tolerances, and standards.
U—Working under specific instructions.
P—Dealing with people.
J —Making judgments and decisions.

In making the essential function determination:

> Evaluate the work activities of the job for applicability of the temperament factors by referring to the definition of the factors. Select those factors considered to be important in relation to the kinds of adjustment which the worker must make for successful job performance. Do not assign temperaments based on incidental work activities. Some simple jobs may require the worker to adjust to only one Temperament factor, while other jobs may require adjustment to several. In item 9 of the JAR (Job Analysis Report) enter the letter designation(s) of

[7] Job Accommodation Network, Facts about Disability (1992).

> Temperament Factor(s) considered to be important in relation to the kinds of adjustments which the worker must make for successful job performance.[8]

Thus, if we know the essential functions of the job and what effect the mental disorder has on the ability to perform the essential functions, we will know whether the employee in question is a "qualified individual with a disability." If the individual cannot perform an essential function of the job because of the individual's impairment, that would end the question of the individual's entitlement.

If the individual is a "qualified individual with a disability," the next question is, can reasonable accommodation be made? In arriving at the answer to this question, consideration must be given to the exact nature of the individual's work limitation and to whether appropriate adjustments in the work assignment or environment can be made without constituting either an undue hardship or a threat to health and safety.

§ 17.3 —Judicial Interpretation of Rehabilitation Act

Although at the time of this writing there are no reported decisions directly applying the provisions of the ADA, there is an essentially similar body of decisions applying the principles of the Rehabilitation Act of 1973.[9] This is the Act that imposes upon employers and educational institutions engaging in federally funded activities obligations with respect to rehabilitation of disabled persons essentially similar to those under the ADA. Thus, the provisions of the Acts are essentially parallel. Equal Employment Opportunity Commission (EEOC) Regulation 1630.1 states in subpart (c): "Except as otherwise provided in this part, this part does not apply a lesser standard than the standards applied under Title V of the Rehabilitation Act of 1973 (29 U.S.C. 790-794 (a)), or the regulations issued by federal agencies pursuant to that title." The appendix to part 1630 further states: "Unless expressly stated otherwise, the standards applied in the ADA are not intended to be lesser than the standards applied under the Rehabilitation Act of 1973."

The following summarizes judicial interpretation of the relevant sections of the Rehabilitation Act of 1973:

Qualified Individual with a Disability

Schmidt v. Bell, 33 Fair Empl. Prac. Cas. (BNA) 839 (1983).

Person suffering from post-traumatic stress disorder found not qualified because he could not perform the essential requirements of the position of

---

[8] Department of Labor, Revised Handbook for Analyzing Jobs 10-5 (1992).

[9] 29 U.S.C. §§ 790–800 (1973).

student loan collector due to his resentment of any type of authority and a volatile explosive personality that was exacerbated under stress. It was found that the position of student loan collector was inherently stressful.

Doe v. New York University, 666 F.2d 761 (2d Cir. 1981).

Medical school applicant for psychiatric training held not qualified because her borderline personality disorder created self-destructive and antisocial behavior that had a bearing on the safety of other students, faculty, and patients to whom she could be exposed.

Doe v. Region 13 Mental Health-Mental Retardation Commission, 704 F.2d 1402 (5th Cir. 1983).

Similar type of case and holding.

Franklin v. United States Postal Service, 687 F. Supp. 1214 (S.D. Ohio 1988).

Paranoid schizophrenic unable to perform essential functions of job because he was dangerous to fellow employees and public and did not take the necessary medication to control his condition.

Matzo v. Postmaster General, 685 F. Supp. 260, 46 Fair Empl. Prac. Cas. (BNA) 869 (D.D.C. 1987).

Not "otherwise qualified" because manic-depressive condition made employee unable to work and stay on duty for duration of work day.

Fields v. Lyng, 48 Fair Empl. Prac. Cas. (BNA) 103 (1988).

Former United States Department of Agriculture labor relations specialist not qualified when borderline personality disorder side effects of anxiety when traveling and kleptomania made him unable to perform work effectively and weakened his credibility for people with whom he was dealing.

Grace Mills v. Derwinski, 56 Fair Empl. Prac. Cas. (BNA) 1592 (1991).

Nurse at Veterans Administration not otherwise qualified when she could not, because of the medication regime necessary for her manic-depressive condition, be on duty before 10:00 a.m. when the regular duties started at 7:00 or 8:00 A.M.

Reasonable Accommodation

Gardner v. Morris, 752 F.2d 1271 (8th Cir. 1985).

Not reasonable accommodation to require Corps of Engineers to provide on-site medical facilities for monitoring medication required for claimant's manic depression when the assignment was in Saudi Arabia at a comparatively isolated desert location. The court made clear that if medical facilities were available under ordinary conditions, the claimant's condition could have been reasonably accommodated merely by his taking appropriate medication, being monitored, and given reasonable opportunity to do so.

Franklin v. United States Postal Service, 687 F. Supp. 1214 (S.D. Ohio 1988).

Paranoid schizophrenic postal worker was reasonably accommodated when he was given a "last chance agreement" to show that he could perform the duties of his occupation when he stayed on his required medication schedule. He failed to maintain the proper medication schedule and had so many altercations with fellow employees and the public that it was considered dangerous to retain him.

Shea v. Tisch, 870 F.2d 786 (1st Cir.), 49 Fair Empl. Prac. Cas. (BNA) 625 (1988).

Not reasonable accommodation to assign worker who had anxiety disorder only to daytime, weekday positions within 15 miles of home because doing so would violate the contract rights of other employees to rotate similar assignments on a seniority basis.

Adams v. General Services Administration, 723 F. Supp. 1531 (D.D.C. 1989).

Not unreasonable accommodation to require agency to transfer employee who suffers from maladaptive reaction to psychic stressors and who had assaulted a supervisor when agency entitled to assign personnel as the needs of the mission dictate.

Lucero v. Hart, 915 F.2d 1367 (9th Cir.), 54 Fair Empl. Prac. Cas. (BNA) 75 (1990).

Employer made reasonable efforts to accommodate emotionally handicapped typist who had stress reaction when she took and failed typing test. A last chance was given her by providing additional opportunities to take the test.

Kimbro v. Atlantic Richfield Co., 889 F.2d 869 (9th Cir.), 57 Fair Empl. Prac. Cas. (BNA) 363 (1989), *cert. denied,* 111 Supreme Court Reporter 53 (1990).

It would have been reasonable accommodation to require employer to give leave to the employee when migraine attacks were coming on and the employee could tell in advance what the pattern of such attacks was. However, the employer was not required to allow employee to take sick leave on particular days or hours when the migraine attack occurred without the employee giving the employer advance notice because it would have been an undue hardship on the employer due to the employer's need to schedule projects in advance.

Baxter v. Wisconsin Department of Natural Resources, 477 N.W.2d 648 (Wis.), 57 Fair Empl. Prac. Cas. (BNA) 740 (1991).

It would have been a reasonable accommodation for an employee who had depression to modify the work schedule sufficiently to allow employee to see a psychiatrist and to have a discussion with the program head regarding his problem, and to be given explicit instructions concerning the job duties. It would not have been a reasonable accommodation to require employer to provide job coach and extend probationary period.

Drabandt v. James River Corp., 56 Fair Empl. Prac. Cas. (BNA) 881 (1991).
Reasonable accommodation required allowing employee to be assigned low-stress job when qualified.

§ 17.4 —Job Analysis Report

The following job analysis report was furnished by Mr. Paul Johnson, a Fairfield, California, vocational consultant who helped prepare the *Report of the Medical Advisory Committee of the California Division of Industrial Accidents: The Evaluation of Permanent Psychiatric Disability.* [10]

As to when such a job analysis report should be prepared, Mr. Johnson says, "If you don't have it before you need it, when you need it, it's too late." Obviously, in a litigation context, required performance standards prepared before the onset of litigation would have much more credibility than such standards prepared later.

For our present purposes, the portion of the report immediately relevant is the description of essential functions 1, 2, and 3. Note that in the section entitled "Required Temperaments Report Summary," the temperament symbols were prepared under the former *Handbook for Analyzing Jobs.* Under the revised handbook, D-DCP is simply called D; J-SJC is J; M-MVC is essentially embraced within J; DEPL is now P; and V-VARCH is V. As far as substance is concerned, there is no essential difference.

Summary Job Analysis (JA) Report
Identifying Information

Report Location and Identification = \word\F129JOB.DOC

ANALYST IDENTIFICATION:

Analyst's Name:	Paul Johnson
Analyst's Firm:	Watters and Associates
Date of JA:	February 19, 1992
Analyst Firm Reviewer:	George Watters

[10] See **App. A.**

ESTABLISHMENT ORGANIZATION:

Establishment Name:
Establishment Reviewer:
Date of JA Review: February 20, 1992

JOB IDENTIFICATION:

Job Title: Administrative Assistant
Job ID Code: 169.167-010

Summary of Task Statements
Essential Functions/Tasks:
Essential Function #1

Essential Task/Function 1 Justification. The reason the position exists is to perform the function; a limited number of employees are available among whom the performance of that job function can be distributed; and the function is highly specialized.

The position of Administrative Assistant is unique within the university system in that those departments that require an Administrative Assistant are assigned only one. The skills, knowledge and abilities required of Administrative Assistants throughout the system vary by department. Each department requires highly specialized backgrounds of administrative staff members to efficiently carry out assignments and achieve necessary department goals.

Essential Function #1 Description

Coordinates office services such as personnel, budget preparation and control, housekeeping, records control and special management studies for the purpose of improving work flow, simplifying reporting procedures and implementing cost reductions, using: (machine/s) computer, printer, 10-key adding machine; (tool/s) pens, pencils, stapler, hole punch, ruler; (equipment) telephone, video display terminal, fax machine, copy machine, electronic calculator; (work aid/s) procedure manuals, technical manuals, maps, charts and tables, and various software programs.

Essential Function #2

Essential Task/Function 2 Justification. The reason the position exists is to perform the function; a limited number of employees are available among whom the performance of that job function can be distributed; and the function is highly specialized.

The position of Administrative Assistant is unique within the university system in that those departments that require an Administrative Assistant are assigned only one. The skills, knowledge and abilities required of Administrative Assistants throughout the system vary by department. Each department requires highly specialized backgrounds of administrative staff members to efficiently carry out assignments and achieve necessary department goals.

Essential Function #2 Description

Analyzes department operating practice such as recordkeeping systems, forms control, office layout, personnel and budgetary requirements, and performance standards for the purpose of creating new systems or revising established procedures, using: (machine/s) computer, printer, 10-key adding machine; (tool/s) pens, pencils, stapler, hole punch, ruler; (equipment) telephone, video display terminal, fax machine, copy machine, electronic calculator; (work aid/s) procedure manuals, technical manuals, maps, charts and tables, various software programs.

Essential Function #3

Essential Task/Function 3 Justification. The reason the position exists is to perform the function; a limited number of employees are available among whom the performance of that job function can be distributed; and the function is highly specialized.

The position of Administrative Assistant is unique within the university system in that those departments that require an Administrative Assistant are assigned only one. The skills, knowledge and abilities required of Administrative Assistants throughout the system vary by department. Each department requires highly specialized backgrounds of administrative staff members to efficiently carry out assignments and achieve necessary department goals.

Essential Function #3 Description

Coordinates collection and preparation of operating reports including time-and-attendance records, terminations, new hires, transfers, budget expenditures and statistical records of performance data for the purpose of preparing reports including conclusions and recommendations for solutions of administrative problems, using: (machine/s) computer, printer, 10-key adding machine; (tool/s) pens, pencils, stapler, hole punch, ruler; (equipment) telephone, video display terminal, fax machine, copy machine, electronic calculator; (work aid/s) procedure manuals, technical manuals, maps, charts and tables, various software programs.

GED Rating Summary

GED Reasoning Level = 5. Defined as the ability to apply principles of logical or scientific thinking to define problems, collect data, establish facts, and draw valid conclusions. Interpret an extensive variety of technical instructions in mathematical or diagrammatic form. Deal with several abstract and concrete variables.

Example of task illustrating level 5 GED Reasoning Development required by the job: Coordinates collection and preparation of operating reports, including time-and-attendance records, terminations, new hires, transfers, budget expenditures and statistical records of performance data for the purpose of preparing reports including conclusions and recommendations for solutions of administrative problems.

GED Math Level = 3. Defined as the ability to compute discount, interest, profit and loss; commission, markup, and selling price; ratio and proportion, and percentage. Calculate surfaces, volumes, weights and measures.

Algebra:

Calculate variables and formulas; monomials and polynomials; ratio and proportion variables; and square roots and radicals.

Geometry:

Calculate plane and solid figures; circumference, area and volume. Understand kinds of angles, and properties of pairs of angles.

Example of task illustrating level 3 GED Mathematical Development required by the job: Coordinates collection and preparation of operating reports, including time-and-attendance records, budget expenditures and statistical records of performance data for the purpose of preparing reports including conclusions and recommendations for solutions of administrative problems.

GED Language Level = 5. Defined as

Reading:

Read literature, book and play reviews, scientific and technical journals, abstracts, financial reports and legal documents.

Writing:

Write novels, plays, editorials, journals, speeches, manuals, critiques, poetry and songs.

Speaking:

Conversant in the theory, principles, and methods of effective and persuasive speaking, voice and diction, phonetics, discussion and debate.

Example of task illustrating level 5 GED Language Development required by the job: Coordinates collection and preparation of operating reports including time-and-attendance records, budget expenditures, and statistical records of performance data for the purpose of preparing reports including conclusions and recommendations for solutions of administrative problems.

Specific Vocational Preparation (SVP) Summary

Level 7—Over 2 years up to and including 4 years.

Skilled Work—includes vocational education, apprenticeship, in-plant, on-the-job, and essential experience gained in other jobs.

Summary of DPT Function Ratings

Data Rating = 1-Coordinating.

Determining time, place and sequence of operations or actions to be taken on the basis of analysis of data; executing determinations and/or reporting on events. Data includes numbers, words, symbols, ideas, concepts and oral verbalizations.

Example of task illustrating level 1 Data Rating required by the job: Coordinates collection and preparation of operating reports including time-and-attendance records, terminations, new hires, transfers, budget expenditures and statistical records of performance data for the purpose of preparing reports including conclusions and recommendations for solutions of administrative problems.

People Rating = 6-Speaking-Signaling.

Talking with and/or signaling people to convey or exchange information. Includes giving assignments and/or directions to helpers or assistants.

Example of task illustrating level 6 People Rating required by the job: Coordinates collection and preparation of operating reports including time-and-attendance records, terminations, new hires, transfers, budget expenditures and statistical records of performance data for the purpose of preparing reports including conclusions and recommendations for solutions of administrative problems.

Things Rating = 7-Handling.

Using body members, hand tools, and/or special devices to work, move or carry objects or materials. Involves little or no latitude for judgment with regard to attainment of standards or in selecting appropriate tool, object or material.

Example of task illustrating level 7 Handling Rating required by the job: Analyzes department operating practices such as recordkeeping systems, forms control, office layout, personnel and budgetary requirements, and performance standards for the purpose of creating new systems or revising established procedures, using: (machine/s) computer, printer, 10-key adding machine; (tool/s) pens, pencils, stapler, hole punch, ruler; (equipment) telephone, video display terminal, fax machine, copy machine, electronic calculator; (work aid/s) procedure manuals, technical manuals, maps, charts and tables, various software programs.

Required Temperaments Report Summary

D-DCP (Direction, Control, and Planning).

Work situations where accepting responsibility for the direction, control or planning of an activity is required. (Consider jobs for this factor when the worker is in a position to negotiate, organize, direct, supervise, formulate practices or make final decisions.)

Example of task illustrating the necessity for adaptability to accepting responsibility for the direction, control and planning of an activity required by the job: Coordinates collection and preparation of operating reports including time-and-attendance records, terminations, new hires, transfers, budget expenditures and statistical records of performance data for the purpose of preparing reports including conclusions and recommendations for solutions of administrative problems.

J-SJC (Sensory or Judgmental Criteria).

Work situations where making generalizations, evaluations, or decisions based on sensory or judgmental criteria is required. (Consider jobs for this factor when the worker relies on one or more of the five physical senses or relies on knowledge gained by experience to make evaluations.)

Example of task illustrating the necessity for adaptability to making generalizations, evaluations or decisions based on sensory or judgmental criteria required by the job: Coordinates office services such as personnel, budget preparation and control, housekeeping, records control and special management studies for the purpose of improving work flow, simplifying reporting procedures and implementing cost reductions.

M-MVC (Measurable or Verifiable Criteria).

Work situations in which making generalizations, judgments, or decisions based on measurable or verifiable criteria is required. (Consider jobs for this factor when the worker makes evaluations on the basis of data.)

Example of task illustrating the necessity for adaptability to making generalizations, judgments, or decisions based on measurable or verifiable criteria required by the job: Coordinates collection and preparation of operating reports including time-and-attendance records, budget expenditures and statistical records of performance data for the purpose of preparing reports including conclusions and recommendations for solutions of administrative problems.

P-DEPL (Dealing with People).

Work situations where dealing with people beyond giving and receiving of instructions is required. (Consider jobs for this factor when the worker must relate to people in situations involving more than giving or receiving instructions.)

Example of task illustrating the necessity for adaptability to dealing with people beyond giving and receiving of instructions required by the job: Coordinates office services such as personnel, budget preparation and control, housekeeping, records control and special management studies for the purpose of improving work flow, simplifying reporting procedures and implementing cost reductions.

V-VARCH (VARiety and CHange).

Work situations where performing a variety of duties, often changing from one task to another of a different nature without loss of efficiency or composure. (Consider jobs for this factor when different skills, knowledge and abilities are required for performing a wide variety of tasks.)

Example of task illustrating the necessity for adaptability to perform a variety of duties, often changing from one task to another of a different nature without loss of efficiency or composure required by the job: Analyzes department operating practices such as recordkeeping systems, forms control, office layout, personnel and budgetary requirements, and performance standards for the purpose of creating new systems or revising established procedures.

Summary of Key Aptitude Ratings

General Intelligence Rating: 2, Above Average Aptitude (67th–90th Percentile). Defined as general learning ability. The ability to "catch on," or understand instructions and underlying principles; the ability to reason and make judgments.

Example of task illustrating highest level of "G" aptitude required by the job: Analyzes department operating practices such as recordkeeping systems, forms control, office layout, personnel and budgetary requirements, and performance standards for the purpose of creating new systems or revising established procedures. Level 2 General Intelligence is required to examine and evaluate established department administrative practices for their adequacy, and to present alternative actions for those practices found to no longer adequately serve their intended purpose.

Verbal Aptitude Rating: 2, Above Average Aptitude (67th–90th Percentile). Defined as the ability to understand the meanings of words and to use them effectively; to comprehend language, understand relationships between words and to understand meanings of whole sentences and paragraphs.

Example of task illustrating highest level of "V" aptitude required by the job: Coordinates collection and preparation of operating reports including time-and-attendance records, terminations, new hires, transfers, budget expenditures and statistical records of performance data for the purpose of preparing reports including conclusions and recommendations for solutions of administrative problems. Level 2 Verbal Aptitude is required to communicate effectively with instructors, managers, and other administrative staff to teach and train them through explanation, demonstration and supervised practice, to implement alternative administrative practices for those that have been found to be inadequate.

Numerical Aptitude Rating: 3, Average Aptitude (33rd–67th Percentile). Defined as the ability to perform arithmetic operations quickly and accurately.

Example of task illustrating highest level of "N" aptitude required by the job: Coordinates collection and preparation of operating reports including time-and-attendance records, terminations, new hires, transfers, budget expenditures and statistical records of performance data for the purpose of preparing reports including conclusions and recommendations for solutions of administrative problems. Level 3 Numerical Aptitude is required to compute, compile and analyze data for the purpose of preparing reports including conclusions and recommendations for solutions of administrative problems.

Clerical Perception Rating: 3, Average Aptitude (33rd–67th Percentile). The ability to perceive detail in verbal or tabular material. The ability to observe differences in copy, to proofread words and numbers, and to avoid perceptual errors in arithmetic computation.

Example of task illustrating highest level of "Q" aptitude required by the job: Coordinates collection and preparation of operating reports including time-and-attendance records, terminations, new hires, transfers, budget expenditures and statistical records of performance data for the purpose of preparing reports including conclusions and recommendations for solutions of administrative problems. Level 3 Clerical Perception is required to copy, compute and compile data and to present appropriate alternative actions in relation to that evaluation.

DOL Summary of Customary Physical Demands of Job

Rating Symbol Key:

NP = Not Present—Does not exist
O = Occasionally—Up to 1/3 of the time
F = Frequently—From 1/3 to 2/3 of the time
C = Constantly—2/3 or more of the time

Physical Demands

1.	STRENGTH:			4.	REACHING	
F						
	A. Standing	20%			HANDLING	
F						
	Walking	40%			FINGERING	
F						
	Sitting	40%			FEELING	NP
	B. Lifting	0	10 lbs.	5.	TALKING:	
	Carrying	0	10 lbs.		Ordinary	
F						
	Pushing	0	12 lbs.		Other	
O						
2.	CLIMBING	0			HEARING:	
	BALANCING	0			Conversations	
F						
					Other Sounds	O
3.	STOOPING	0		6.	SEEING:	
	KNEELING	0			Acuity, Near	C
	CROUCHING	0			Acuity, Far	F
	CRAWLING	NP			Depth Perception	O
					Accommodation	O
					Color Vision	O
					Field of Vision	O

7. PHYSICAL DEMANDS RATING SUMMARY: Light Work: (2) (3) (4) (5) (6) (DOL Physical Demand Categories 1 to 6 are very significant to the customary performance of the job if contained in parenthesis.)

8. PHYSICAL DEMAND COMMENTS: This position is amenable to many modes of reasonable accommodation.

Customary Environmental Conditions of Job

1. ENVIRONMENT:

   Inside 95%   Outside 5%

2. EXTREME COLD NP
3. EXTREME HEAT NP
4. WEST/HUMID NP
5. NOISE (IN DECIBELS): 70 decibels
   VIBRATION NP

Comments Regarding "Noise": Normal conversational speech.

6. HAZARDS
   - Mechanical NP
   - Explosives NP
   - Electrical NP
   - Radiant Energy NP
   - Burns NP
   - Other Hazard/s NP
7. ATMOSPHERIC CONDITIONS:
   - Fumes NP
   - Mists NP
   - Odors NP
   - Gases NP
   - Dusts NP
   - Poor Ventilation NP
   - Other Atmospheric Hazards NP
8. PROTECTIVE CLOTHING—DEVICES:
9. E.C. SUMMARY: Inside Work 2 3 4 5 6 7
10. SUMMARY ENVIRONMENTAL COMMENTS: This position performs all essential functions in an office environment that is well ventilated, temperature controlled and adequately lit.

Analyst Comments

This position is amenable to various methods of reasonable accommodation.

§ 17.5 —Summary of Opinions

This section summarizes Mr. Johnson's opinions on the subject of reasonable accommodation with respect to the job analysis in **§ 17.4**. Assume that an employee of the company for which the job analysis was prepared is seriously disturbed when a new supervisor replaces the former supervisor with whom the employee had comfortable relations. The employee has difficulties with the new supervisor, and because of preexisting vulnerabilities, suffers either a major depression or general anxiety disorder (because most of the nonpsychotic disorders would fall into these categories, we can discuss reasonable accommodation with respect to each). We will assume that the employee is unable to carry out her duties and, therefore, is terminated. After a period of psychiatric treatment, the employee feels that she is now capable of returning to this employment, and upon hearing that the former supervisor has now left the company, applies for reinstatement. We will assume that the employee still suffers from some residuals of a mental condition consisting of the following:

If major depression: depressed mood, markedly diminished interest or pleasure in activities, fatigue or a loss of energy, diminished ability to think or concentrate, or indecisiveness.

If general anxiety disorder: difficulty concentrating, hypervigilance, irritability, feeling keyed up or on edge.

It was Mr. Johnson's feeling that in most situations, the employee could handle essential functions 1 and 3 from the start, although he would advise that the psychiatrist have a meeting with the supervisor simply to make suggestions as to the nature of the employee's then limitations and the best way to be sure that the work environment could accommodate them. The main point is that functions 1 and 3 do not require the investment of one's ego in a manner similar to that required by function 2 because they simply require performing in accordance with previously set standards and performing functions which, under the assumptions of our situation, this employee at one time performed successfully.

The reasonable accommodation required for function 2 would be simply to ease the employee into it. This is because function 2 demands a degree of creativity due to the requirement of considering the creation of new systems or revising established procedures. At the outset, this can involve situations in which, in effect, one lays one's ego on the line in making recommendations for new ways of doing things. For example, one may have to defend proposals. The easing in could be facilitated by, with respect to essential function 3, which involves conclusions and recommendations for solving administrative problems, having the supervisor assist and stimulate the employee to make such conclusions by a conference or two with her on such matters. That would probably be sufficient emotional support for this type of employee.

As to function 2, the reasonable accommodation would simply be to have a probationary period lasting up to approximately six months in which the employee would be given an opportunity to find that she could perform functions 1 and 3 capably and then would be emboldened to proceed on with returning to the exercise of essential function 2, namely recommending new and improved procedures. Mr. Johnson estimates that approximately six months would be reasonable for this purpose.

In considering the appropriateness of this recommendation, recall **Chapters 1** and **2** concerning the DSM-III-R diagnostic criteria. Under "Course," it is stated that the duration of a major depressive episode is variable. Untreated, the episode typically lasts six months or longer. Usually there is a complete remission of symptoms and general functioning returns to the premorbid level, though in a large proportion of cases some symptoms persist for as long as two years. This would appear to indicate that when the employee has undergone a course of treatment, the suggested six months of reasonable accommodation would be appropriate.[11]

With regard to general anxiety disorder, DSM-III-R says that "impairment in social or occupational functioning is rarely more than mild."[12] This provides additional reason to believe the suggested reasonable accommodation would be appropriate. Thus, a reasonable accommodation would appear to be beneficial for all concerned.

§ 17.6 Sexual Harassment Issues

This is a rapidly growing specialized field of litigation given impetus by the Clarence Thomas-Anita Hill hearings.[13]

The Civil Rights Act of 1991[14] provides for the right to recover compensatory damages and punitive damages for violation of the right to be free from sexual harassment. Sexual harassment as such has been unlawful since the Civil Rights Act of 1964.[15] By regulation, the EEOC provided that sexual harassment could consist of the following:

> Unwelcome sexual advances, request for sexual favors, and other verbal or physical conduct of a sexual nature when submission to such conduct is made either explicitly or implicitly, a term or condition of an individual's employment, (2) submission to or rejection of such conduct by an individual is used as the basis for employment decisions affecting such an individual or (3) such conduct has the purpose or effect of unreasonably interfering with an individual's work performance or creating an intimidating, hostile or offensive working environment.[16]

The United States Supreme Court further delineated these concepts in the case of *Meritor Savings Bank v. Vincent.*[17] There it distinguished between two types of sexual harassment: *quid pro quo* harassment and *hostile working environment*

---

[11] Am. Psychiatric Ass'n, Diagnostic and Statistical Manual of Mental Disorders 220–21 (3d ed., rev. 1987).

[12] *Id.* at 251.

[13] *See* A. Conte, Sexual Harassment in the Workplace (John Wiley & Sons 1990).

[14] 42 U.S.C. § 1981(A) (1988).

[15] *Id.* § 2000(e)-(a)(1).

[16] 29 C.F.R. § 1604.11(a) (1980).

[17] 477 U.S. 57 (1986).

harassment. *Quid pro quo* harassment involves an explicit or implicit trade of sexual favors in exchange for some job benefit, such as a promotion or a raise, or to prevent a job detriment, such as a termination or demotion. *Hostile working environment* harassment does not require such a trade-off. The victim must show only that the harassment was "sufficiently severe or pervasive" so as to "alter the conditions of [the victim's] employment and create an abusive working environment."[18] A recent article in the *Journal of Psychiatry and Law* suggests that the latter category can usefully be subdivided into two further types of sexual harassment: (1) the type that involves sexual assault or other criminal behavior, and (2) the type that involves harassment of a less serious nature, such as sexual propositions, epithets, dirty jokes, and visual displays that produce only psychological distress and are generally not criminal in nature. The article states that the latter type is the type most commonly seen and the type most difficult to define, prove, or disprove.[19]

A recent judicial development highlights the importance of the forensic psychological aspects of these cases. In *Ellison v. Brady,*[20] the court stated a doctrine that explicitly underlines the relevance of the previous mental condition of a plaintiff in this type of litigation. That decision adopted a "reasonable woman" standard for determining whether a liability-creating abusive working environment exists. In doing so, the court said that "evaluating the severity and pervasiveness of sexual harassment, we should focus on the perspective of the victim" and

> in order to shield employers from having to accommodate the idiosyncratic concerns of the rare hypersensitive employee, we hold that a female plaintiff states a prima facie case of hostile environment sexual harassment when she alleges conduct which a reasonable woman would consider sufficiently severe or pervasive to alter the conditions of employment and create an abusive working environment.[21]

Thus, the psychiatric doctrines discussed in **Chapters 1** and **2** dealing with mental disorders and personality disorders are of crucial importance for determining the existence of preexisting conditions.

The required forensic evaluation for such cases focuses upon two areas. The first relates to the liability aspects; second are the damages aspects.

---

[18] *Id.* at 67.

[19] Feldman-Schorrig & McDonald, *The Role of Forensic Psychiatry in the Defense of Sexual Harassment Cases,* 20 J. Psychiatry & L. 5 (1992). Dr. Schorrig is a psychiatrist and Mr. McDonald is an attorney, both of whom practice in the Los Angeles area. This author is substantially indebted to the writers of this article for much of the information on this topic.

[20] 925 F.2d 872 (9th Cir. 1991).

[21] *Id.* at 879.

Liability Aspects

There are three basic categories here for which psychiatric evaluation can give important assistance. These are the issues of credibility, hypersensitivity, and invitation or welcoming conduct.[22]

Dr. Feldman-Schorrig's article refers to studies indicating that women who file sexual harassment claims often have a history of victimization, either through incest or rape. Such a person might be hypersensitive.

Another doctrine referred to is *repetition compulsion,* or the tendency of individuals to repeat past behavior. Dr. Feldman-Schorrig states that there is strong evidence that a substantial proportion of women who file such claims are not only hypersensitive, but also may be driven to seek out and manufacture situations similar to past experiences, which they later label as harassment. It is theorized that the tendency of individuals to repeat such behavior is an attempt to gain mastery over the original trauma that generated the compulsion.

Certain personality disorders may be conducive to claims of sexual harassment. The article suggests that there is a significant degree of correlation between a history of childhood abuse and a diagnosis of borderline personality disorder. See **Chapter 2**. In a very broad summary, a borderline personality disordered individual is likely to be dishonest.

Another common personality disorder found among women with sexual abuse histories is histrionic personality. Dr. Feldman-Schorrig's article states:

> Women with histrionic personality disorders are easily recognized by their inappropriately seductive appearance or behavior. They are dramatic and expressionistic and prone to exaggeration. They experience flights into romantic fantasy and their relationships with men are typically controlling or dependent, and they often act out a role such as "victim" or "princess."[23]

Another psychiatric syndrome referred to is *displacement.* This term applies to a situation in which a victim of abuse, as an unconscious effort to find a safer outlet for anger felt toward an abusive partner or spouse, might displace the anger to a more available but less threatening target. In one example, the claimant alleged that a coworker screamed at her frequently, carried a .357 magnum gun, and referred to her in foul language. Records of her court divorce proceedings revealed that she had accused her estranged husband of identical behavior.

The foregoing illustrate types of mental conditions that can lead a claimant, through unconscious motivation, to falsely accuse someone of harassment, or to find offensive behavior that the "reasonable woman" would not find offensive.

---

[22] The cases make clear that the sexual conduct in the workplace must be unwelcomed to be actionable. *See* 29 C.F.R. § 1604.11(a) (1980) and Meritor Sav. Bank v. Vincent, 477 U.S. 57, 68 (1986).

[23] Feldman-Schorrig & McDonald, *The Role of Forensic Psychiatry in the Defense of Sexual Harassment Cases,* 20 J. Psychiatry & L. 14 (1992).

This points up the importance of discovery in such a case regarding the claimant's family relationships, happiness or unhappiness, childhood, developmental functioning, and adult history. All are essential. See **Chapter 16**. Although the discussion has focused on the defense, absence of such indications of unreliability can help a plaintiff's affirmative showing. See **Chapters 11** and **12** for a discussion of tests of credibility.[24]

Damages Inquiry

If a mental injury is established, the damages claimed would involve an assertion that the plaintiff had suffered a mental disorder as the result of the defendant's behavior. To the extent that the law would compensate for mental suffering, a jury could award some amount of damages regardless of whether a bona fide mental disorder was sustained. However, for any substantial damages to be awarded, some type of lasting mental injury would need to be established according to DSM-III-R criteria. Conversely, the lack of such an injury should minimize the degree of damages.

§ 17.7 Civil Child Abuse and Sexual Assault Cases

Cases of child abuse, battered wives, and sexual assault also involve claims of mental disorders and vocational impairment. In her book, *Making the Connections: Women, Work and Abuse,* Patricia A. Murphy discusses the similarities of the types of vocational impairment found in such victims. Cases range from actions by a "now mature" child against the abusing parent (although the parents' ability to respond in damages may be limited) and claims made in connection with divorce proceedings, in which the wife asserts an additional right to compensation on account of battering, over and above rights to division of the marital estate. The resolution of such issues in litigation requires the determination of whether the plaintiff sustained a mental disorder and whether its effects were such as to impair significant temperament capacities involved in performing the basic work functions. See **Chapter 7**. Ms. Murphy's book relies on similarities between the effects of post-traumatic stress disorder and the effects on abuse and assault victims. Thus, she refers to a *rape trauma syndrome* that creates sleep and eating disorders, phobias, intrusive thoughts about the trauma, and flashbacks.

---

[24] Additional specific studies of malingering include Lees-Haley, *1989 F and F – K Scales, Questionable Indices of Malingering,* 7 Am. J. Forensic Psychol. 81–84 (1989); Lees-Haley, *Malingering Post Traumatic Stress Disorder on the MMPI,* 2 1989 Forensic Reps. 89-81 (1990); Lees-Haley, *Provisional Normative Data for a Credibility Scale for the Evaluation of Personal Injury Claimants,* 66 Psychol. Reps. 1355–60 (1989).

However, in assessing the significance of this contention from a practical litigation standpoint, note that DSM-III-R does not presently recognize the existence of rape trauma syndrome. If the particular issue is litigated, one can foresee a contest of experts, with a judge or jury having to decide on the reasonableness of the data supporting plaintiff's claim of such a syndrome as against the fact that the American Psychiatric Association has not recognized it.

§ 17.8 Emotional Distress and Wrongful Termination

The tort of infliction of emotional distress is defined as intentional or reckless conduct that is outrageous and inflicts severe emotional distress.[25]

Emotional distress issues can arise as a part of general damages in ordinary tort claims and are ordinarily joined with claims for punitive damages in wrongful termination litigation. In the wrongful termination cases, these damage claims typically are made in connection with a cause of action for intentional or negligent infliction of emotional distress.

Ordinarily, damages for noneconomic losses are not recoverable for a wrongful discharge in breach of contract. There is variation among the authorities as to whether they are recoverable for a wrongful discharge in violation of public policy.[26]

As discussed in **§ 17.7**, a claim that mental suffering caused a lasting effect is much more substantial if established by proof of a DSM-III-R mental disorder, conversely if not. In this situation, a preexisting mental disorder can be a two-edged sword. If loss of earning capacity is claimed, then proof of a preexisting personality disorder could involve showing the existence of temperament deficits that reduce the claimed loss of earning capacity. However, in a jurisdiction in which proof of outrageous conduct is required to establish recovery for infliction of emotional distress, mistreatment may be a significant factor in determining whether the defendant's conduct was outrageous.[27] This could require an investigation of whether the claimant in fact had a preexisting mental disorder and whether the employer had reason to be aware of its existence.[28]

The significance of DSM-III-R in its definitions of Axis I, Mental Disorders, and Axis II, Personality Disorders, is illustrated by the case of *Spackman v. Good.*[29] In that case, although children were found to have been sexually abused by a third party, the fact that they were psychopaths as the result of sexual

---

[25] Restatement (Second) of Torts § 46 (1965).

[26] *See* 30 C.J.S. *Employer-Employee* § 100 (1992).

[27] Bundren v. Superior Court, 193 Cal. Rptr. 671 (Ct. App. 1983); Fletcher v. Western Nat'l Life Ins. Co., 689 Cal. Rptr. 78 (Ct. App. 1970).

[28] *See* 30 C.J.S.2d *Employer-Employee* § 100 (1992).

[29] 54 Cal. Rptr. 78 (1966).

trauma from a bad home environment with their own parents prevented the establishment of the requisite causation for recovery against the defendant.

Finally, in a claim for wrongful termination damages, there is a duty of mitigation imposed upon the plaintiff. This means that the plaintiff is required to use reasonable efforts to seek other employment.[30] If an employee contends that her inability to mitigate damages stemmed from the effects of a mental injury caused by the employer's behavior, the same techniques of disability evaluation discussed in **Chapters 7** and **8** would be relevant. Thus, the inquiry would have to be made as to what mental disorder was sustained, what impairment was sustained as a result of the mental disorder (according to DSM-III-R diagnostic criteria), and what the vocational expert's testimony would be with respect to the effect of such impairments on the ability to compete in the labor market.

§ 17.9 Disability Evaluation under Social Security

Claims under the Social Security Act for total disability will not be discussed here because of the fact that the Social Security Administration has its own very similar procedures for evaluating disability.[31] The descriptions used to identify the existence of relevant mental disorders are essentially based on DSM-III-R. The other aspect of Social Security disability litigation procedure is the presentation of vocational experts. Their testimony is based upon the principles discussed in **Chapters 7** and **8**. The only difference between this type of litigation and all the others is that only total disability is considered as entitling the recipient to benefits under the Social Security Act.[32]

---

[30] 30 C.J.S.2d *Employer-Employee* § 104 (1992).

[31] *See* 20 C.F.R. §§ 400–499 (1992).

[32] 29 U.S.C. §§ 301–1397 (1988).

APPENDIXES

A. Report of the Medical Advisory Committee of the California Division of Industrial Accidents: The Evaluation of Permanent Psychiatric Disability

B. Appellate Decisions Citing DSM-III-R

C. Investigation and Discovery Documents

D. Report on Privilege Between Patient and Clinician

APPENDIX A

REPORT OF THE MEDICAL ADVISORY COMMITTEE OF THE CALIFORNIA DIVISION OF INDUSTRIAL ACCIDENTS

THE EVALUATION OF PERMANENT PSYCHIATRIC DISABILITY

STATE OF CALIFORNIA GEORGE DEUKMEJIAN, Governor

DEPARTMENT OF INDUSTRIAL RELATIONS
DIVISION OF INDUSTRIAL ACCIDENTS—WORKERS' COMPENSATION APPEALS BOARD
525 GOLDEN GATE AVENUE
SAN FRANCISCO 94102

(415) 557-3542

ADDRESS REPLY TO:
P.O. BOX 603
SAN FRANCISCO, CA 94101

August 12, 1987

TO: WORKERS' COMPENSATION COMMUNITY

The following guidelines, which will become effective August 1, 1987, represent countless hours of dedicated work by the Sub-Committee on Permanent Psychiatric Disability and its respective consultants. It also represents the tireless efforts of the workers' compensation community who assisted in their development.

The guidelines provide a basis for objective evaluation of work-related psychiatric disability, which represents an immense step forward in reasonable and consistent psychiatric disability rating.

I want to take this opportunity to express my appreciation to both the committee, its respective consultants and those members of the workers' compensation community that are responsible for the successful completion of this project.

BARRY F. CARMODY
Deputy Director/
Administrative Director

BFC/af

THE EVALUATION OF PERMANENT PSYCHIATRIC DISABILITY

A Report to the Medical Advisory Committee of the
California Division of Industrial Accidents

Prepared by the
SUBCOMMITTEE ON PERMANENT PSYCHIATRIC DISABILITY

Allen J. Enelow, M.D., Chairman
Leta McKinney Adler, Ph.D.
David Braff, M.D.
J. Brand Brickman, M.D.
Arnold E. Herrera, Ph.D.
Herbert Lasky, Judge (Retired)
Melvin Lipsett, M.D.
Michael P. Maloney, Ph.D.
Michael Ward, Ph.D.

With consultation from:
William L. Clark, M.D., Former Medical Director,
California Division of Industrial Accidents
Paul D. Johnson, M.A., Job Analyst/Vocational Consultant
Far West Vocational Management
Jacob P. Panzarella, Ph.D.
Pacific Presbyterian Medical Center

And:
Workers' Compensation Consultants
Disability Evaluators
Don Petersen, Bureau Chief (I&A)
Del Gaines, Area Supervisor, North
Alvin Hecht, Area Supervisor, South
Sharon Collins
Margaret Easton

And the following psychologists:
Herbert N. Weissman, Ph.D.
Alexander B. Caldwell, Ph.D.
Philip Erdberg, Ph.D.
James A. Moses, Ph.D.
Thomas L. Morrison, Ph.D.
Irla Zimmerman, Ph.D.

<u>Effective August 1, 1987</u> (2nd Printing)

TABLE OF CONTENTS

FOREWORD

The Subcommittee on Permanent Psychiatric Disabilty, which authored this report, consists of four forensic psychiatrists, three clinical and forensic psychologists, and a medical sociologist familiar with psychiatric nomenclature and measurement problems, joined by a Workers' Compensation Judge. The Subcommittee reviewed legislation, regulations, and case law pertaining to workers' compensation, especially that related to compensation for work-related psychiatric injury in California. The Subcommittee also reviewed published and unpublished papers which discussed problems related to the evaluation of claims arising from alleged work-related psychiatric injury in the California workers' compensation system. A limited review of existing systems for evaluating psychiatric disorder and psychiatric disability was carried out, and a small number of personal communications with attorneys and forensic clinicians were most helpful.

The Subcommittee was greatly assisted by its consultants. William L. Clark, M.D., Medical Director, Division of Industrial Accidents, and Herbert Lasky, Judge of the Workers' Compensation Appeals Board, were extremely helpful in providing information about the California Workers' Compensation system. Paul D. Johnson, M.A., has assisted the Subcommittee to conceptualize work functions and provided useful information about occupational adjustment. Jacob P. Panzarella, Ph.D., provided the Subcommittee with a detailed criticism of an earlier draft of its work. The Worker's Compensation Consultants, Disability Evaluators, Don Petersen, Del Gaines, Alvin Hecht, Sharon Collins, and Margaret Easton, provided valuable contributions.

A group of academic and forensic psychologists conducted a preliminary review of the psychological assessment literature related to the evaluation of industrial injury. They recommended psychological tests which they considered to be conceptually and empirically well-grounded and suggested initial quantitative criteria for these tests.

After review by expert forensic psychiatrists and psychologists, applicant and defense attorneys, claims adjusters, and the general public, Chapters I, II, and III were extensively modified and are being proposed for adoption. Chapter IV, which established quantitative criteria for psychological list findings, will be subject of further study.

Chapter I
INTRODUCTION AND RATIONALE

A. Introduction

This report was prepared in response to the controversy and delayed case resolution of workers' compensation claims based on alleged psychiatric injury. The controversy and delay have become increasingly significant because the number of such claims has risen dramatically in recent years. The evaluation and adjudication of these claims have been especially problematic when the alleged psychiatric injury is associated with work stress rather than physical injury and when the claim involves a possible finding of permanent disability.

One California Workers' Compensation Judge has criticized the "legal rules and current practice techniques" in the handling and resolution of psychiatric injury claims as follows:

> Legal rules fall short in several major respects: 1) psychiatric injuries are not defined in medically meaningful terms; 2) adequate data supporting the legal conclusions which determine the existence or nonexistence of liability are not required; and 3) the rationale underlying the rules is not explained in terms of diminished ability to compete in the open labor market, the fundamental of the entire system.
> (Lasky 1980)

The Subcommittee on Permanent Psychiatric Disability endeavored to clarify these and other issues by applying the concepts and methods of the behaviorial sciences to the procedures by which permanent partial disability is evaluated. Its work consisted in developing: (1) model outlines of the clinical examiner's evaluation report and of the psychological assessment report which provide judges with the detailed data on which the examiner's judgments are based (Chapter II), and (2) guidelines for the clinical evaluation of psychiatric disability (Chapter III). The ultimate objective is to increase consistency in the evaluation of the extent of permanent disability.

B. Principles Underlying the California Permanent Disability Rating System

Since the Disability Schedules presented here are assimilated into the California permanent disability rating system, which is presented in "percentage disability", it is important to recapitulate the underlying principles of that system. Permanent disability has been defined as follows: "any impairment of bodily or mental function which remains after maximum recovery has been attained from the effects of injury, and which causes impairment of earning capacity, impairment of the normal use of a member, or a competitive handicap in the open labor market" (Hanna, California Law of Employee Injuries and Workmen's Compensation (1986 ed.) Section 14.0 (2) (a). (See also: State Compensation Insurance Fund v. Industrial Accidents Commission (Hutchinson) (1963) 59 Cal. 2d 45, 27 Cal. Rptr. 702 28 C.C.C. 20.) Actually, the underlying principle has always been a rehabilitation concept, although rehabilitation in this connection does not have its modern meaning of specialized rehabilitation services. The original framers of the "Schedule for Rating Permanent Disability" assumed that one who sustained a permanent injury on the job would need payment for a period of time to readjust to the job market—either to find a new occupation appropriate to the disability or to acquire skills necessary to compensate for the injury in an old job.

It was assumed that the more serious the injury, the longer it would take to readjust. For example, it would take someone who lost an arm longer to readjust than someone who lost a finger. The length of time was expressed in percentages by allowing four weeks for every one percent of disability. Thus 25 percent disability originally equated to 100 weeks of payments. This computation procedure has been amended so that the number of weeks is less than four for lower percentages of disability and greater than four for higher percentages of disability. (E.g., for disability less than 10 percent, three weeks are now allowed for each one percent, but for 30 percent or greater disability, more than four weeks are allowed, increasing as the percent disability increases.) (See Labor Code Section 4658.)

Disability payments were set on the basis of two thirds of average earnings up to a maximum, currently $140 per week. This amount was designed to tide the employee over in his period of readjustment but not to make up totally for loss of past earning capacity. Thus, the worker was given an incentive to return to work.

The system was further fine-tuned by adjusting for age and occupation. The California Labor Code requires that "In determining the percentage of permanent disability, account shall be taken of the nature of the physical injury or disfigurement, the occupation of the injured, and his age at time of such injury, consideration being given to the diminished ability of such injured employee to compete in the open labor market" (Section 4660 (a)). Various injuries affect different occupations in different ways; e.g., loss of a finger affects a violinist or carpenter differently from a clerk. Similarly, it was assumed that the readjustment period is longer past the age of 39 years. Adjustments for age and occupation are made by the Disability Evaluation Bureau.

It was early understood that the system could not be tailor-made to include all factors which affect adjustment in the labor market. As stated in the report of Senate Interim Committee on Workmen's Compensation Benefits (California 1953),

> Among those which have to be omitted are: make up of the man, his personal or inherent adaptability, nervous temperament, ambition or desire to recover, intelligence, education and mentality, aptitudes, general health and physical strength, reading habits, appearance and personal care, race or nationality, family relations and family support, surroundings, attitude of employer, opportunities for employment through family or friends, union membership, occupational license, affiliations, all previous occupations or employments, geographical restrictions of employment, general economic conditions and economic cycles of industrial activities.

C. Professional Standards for Examiners

Examiners for Workers' Compensation are expected to adhere to professional standards of competent practice and to codes of professional, ethical, and legal conduct defined by both the American Psychiatric and American Psychological Associations, as well as by the appropriate State Licensing Boards.

The examiner must be aware of the legal issues defined by Workers' Compensation law and legal standards of evidence and proof. In the adjudication of the compensation claim, it is necessary to determine: (1) whether or not there is mental or emotional disability and, if any, the nature of the disability; (2) whether or not a work place injury played a role in producing any observed disability; and (3) whether or not observed disability has resulted in diminished ability to compete in the open labor market. The expert's duty is to describe findings and to provide and document an expert opinion on the above issues that meets the reasonable medical-legal standard ("reasonably medically probable"). Furthermore, the clinical procedures and assessment measures utilized in forming the expert opinion must be generally accepted in the expert's scientific community (Frye v. U.S. 293F. 103 D.C. Cir. 1923).

In short, the examiner's value to the Court is greatest when:

1. The examiner's report fully documents information obtained by observation, interview, psychological assessment (including test scores) of the applicant; by a thorough review of medical records, employment and personnel records, and referral documents; by collateral interviews, when possible; and other information available for a comprehensive case review.

2. The examiner's opinion with respect to the legal issues is expressly related to the documented information, the sources of that information are provided, and the conclusions reached on the basis of the data meet the standard of reasonable medical probability.

Chapter II
OUTLINES OF EVALUATION REPORTS

As a means of introducing some standardization to the contents of evaluation reports, two model outlines are presented in this Section. Outline A, the Evaluation Report for Psychiatric Disability, is a guide for the independent examiner, who may be either a psychiatrist or psychologist. It assures that the clinician has provided all the information and opinions required by W.C.A.B. Rules of Practice and Procedure Section 10606 (1973). Outline B, the Psychological Assessment Report, is a guide for the psychologist in those instances where the psychologist's role is to provide psychological assessment as part of a collaborative evaluation. The latter's findings are to be assimilated into the evaluation report of the independent examiner, supported in detail by a complete psychological assessment report which includes test scores.

The psychiatrist or psychologist who examines an applicant for Workers' Compensation on the basis of alleged psychiatric injury should conduct a careful interview of the applicant addressing elements of the outline for the evaluation report. To complete the interview almost always will require at least one and a half to two hours of direct contact with the applicant by the examiner. Registered psychological assistants may be used to obtain relevant background information and/or to administer various tests. Their specific role in the evaluation procedure should be delineated in the report. Extensive dependence on material obtained by ancillary personnel is undesirable except in the case of applicants who have significant expressive/receptive English language deficits. It is preferable that such applicants be evaluated by examiners who can speak and also administer psychological tests in the primary language. The use of interpreters may lead to distortion of the facts and misinterpretation of the data.

The examiner should conduct such interviews as may be appropriate and possible and should review the psychological assessment findings, the medical and employment and other documents or records[1] of the applicant, and other referral documents. When all this information is assembled, it should be documented in the report with a detailed description of the cognitive, affective, and behavioral signs/symptoms of the applicant, as well as the psychological assessment scores and interpretations.

It should be noted that the following outlines are more suggestive than prescriptive. The content of reports will vary with the referral questions, the nature of the applicant's presenting problems, and, to some extent, the practice of individual clinicians. The suggested headings are not required, but a systematic, quasi-standardized report including all the relevant facts is likely to be most useful to judges.

FN1 Employment and other documents or records, if reviewed, should be made available to applicant or his or her counsel at the same time.

A. EVALUATION REPORT FOR PSYCHIATRIC DISABILITY

(To be used by psychiatrist and psychologist examiners.)

I. Identifying information

A. Date, place, and duration of examination

B. Reason for referral and referral questions

C. Names and functions of others taking part in the examination, including use of interpreter

D. Applicant (patient/client)

1. Date of birth
2. Date of alleged industrial injury
3. Date last worked

E. Sources of facts (Include collaterals, if interviewed)

II. Description of applicant at interview

A. Appearance (Do not omit obvious physical aberrations.)

B. Demeanor, general behavior

C. Apparent affective state, based on observation

D. Stream of speech

E. Interaction with interviewer

III. Description of applicant's current complaints

A. Subjective complaints

B. Applicant's view of the impairment created by the complaints

IV. History of present illness

A. Applicant's description of industrial stressors, onset of complaints, and alleged injuries or illness associated with onset

B. **Psychological response to alleged injury situation**

C. History of mental health problems since alleged injury

D. History of treatment since alleged injury

E. Current treatment and medication, including medication taken on day of interview

V. **Occupational history** (Distinguish baseline, injury concurrent, and postinjury events.)

A. Educational level and professional, technical, or vocational training

B. Sequential description of occupations pursued (including military service)

1. Training and skills required
2. Supervisory responsibilities
3. Career mobility (upward, downward, lateral)

C. Difficulties and/or accomplishments in each occupational setting

D. Previous occupational injuries, time lost, and outcome

VI. **Past mental health history and relevant medical history**

VII. **Family history**

A. Family of origin

1. Parents' age, education, occupational history
2. Siblings' age, education, occupational history
3. Composition of family during applicant's childhood and youth
4. Mental health history and relevant medical history of family members
5. Family response to illness
6. Relevant social history of family members
7. Quality of family relations

B. Family of procreation

1. Present marital status
2. Spouse's age, education, occupational history

3. Number of offspring (Obtain same data for adult offspring as for spouse.)
4. Mental health history and relevant medical history of family members
5. Relevant social history of family members
6. Quality of family relations

C. History of previous marriages

VIII. Developmental history

IX. Social History (Distinguish baseline, injury concurrent, and postinjury findings.)

A. Interpersonal relationships

B. Previous life changes (external stresses and losses) and response to these

C. Educational history

D. Legal history, when applicable (Include previous workers' compensation and personal injury claims, with the circumstances and outcome.)

E. Criminal history which is relevant to diagnosis and/or disability

F. Substance use and abuse

G. Applicant's description of a typical day

X. MENTAL STATUS EXAMINATION (Include relevant negative findings.)

A. Level of consciousness

B. Mood, e.g.:

1. Depression
2. Lability
3. Elation
4. Anxiety
5. Inapppropriateness

C. Cognition/thinking

1. Orientation
2. Estimation of intelligence

3. Memory dysfunction
   a. Recall/short-term memory
   b. Remote memory
4. Perceptual and communication disorders (agnosias and aphasias)
5. Thought content
6. Thought disorder, e.g.:
   a. Ideas of reference
   b. Looseness of associations
   c. Delusions
   d. Perceptual disorders, including hallucinations
   e. Intrusive thought/obsessive thinking
7. Evidence of deficit in
   a. Learning
   b. Problem solving
   c. Judgment
8. Insight (Include applicant's perception of relationship between injury and psychological condition.)

D. Behavior

1. Motor: Retardation or hyperactivity
2. Appropriateness in interview

E. Evidence of physiologic disturbance

1. Skeletal muscle system
2. Autonomic
3. Somatoform or conversion symptom

XI. Findings from psychological assessment (Attach complete psychological report.)

XII. Review of medical record

XIII. Interviews with collateral sources and Review of Employment or Personnel Records (Compare description of industrial stressor with applicant's account.)

XIV. Diagnosis using DSM-III terminology and criteria

XV. Summary and conclusions (Provide sources for all information cited as evidence.)

A. Brief summary of relevant history and findings

12

B. If any disability, present and justify an opinion concerning the current cause(s), whether or not they are related to the work place. Consider:

1. The relationship of work exposure to disability
2. Nonindustrial causes of disability, including pre-existing causal factors
3. Aggravating or accelerating factors (industrial and nonindustrial)
4. Natural progression of pre-existing disorder
5. Active or passive contribution of the workplace to the disability. (See Twentieth Century Fox Film Corporation v. W.C.A.B. and Kevin Conway (1983) 141 C.A. 3rd 778, 190 CAL Rptr 560, 48 C.C.C. 275 and also Georgia Pacific Corporation v. W.C.A.B. and Robert H. Byrne (1983) 144 C.A. 3rd 72, 192 Rptr. 643, 48 C.C.C. 443.)
6. Applicant's subjective reaction to stress at work, if relevant. (See Albertson's Inc. v. W.C.A.B. (Bradley) (1982) 131 Cal.App.3d 308, 182 Cal. Rptr. 304, 47 C.C.C. 460.)

C. Indicate diagnostic entities which were work-disabling prior to the alleged industrial injury and provide evidence.

D. State whether the disability is temporary or has reached a permanent and stationary status and cite evidence. If the condition is permanent and stationary, state on what date it became so and cite evidence. Consider the natural history of the disorder, the response to treatment. If the condition is not yet permanent and stationary, state when you expect it will be so. If you think further reasonable medical treatment will improve the condition, describe the treatment and its expected benefits.

E. If the disability is permanent and stationary, present an opinion regarding the nature and severity of the disability. Describe the disabling symptoms (subjective and objective factors in disability) according to Schedule A in Chapter III. Complete the Work Function Impairment Form shown on page 15 citing symptoms, mental status findings, psychological test data, and history as supporting data. (Descriptions of work functions appear on pages 16, 17 and 18.) If there is a non-psychiatric disability, a specialist in the area affected shall present an opinion regarding the nature and severity of the organ system affected.

F. Make an advisory apportionment of disability. In order to do this, describe the disability that would exist at this time in the absence of the work place injury. Cite the evidence on which the estimated preinjury level is based. Use a separate Work Function Impairment Form.

G. Indicate recommended treatment and/or rehabilitation, if any. State whether the employee, the effects of whose injury, whether or not combined with the effects of a prior injury or disability, if any, is permanently precluded or likely to be precluded from engaging in his or her usual and customary occupation or the position in which he or she was engaged at the time of injury.

H. Respond to all referral questions and/or to questions and issues raised in referral reports.

WORK FUNCTION IMPAIRMENT FORM

	WORK FUNCTION	LEVEL OF IMPAIRMENT	SUPPORTING DATA (Cite Findings)
1.	Ability to comprehend and follow instructions		
2.	Ability to perform simple and repetitive tasks		
3.	Ability to maintain a work pace appropriate to a given work load		
4.	Ability to perform complex or varied tasks		
5.	Ability to relate to other people beyond giving and receiving instructions		
6.	Ability to influence people		
7.	Ability to make generalizations, evaluations or decisions without immediate supervision		
8.	Ability to accept and carry out responsibility for direction, control and planning		

NOTE:

When completing this form consideration is to be given to Descriptions of Work Functions - Functional Manifestations (see pages 16, 17 and 18 following).

DESCRIPTIONS OF WORK FUNCTIONS

FUNCTIONAL MANIFESTATIONS

The following is a list of the functional manifestations of each of the eight work functions to be evaluated. The examiner should consider these factors in evaluating each work function, using clinical observations and objective supporting data.

1. **Ability to comprehend and follow instructions**

   Consider:

   the ability to maintain attention and concentration for necessary periods;

   the ability to understand written or oral instructions; and

   the ability to do work requiring set limits, tolerances or standards.

2. **Ability to perform simple and repetitive tasks**

   Consider:

   the ability to ask simple questions or request assistance;

   the ability to perform activities of a routine nature; and

   the ability to remember locations and work procedures.

3. **Ability to maintain a work pace appropriate to a given work load**

   Consider:

   the ability to perform activities within a schedule, maintain regular attendance and be punctual; and

   the ability to complete a normal work day and/or work week and perform at a consistent pace.

4. **Ability to perform complex and varied tasks**

   Consider:

   the ability to synthesize, coordinate, and analyze data; and the ability to perform jobs requiring precise attainment of set limits, tolerances, or standards.

5. **Ability to relate to other people beyond giving and receiving instructions**

Consider:

the ability to get along with co-workers or peers;

the ability to perform work activities requiring negotiating with, explaining, or persuading; and

the ability to respond appropriately to evaluation or criticism.

6. **Ability to influence people**

Consider:

the ability to convince or direct others;

the ability to understand the meaning of words and to use them appropriately and effectively; and

the ability to interact appropriately with people.

7. **Ability to make generalizations, evaluations or decisions without immediate supervision**

Consider:

the ability to recognize potential hazards and follow appropriate precautions;

the ability to understand and remember detailed instructions;

the ability to make independent decisions or judgments based on appropriate information; and

the ability to set realistic goals or make plans independent of others.

8. Ability to accept and carry out responsibility for direction, control and planning

Consider:

the ability to set realistic goals or make plans independently of others;

the ability to negotiate with, instruct or supervise people; and

the ability to respond appropriately to changes in the work conditions.

B. PSYCHOLOGICAL ASSESSMENT REPORT FOR PSYCHIATRIC DISABILITY

(To accompany an Evaluation Report for Psychiatric Disability)

I. Identifying information

A. Applicant's name, age, birthdate, phone number, and social security number

B. Date of alleged injury or exposure

C. Date last worked

D. Description of alleged injury or exposure

II. Referral information

A. Date of referral

B. Referral source: name and role in evaluation/litigation process

C. Nature of referral and referral questions

III. Behavioral observation and personal characteristics

A. Description of physical appearance, mode of dress

B. Speech, hearing, vision, R/L handedness

C. Other apparent physical cognitive or emotional impairments, including history of unconsciousness, high or protracted fever, seizure activity

D. Literacy, educational level, and whether English is first language

E. Ethnic origin, marital status, occupation, socioeconomic status

F. Self-presentation of applicant supported by relevant observations, test scores, and history (Comment on such qualities as motivation, candor, spontaneity, reliability, consistency of performance, tendency to exaggerate or malinger, and presentation of self in an overly positive light.)

IV. Clinical interview (Cf. Outline A, the Evaluation Report for Psychiatric Disability, Sections II-IX, pages 9-11) Since this Psychological Assessment Report accompanies an Evaluation Report for Psychiatric Disability, a brief review of relevant history is sufficient.

V. Records available/reviewed. Including job descriptions and performance evaluations.
(Identify as to before or after alleged injury/exposure.)

VI. Prior psychological assessments (from records). List, including:

A. Date

B. Examiner

C. Test (Include form used.)

D. Scores and interpretation

VII. Evaluation procedures. List instruments when used in the following order. Indicate date and total administration time. (This is a reporting format and does not necessarily imply that procedures be administered in this order.)

A. Objective tests measuring general cognition

B. Neuropsychological tests if indicated

C. Objective (standardized and normed) tests relating to personality and emotional state

D. Self-report inventories relating to emotional state

E. Projective devices

F. Interview

VIII. Results and discussion

A. Describe assessment findings, providing test scores and documentation sufficient to permit other psychological examiners to review the issues raised and opinions rendered. (Indicate if computer scored/interpreted and give score.) Relate test findings to observations and relevant history, with emphasis on the vocational sphere.

B. Relate all assessment findings to DSM-III diagnosis on Axis I, Axis II and, when appropriate, Axis III. (Note: It is inappropriate for a psychologist to offer independent Axis III diagnosis.)

C. Current findings and inferences relative to work place injury and job-related impairments. (The psychologist should follow "XV. Summary and Conclusions" in the Evaluation Report for Psychiatric Disability, but should include the additional information below.)

1. Distinguish between transient/situational conditions and enduring/permanent conditions.

2. Where appropriate describe and document with test findings and range and severity of psychological impairment with respect to ability to work in the same job or to compete on the open job market.

3. Describe and document with test findings what types of intervention are required to return applicant to the same job or to rehabilitate applicant for other employment, with amounts of time involved.

Chapter III

CLINICAL EVALUATION OF PERMANENT PSYCHIATRIC DISABILITY

In evaluating an applicant with an alleged psychiatric disability, the examiner should first decide: (1) whether or not there is any emotional or mental condition which handicaps the applicant in competing on the open job market, (2) whether or not this disability is to any degree work-related, and (3) whether or not the disability is permanent and stationary, that is, whether or not the applicant can receive further benefit from treatment at this time. If it is the examiner's opinion that there is psychiatric disability which is to some degree work-related and that maximum benefit from treatment has been reached, then the applicant may be evaluated for permanent psychiatric disability. (California Casualty Ins. Co. v. W.C.A.B. (Jackson) (1985) 50 C.C.C. 262, 265; 167 Cal. App. 470, 476; 213 Cal. Rptr. 420) The examiner will proceed to evaluate the extent and nature of the disability and to describe the prognosis according to the guidelines presented in this section.

The guidelines ask the examiner (1) to diagnose the applicant according to DSM-III[2], (2) to evaluate the applicant's ability to perform specific work functions, and (3) to provide information concerning the applicant's prognosis. To assist the examiner and the court, schedules for summarizing relevant information are provided. The values in these schedules are not substitutes for the discussion described in the Summary and Conclusions Section of the Evaluation Report on pages 12, 13 and 14. They are values to be used in documenting or supporting the conclusions.

FN2 The use of Diagnostic and Statistical Manual of Mental Disorders 3rd Edition (DSM-III) includes referral to all subsequent revisions and/or editions as they become available and appropriate to the evaluation.

A. Evaluation of the Nature and Severity of Impairment

Schedule A provides the examiner an outline with which to describe the nature and severity of the applicant's mental or emotional impairment. The Schedule provides for Axis I and Axis II diagnoses, and also an Axis III diagnosis when appropriate. The examiner should indicate whether or not these diagnoses were occupationally disabling prior to the alleged injury and support the opinion.

Schedule A also provides that the examiner list all symptoms related to the Axis I diagnosis or diagnoses and to state whether they are constant, intermittent, or occasional. Next the examiner is asked to evaluate the level of impairment in the applicant's ability to perform eight work functions. The Work Functions Impairment Form (page 15) provides a convenient way to summarize this information. The eight work functions are listed in Schedule A and described on pages 16, 17 and 18. The evaluation is performed as if there were no question of apportionment, even when apportionment is suggested by the examiner's assessment of the etiology.

Schedule A. EVALUATION OF THE NATURE AND SEVERITY OF THE DISABILITY

I. DSM-III diagnosis

A. Axis I

B. Axis II

C. Axis III

II. List all disabling symptoms and state whether each is constant, intermittent, or occasional. ("Intermittent" means present half the time; "occasional", less than half the time.)

III. Using the levels defined in A below, describe the extent to which disabling symptom leads to impairment on the eight work functions shown in B below.

A. Level of impairment

1. Minimal (discomfort, but not disabling)
2. Very slight (detectable impairment)
3. Slight (noticeable impairment)
4. Moderate (marked impairment)
5. Severe (unable to perform work function)

B. Work function: Document those symptoms which impair each of the following work functions and the levels of impairment on the Work Function Impairment Form on page 15. (See pages 16, 17 and 18 for descriptions of the work functions.)

1. Ability to comprehend and follow instructions
2. Ability to perform simple and repetitive tasks
3. Ability to maintain a work pace appropriate to a given workload
4. Ability to perform complex or varied tasks
5. Ability to relate to other people beyond giving and receiving instructions

6. Ability to influence people

7. Ability to make generalizations, evaluations or decisions without immediate supervision

8. Ability to accept and carry out responsibility for direction, control, and planning

Information on severity of symptoms in Schedule A will assist the Court to determine the level of severity of impairment of work function (factors of disability).

DIVISION OF INDUSTRIAL ACCIDENTS
ADMINISTRATIVE DIRECTOR
ADMINISTRATIVE RULES

CHAPTER 4.5
Division of Industrial Accidents
Subchapter 1
Administrative Director
Administrative Rules

Article 2, Disabilitites, Description of, of the Administrative Rules of the Administrative Director is added to read as follows:

Article 2. Disabilities, Description of

Section 97265 of the Administrative Rules of the Administrative Director is amended to read as follows:

9726 Method of Measurement (Psychiatric)

The method of measuring the psychiatric elements of a disability ~~should~~ shall follow the Report of the Subcommittee on Permanent Psychiatric Disability to the Medical Advisory Committee of the California Division of Industrial Accidents, entitled "The Evaluation of Permanent Psychiatr Disability", adopted, fowarded for adoption on July 10, 1987, and subsequent amendments and/or revisions thereto adopted after a public hearing.

Authority cited: Sections 4660 and 5307.3 Labor Code
Reference: Section 4660, Labor Code

Note: The Report (which contains these Protocols) of the Subcommittee on Permanent Psychiatric Disability, as adopted, will not appear as a printed part of the Administrative Director's Regulations (8 CAC Admin Code Section 9726); copies will be available through the Medical Director of the Division of Industrial Accidents.

THIS ENTIRE PAGE IS NEW AND WILL CONSTITUTE AN ADDITION TO THE SCHEDULE FOR RATING PERMANENT DISABILITIES

1-B **1.4-- PSYCHIATRIC DISABILITIES - STANDARD RATING**

Level of Impairment*	Work Function Impairment Values							
	Group I Work Functions*			Group II Work Functions*				
	1	2	3	4	5	6	7	8
Minimal	0%	0%	0%	0%	0%	0%	0%	0%
Very Slight	5	5	5	2	4	1	2	1
Slight	10	10	10	3	8	2	3	2
Slight to Moderate	20	20	20	8	19	4	8	4
Moderate	30	30	30	12	29	6	12	6
Moderate to Severe	40	40	40	16	40	8	16	8
Severe	50	50	50	20	50	10	20	10

To obtain standard rating where only one work function impairment exists:

(1) Refer to Chart above.

To obtain standard rating where multiple work function impairments exist:

(1) For impairments within Group I, use the greatest value plus one-half the sum of the lesser values.

(2) For impairments within Group II, use the greatest value plus one-fifth the sum of the lesser values.

(3) For impairments within both groups, combine Steps (1) and (2) using the formula:

$$\text{Group I Total} + \left[\left[.45 - \left(\frac{\text{Group I Total}}{300}\right)\right] \times \text{Group II Total}\right]$$

(a) The result obtained shall be taken at not less than that obtained in Step (2).

(4) Round off only the final result obtained in Step (1), (2), or (3). Round only to the values of 1, 2, 3, 5, 8, 10, 13, 15, and multiples of 5% thereafter.

When warranted by facts and evidence, a deviation from the foregoing may be employed.

*See "Psychiatric Protocols" for definitions (AD Rule 9726).

LIST OF DISABILITIES AND STANDARD RATINGS

DISABILITY NUMBER	DISABILITY	STANDARD RATING
	1.— BRAIN AND NERVOUS SYSTEM	
1.1—	PARALYSIS*	
	PARALYSIS ONE SIDE OF BODY:	
1.121	SLIGHT..................................	20%
1.141	MODERATE..................................	60%
1.161	SEVERE..................................	100%
1.183	SEVERE PARALYSIS BOTH LOWER EXTREMITIES (SEE ALSO DISABILITY NUMBER 18.313).........	100%
1.3—	EPILEPSY*: (SEE NOTE 1.)	
1.32	SLIGHT..................................	25%
1.33	SLIGHT TO MODERATE..........................	50%
1.34	MODERATE..................................	75%
1.36	SEVERE..................................	100%
	PSYCHIATRIC DISABILITIES: SEE PAGE 1-B.	
1.4—	~~NEUROSIS*:~~	
~~1.41~~	~~VERY SLIGHT..............................~~	~~10%~~
~~1.42~~	~~SLIGHT..................................~~	~~20%~~
~~1.44~~	~~MODERATE..................................~~	~~50%~~
~~1.46~~	~~SEVERE..................................~~	~~65%~~
~~1.47~~	~~PRONOUNCED..............................~~	~~100%~~

DISABILITY NUMBER	DISABILITY	STANDARD RATING
1.5—	POST-TRAUMATIC HEAD SYNDROME*: (SEE NOTE 2.)	
1.52	SLIGHT	20%
1.54	MODERATE..................................	50%
1.56	SEVERE..................................	100%
1.6—	VERTIGO*:	
1.62	SLIGHT..................................	10%
1.64	MODERATE..................................	50%
1.66	SEVERE..................................	100%
1.7—	HEADACHES*:	
1.72	SLIGHT..................................	5%
1.74	MODERATE..................................	15%
1.76	SEVERE..................................	60%
1.77	PRONOUNCED..............................	100%
1.8—	MENTAL DETERIORATION*:	
1.82	SLIGHT..................................	20%
1.84	MODERATE..................................	50%
1.86	SEVERE..................................	75%
1.87	PRONOUNCED..............................	100%

NOTES: EPILEPSY

(1) THE INFORMATION FURNISHED SHOULD INCLUDE – FREQUENCY, TYPE, AND SEVERITY OF EPISODES; FREQUENCY AND DURATION OF LOSS OF CONSCIOUSNESS; EXTENT OF MENTAL IMPAIRMENT; TYPE AND SEVERITY OF OTHER SYMPTOMS; PRESENCE OR ABSENCE OF AURA; EFFECT OF MEDICATION IN CONTROLLING SEIZURES; PROGNOSIS.

POST-TRAUMATIC HEAD SYNDROME

(2) MAY INCLUDE THE FOLLOWING FACTORS – VERTIGO, IMPAIRMENT OF MEMORY, IMPAIRMENT OF CONCENTRATION, HEADACHES, FATIGABILITY, NERVOUSNESS, IRRITABILITY, MENTAL DETERIORATION.

*THE RATING MAY BE INCREASED OR DECREASED FROM THE SCHEDULED RATING WHERE THE DEGREE OF DISABILITY SO WARRANTS.

35

COLUMN FOR DISABILITY–OCCUPATION COMBINATION

DISABILITY NUMBER		GROUP NUMBER																													
		1	*1A*	2	3	4	5	6	7	8	9	10	11	12	13	14	15	16	17	18	19	20	21	22	23	24	25	26	27	28	29	30
1.— BRAIN AND NERVOUS SYSTEM																																
1.1–	1.121	G	*G*	F	D	E	E	E	G	F	C	H	D	G	F	G	G	C	F	D	E	F	G	D	F	G	F	H	G	H	J	J
	1.141	G	*G*	F	D	E	E	E	G	F	C	H	D	G	F	G	G	C	F	D	E	F	G	D	F	G	F	H	G	H	J	J
	1.161	100	*100*	100	100	100	100	100	100	100	100	100	100	100	100	100	100	100	100	100	100	100	100	100	100	100	100	100	100	100	100	100
	1.183	100	*100*	100	100	100	100	100	100	100	100	100	100	100	100	100	100	100	100	100	100	100	100	100	100	100	100	100	100	100	100	100
1.3–	1.32	F	*F*	F	F	F	D	H	F	H	C	F	F	F	F	C	F	C	G	G	H	H	D	H	G	H	I	I	G	F	L	K
	1.33	F	*F*	F	F	F	D	H	F	H	C	F	F	F	F	C	F	C	G	G	H	H	D	H	G	H	I	I	G	F	L	K
	1.34	F	*F*	F	F	F	D	H	F	H	C	F	F	F	F	C	F	C	G	G	H	H	D	H	G	H	I	I	G	F	L	K
	1.36	100	*100*	100	100	100	100	100	100	100	100	100	100	100	100	100	100	100	100	100	100	100	100	100	100	100	100	100	100	100	100	100
1.4–	~~1.41~~	B	*B*	D	D	F	D	G	D	G	D	F	E	F	E	B	H	F	H	F	F	F	D	G	H	G	I	I	H	G	K	K
	~~1.42~~	~~B~~	~~*B*~~	~~D~~	~~D~~	~~F~~	~~D~~	~~G~~	~~D~~	~~G~~	~~D~~	~~F~~	~~E~~	~~F~~	~~E~~	~~B~~	~~H~~	~~F~~	~~H~~	~~F~~	~~F~~	~~F~~	~~D~~	~~G~~	~~H~~	~~G~~	~~I~~	~~I~~	~~H~~	~~G~~	~~K~~	~~K~~
	~~1.44~~	~~B~~	~~*B*~~	~~D~~	~~D~~	~~F~~	~~D~~	~~G~~	~~D~~	~~G~~	~~D~~	~~F~~	~~E~~	~~F~~	~~E~~	~~B~~	~~H~~	~~F~~	~~H~~	~~F~~	~~F~~	~~F~~	~~D~~	~~G~~	~~H~~	~~G~~	~~I~~	~~I~~	~~H~~	~~G~~	~~K~~	~~K~~
	~~1.46~~	~~B~~	~~*B*~~	~~D~~	~~D~~	~~F~~	~~D~~	~~G~~	~~D~~	~~G~~	~~D~~	~~F~~	~~E~~	~~F~~	~~E~~	~~B~~	~~H~~	~~F~~	~~H~~	~~F~~	~~F~~	~~F~~	~~D~~	~~G~~	~~H~~	~~G~~	~~I~~	~~I~~	~~H~~	~~G~~	~~K~~	~~K~~
	~~1.47~~	~~100~~	*100*	~~100~~	~~100~~	~~100~~	~~100~~	~~100~~	~~100~~	~~100~~	~~100~~	~~100~~	~~100~~	~~100~~	~~100~~	~~100~~	~~100~~	~~100~~	~~100~~	~~100~~	~~100~~	~~100~~	~~100~~	~~100~~	~~100~~	~~100~~	~~100~~	~~100~~	~~100~~	~~100~~	~~100~~	~~100~~
1.5–	1.52	D	*D*	E	D	F	D	F	E	F	D	G	F	F	F	D	G	E	G	F	F	F	E	F	F	G	H	H	G	G	K	K
	1.54	D	*D*	E	D	F	D	F	E	F	D	G	F	F	F	D	G	E	G	F	F	F	E	F	F	G	H	H	G	G	K	K
	1.56	100	*100*	100	100	100	100	100	100	100	100	100	100	100	100	100	100	100	100	100	100	100	100	100	100	100	100	100	100	100	100	100
1.6–	1.62	F	*F*	F	D	F	D	F	F	F	D	H	F	F	H	F	F	C	F	F	F	F	F	E	E	H	F	H	F	H	L	K
	1.64	E	*F*	F	D	F	D	F	F	F	D	H	F	F	H	F	F	C	F	F	F	F	F	E	E	H	F	H	F	H	L	K
	1.66	100	*100*	100	100	100	100	100	100	100	100	100	100	100	100	100	100	100	100	100	100	100	100	100	100	100	100	100	100	100	100	100
1.7–	1.72	D	*D*	E	D	F	D	F	E	F	D	G	F	F	F	D	G	E	G	F	F	F	E	F	F	G	H	H	G	G	K	K
	1.74	D	*D*	E	D	F	D	F	E	F	D	G	F	F	F	D	G	E	G	F	F	F	E	F	F	G	H	H	G	G	K	K
	1.76	D	*D*	E	D	F	D	F	E	F	D	G	F	F	F	D	G	E	G	F	F	F	E	F	F	G	H	H	G	G	K	K
	1.77	100	*100*	100	100	100	100	100	100	100	100	100	100	100	100	100	100	100	100	100	100	100	100	100	100	100	100	100	100	100	100	100

* *Entries in this type face apply to injuries occurring on and after January 1, 1961.*

36

DISABILITY NUMBER		GROUP NUMBER																													
		31	32	33	34	35	36	37	38	39	40	41	42	43	44	45	46	47	48	49	50	51	52	53	54	55	56	57	58	59	60
1.—	BRAIN AND NERVOUS SYSTEM																														
1.1—	1.121	J	J	J	I	G	D	F	F	D	F	D	D	H	I	G	H	H	J	H	D	E	G	F	I	D	D	F	G	K	G
	1.141	J	J	J	I	G	D	F	F	D	F	D	D	H	I	G	H	H	J	H	D	E	G	F	I	D	D	F	G	K	G
	1.161	100	100	100	100	100	100	100	100	100	100	100	100	100	100	100	100	100	100	100	100	100	100	100	100	100	100	100	100	100	100
	1.183	100	100	100	100	100	100	100	100	100	100	100	100	100	100	100	100	100	100	100	100	100	100	100	100	100	100	100	100	100	100
1.3—	1.32	J	H	I	F	I	I	H	F	G	J	I	F	I	F	J	J	I	L	L	I	I	I	J	G	G	D	J	G	L	F
	1.33	J	H	I	F	I	I	H	F	G	J	I	F	I	F	J	J	I	L	L	I	I	I	J	G	G	D	J	G	L	F
	1.34	J	H	I	F	I	I	H	F	G	J	I	F	I	F	J	J	I	L	L	I	I	I	J	G	G	D	J	G	L	F
	1.36	100	100	100	100	100	100	100	100	100	100	100	100	100	100	100	100	100	100	100	100	100	100	100	100	100	100	100	100	100	100
1.4—	~~1.41~~	I	H	H	F	J	I	K	G	I	K	L	E	I	H	I	I	H	J	I	H	J	I	J	H	D	D	K	G	L	E
	~~1.42~~	~~I~~	~~H~~	~~H~~	~~F~~	~~J~~	~~I~~	~~K~~	~~G~~	~~I~~	~~K~~	~~L~~	~~E~~	~~I~~	~~H~~	~~I~~	~~I~~	~~H~~	~~J~~	~~I~~	~~H~~	~~J~~	~~I~~	~~J~~	~~H~~	~~D~~	~~D~~	~~K~~	~~G~~	~~L~~	~~E~~
	~~1.44~~	~~I~~	~~H~~	~~H~~	~~F~~	~~J~~	~~I~~	~~K~~	~~G~~	~~I~~	~~K~~	~~L~~	~~E~~	~~I~~	~~H~~	~~I~~	~~I~~	~~H~~	~~J~~	~~I~~	~~H~~	~~J~~	~~I~~	~~J~~	~~H~~	~~D~~	~~D~~	~~K~~	~~G~~	~~L~~	~~E~~
	~~1.46~~	~~I~~	~~H~~	~~H~~	~~F~~	~~J~~	~~I~~	~~K~~	~~G~~	~~I~~	~~K~~	~~L~~	~~E~~	~~I~~	~~H~~	~~I~~	~~I~~	~~H~~	~~J~~	~~I~~	~~H~~	~~J~~	~~I~~	~~J~~	~~H~~	~~D~~	~~D~~	~~K~~	~~G~~	~~L~~	~~E~~
	~~1.47~~	~~100~~	~~100~~	~~100~~	~~100~~	~~100~~	~~100~~	~~100~~	~~100~~	~~100~~	~~100~~	~~100~~	~~100~~	~~100~~	~~100~~	~~100~~	~~100~~	~~100~~	~~100~~	~~100~~	~~100~~	~~100~~	~~100~~	~~100~~	~~100~~	~~100~~	~~100~~	~~100~~	~~100~~	~~100~~	~~100~~
1.5—	1.52	J	H	I	G	H	H	J	F	H	H	I	D	H	H	H	H	G	J	J	G	H	G	I	H	D	E	J	F	L	G
	1.54	J	H	I	G	H	H	J	F	H	H	I	D	H	H	H	H	G	J	J	G	H	G	I	H	D	E	J	F	L	G
	1.56	100	100	100	100	100	100	100	100	100	100	100	100	100	100	100	100	100	100	100	100	100	100	100	100	100	100	100	100	100	100
1.6—	1.62	J	I	J	H	F	D	G	F	C	C	F	C	G	H	G	G	G	I	J	G	C	D	D	I	D	E	H	F	L	K
	1.64	J	I	J	H	F	D	G	F	C	C	F	C	G	H	G	G	G	I	J	G	C	D	D	I	D	E	H	F	L	K
	1.66	100	100	100	100	100	100	100	100	100	100	100	100	100	100	100	100	100	100	100	100	100	100	100	100	100	100	100	100	100	100
1.7—	1.72	J	H	I	G	H	H	J	F	H	H	I	D	H	H	H	H	G	J	J	G	H	G	I	H	D	E	J	F	L	G
	1.74	J	H	I	G	H	H	J	F	H	H	I	D	H	H	H	H	G	J	J	G	H	G	I	H	D	E	J	F	L	G
	1.76	J	H	I	G	H	H	J	F	H	H	I	D	H	H	H	H	G	J	J	G	H	G	I	H	D	E	J	F	L	G
	1.77	100	100	100	100	100	100	100	100	100	100	100	100	100	100	100	100	100	100	100	100	100	100	100	100	100	100	100	100	100	100

APPENDIX B

APPELLATE DECISIONS CITING DSM-III-R

Federal

Knock v. Sullivan, 952 F.2d 405 (7th Cir. 1992).

Brown v. Secretary of Health & Human Services, 948 F.2d 268 (6th Cir. 1991).

Henderson v. Sullivan, 930 F.2d 19 (8th Cir. 1991).

Kennedy v. Sullivan, 919 F.2d 144 (8th Cir. 1990).

Harris v. Vasquez, 913 F.2d 606 (9th Cir. 1990).

Harris v. Vasquez, 943 F.2d 930 (9th Cir. 1990).

Harris v. Vasquez, 949 F.2d 1497 (9th Cir. 1990).

United States v. Oshatz, 912 F.2d 534, 31 Fed. R. Evid. Serv. (Callaghan) 558 (2d Cir. 1990).

Morgan v. Sullivan, 908 F.2d 1426 (9th Cir. 1990).

Pieper v. Bowen, 904 F.2d 710 (9th Cir. 1990).

In re Petition of Sullivan, 904 F.2d 826 (3d Cir. 1990).

United States v. Whitehead, 896 F.2d 432 (9th Cir. 1990).

United States v. Watson, 893 F.2d 970 (8th Cir. 1990).

Perez Torres v. Secretary of Health & Human Services, 890 F.2d 1251 (1st Cir. 1989).

Buck v. Bowen, 885 F.2d 451 (8th Cir. 1989).

Bryant v. Bowen, 882 F.2d 1331 (8th Cir. 1989).

Foster v. Bowen, 853 F.2d 483 (6th Cir. 1988).

Harris v. Pulley, 852 F.2d 1546 (9th Cir. 1988).

Harris v. Pulley, 885 F.2d 1354 (9th Cir. 1988).

Harich v. Dugger, 844 F.2d 1464 (11th Cir. 1988).

Pesta v. Secretary of Health & Human Services, 829 F.2d 1126 (6th Cir. 1987).

Bailey v. Bowen, 827 F.2d 368 (8th Cir. 1987).

Poulin v. Bowen, 817 F.2d 865 (D.C. Cir. 1987).

United States v. Aders, 816 F.2d 673 (4th Cir. 1987).

Metcalf v. Heckler, 800 F.2d 793 (8th Cir. 1986).

Burns v. Clusen, 798 F.2d 931, 21 Fed. R. Evid. Serv. (Callaghan) 481 (7th Cir. 1986).

United States v. Gillis, 773 F.2d 549 (4th Cir. 1985).

United States v. Davis, 772 F.2d 1339, 18 Fed. R. Evid. Serv. (Callaghan) 905 (7th Cir. 1985).

Wilson v. Sears, Roebuck & Co., 757 F.2d 948 (8th Cir. 1985).

United States v. Gould, 741 F.2d 45, 16 Fed. R. Evid. Serv. (Callaghan) 116 (4th Cir. 1984).

Parsons v. Heckler, 739 F.2d 1334 (8th Cir. 1984).

United States v. Torniero, 735 F.2d 725, 15 Fed. R. Evid. Serv. (Callaghan) 1214 (2d Cir. 1984).

United States v. Lyons, 731 F.2d 243, 15 Fed. R. Evid. Serv. (Callaghan) 859 (5th Cir. 1984).

Rowland v. Mad River Local School District, 730 F.2d 444 (6th Cir. 1984).

United States v. Lewellyn, 723 F.2d 615 (8th Cir. 1983).

Granville House, Inc. v. Department of Health & Human Services, 715 F.2d 1292 (8th Cir. 1983).

Protection & Advocacy, Inc. v. Murphy, No. 90C 569, 1992 WL 59100 (N.D. Ill. Mar. 16, 1992).

Drenkhahn v. Derwinski, 2 Vet. App. 207 (1992).

In re Crescenzi, No. 91 CIV. 8045 (PKL), 1992 WL 30615 (S.D.N.Y. Feb. 5, 1992).

Soto v. Sullivan, No. CIV. A. 91-47-CMW, 1991 WL 226776 (D. Del. Oct. 31, 1991).

Phillips v. Lincoln National Life Insurance Co., 774 F. Supp. 495, 14 Employee Benefits Cas. (BNA) 1708 (N.D. Ill. 1991).

Washington v. Derwinski, 1 Vet. App. 459 (1991).

United States v. Dzialo, 773 F. Supp. 21 (E.D. Mich. 1991).

Rankel v. Tracey, No. 84 CIV. 3412, 1991 WL 156324 (S.D.N.Y. Aug. 2, 1991).

Johnson v. Johnson, 766 F. Supp. 662 (N.D. Ill. 1991).

In re Connecticut Prison Overcrowding & Aids Cases, No. H-80-506, CIV. H-88-562, 1990 WL 261348 (D. Conn. Dec. 6, 1990).

Johnson v. Sullivan, No. 87-4266-CV-C-9, 1990 WL 212095 (W.D. Mo. Nov. 28, 1990).

Abdulghani v. Virgin Islands Seaplane Shuttle, Inc., 746 F. Supp. 583 (D.V.I. 1990).

United States v. Beane, No. CIV. A. 88-8488, 1990 WL 63603 (E.D. Pa. May 7, 1990).

Rosenthal v. Mutual Life Insurance Co., 732 F. Supp. 108 (S.D. Fla. 1990).

Phillips v. Michigan Department of Corrections, 731 F. Supp. 792 (W.D. Mich. 1990).

Irwin ex rel. Irwin v. Sullivan, No. 89-1421, 1989 WL 281964 (W.D. Pa. Dec. 18, 1989).

Johnson v. Sullivan, No. CIV. 89-473-D, 1989 WL 280315 (W.D. Okla. Oct. 6, 1989).

Buttrum v. Black, 721 F. Supp. 1268 (N.D. Ga. 1989).

Wilkerson v. Sullivan, 727 F. Supp. 925 (E.D. Pa. 1989).

Ellingson v. Sullivan, No. CIV. 88-6146-FR, 1989 WL 69959 (D. Or. June 21, 1989).

Bullock v. Sullivan, No. CIV. A. 88-8694, 1989 WL 56381 (E.D. Pa. May 25, 1989).

Fairchild v. Lockhart, 744 F. Supp. 1429 (E.D. Ark. 1989).

Gibson v. City of Chicago, 701 F. Supp. 666 (N.D. Ill. 1988).

Johnson v. Johnson, 701 F. Supp. 1363 (N.D. Ill. 1988).

Graham v. Turnage, No. CIV. A. 88-0793, 1988 WL 71275 (E.D. Pa. June 30, 1988).

Spencer v. General Electric Co., 688 F. Supp. 1072, 49 Empl. Prac. Dec. (CCH) ¶ 38,750, 26 Fed. R. Evid. Serv. (Callaghan) 198 (E.D. Va. 1988).

Cintron v. Bowen, 686 F. Supp. 522 (E.D. Pa. 1988).

Rezza v. United States Department of Justice, 56 U.S.L.W. 2686, 46 Empl. Prac. Dec. (CCH) ¶ 37,976 (1988).

United States v. State, 680 F. Supp. 928 (W.D. Mich. 1987).

Scacchetti v. Secretary of Health & Human Services, No. CIV.-83-299T, 1987 WL 9739 (W.D.N.Y. Feb. 27, 1987).

Gray v. Sencer, No. 84 CIV. 7923 (LLS), 1987 WL 7029 (S.D.N.Y. Feb. 19, 1987).

Lingo v. Secretary of Health & Human Services, 658 F. Supp. 345, 17 Soc.Sec.Rep.Ser. 808 (N.D. Ohio 1986).

Sterling v. Velsicol Chemical Corp., 647 F. Supp. 303, 24 Env't Rep. Cas. (BNA) 2017, 17 Envtl. L. Rep. (Envtl. L. Inst.) 20,081 (W.D. Tenn. 1986).

Moro Arroyo v. Secretary of Health & Human Services, 622 F. Supp. 1579 (D.P.R. 1985).

United States v. Shorter, 618 F. Supp. 255, 85-2 U.S. Tax Cas. (CCH) ¶ 9673, 18 Fed. R. Evid. Serv. (Callaghan) 1314 (D.D.C. 1985).

Black v. Heckler, 588 F. Supp. 1355 (N.D. Ill. 1984).

Kramer v. United States, 579 F. Supp. 314 (D. Md. 1984).

Ulane v. Eastern Airlines, Inc., 581 F. Supp. 821, 35 Fair Empl. Prac. Cas. (BNA) 1332, 34 Empl. Prac. Dec. (CCH) ¶ 34,334 (N.D. Ill. 1983).

United States v. Torniero, 570 F. Supp. 721, 13 Fed. R. Evid. Serv. (Callaghan) 1955 (D. Conn. 1983).

Dumas v. Agency for Child Development-New York City Head Start, 569 F. Supp. 831, 32 Fair Empl. Prac. Cas. (BNA) 1365 (S.D.N.Y. 1983).

United States v. Shakur, 560 F. Supp. 318 (S.D.N.Y. 1983).

Granville House, Inc. v. Department of Health & Human Services, 550 F. Supp. 628 (D. Minn. 1982).

In re Irvin, 31 B.R. 251, Bankr. L. Rep. (CCH) ¶ 69,282, 13 Fed. R. Evid. Serv. (Callaghan) 1428 (D. Colo. 1983).

Ferrell v. United States, 23 Cl. Ct. 562 (1991).

Kirwin v. United States, 23 Cl. Ct. 497 (1991).

Pope v. United States, 16 Cl. Ct. 637 (1989).

Grant Associates, Inc. v. United States, 11 Cl. Ct. 816 (1987).

United States v. Bell, 34 M.J. 937 (A.F.C.M.R. 1992).

United States v. Bell, No. ACM 28482, 1992 WL 30417 (A.F.C.M.R. Feb. 12, 1992).

United States v. Lewis, 34 M.J. 745 (N.M.C.M.R. 1991).

United States v. Mansfield, 33 M.J. 972 (A.F.C.M.R. 1991).

United States v. Benedict, 27 M.J. 253 (C.M.A. 1988).

United States v. Bono, 26 M.J. 240 (C.M.A. 1988).

United States v. Rivera, 26 M.J. 638 (A.C.M.R. 1988).

United States v. Carter, 22 M.J. 771 (A.C.M.R. 1988).

United States v. Baasel, 22 M.J. 505 (A.F.C.M.R. 1986).

United States v. Eastman, 20 M.J. 948 (A.F.C.M.R. 1985).

Alabama

Barnett v. State, 540 So. 2d 810 (Ala. 1988).

Arizona

State v. Zmich, 160 Ariz. 108, 770 P.2d 776 (1989).

State v. Motijo, 160 Ariz. 576, 774 P.2d 1366 (1989).

In re Appeal in Maricopa County Juvenile Action, 143 Ariz. 178, 692 P.2d 1027 (1984).

In re Appeal in Maricopa County Juvenile County Action, 142 Ariz. 515, 690 P.2d 816 (1984).

In re Ronwin, 139 Ariz. 576, 680 P.2d 107 (1983).

California

People v. Bean, 46 Cal. 3d 919, 760 P.2d 996, 251 Cal. Rptr. 467 (1988).

People v. Jeff, 204 Cal. App. 3d 309, 251 Cal. Rptr. 135 (1988).

People v. Superior Court (Williams), 233 Cal. App. 3d 477, 284 Cal. Rptr. 601 (1991).

In re Conservatorship of Daigle, 269 Cal. Rptr. 770, Ordered Not Published (Rule 976, Cal. Rule of Ct.) (1990).

People v. Aris, 215 Cal. App. 3d 1178, 264 Cal. Rptr. 167 (1989).

People v. Rich, 45 Cal. 3d 1036, 755 P.2d 960, 248 Cal. Rptr. 510 (1988).

People v. Babbitt, 45 Cal. 3d 660, 755 P.2d 253, 248 Cal. Rptr. 69 (1988).

People v. Williams, 44 Cal. 3d 883, 751 P.2d 395, 245 Cal. Rptr. 336 (1988).

People v. Coleman, 38 Cal. 3d 69, 695 P.2d 189, 211 Cal. Rptr. 102 (1985).

In re Appeal in Maricopa County Juvenile Action, 143 Ariz. 178, 692 P.2d 1027 (1984).

People v. Fields, 35 Cal. 3d 329, 673 P.2d 680, 197 Cal. Rptr. 803 (1983).

People v. Superior Court, 148 Cal. App. 3d 990, 196 Cal. Rptr. 431 (1983).

Money v. Krall, 128 Cal. App. 3d 378, 180 Cal. Rptr. 376 (1982).

Colorado

People v. Fasy, 1992 WL 103611 (May 18, 1992).

In re Romero, 790 P.2d 819 (Colo. 1990).

People ex rel. C.B., 740 P.2d 11 (Colo. 1987).

Delaware

State v. Red Dog, 1992 WL 92385 (Apr. 1992).

District of Columbia

In re Shorter, 570 A.2d 760 (D.C. 1990).

Georgia

Brandvain v. Ridgeview Institute, Inc., 188 Ga. App. 106, 372 S.E.2d 265 (1988).

Fleming v. Zant, 259 Ga. 687, 386 S.E.2d 339 (1989).

Idaho

State v. Roles (Raymond Allen), 1992 WL 9758 (Jan. 27, 1992).

Illinois

People v. Douglas, 183 Ill. App. 3d 241, 538 N.E.2d 1335 (1989).

People v. Shukovsky, 128 Ill. 2d 210, 538 N.E.2d 444 (1988).

Cohen v. Washington National Insurance Co., 175 Ill. App. 3d 517, 529 N.E.2d 1065 (1988).

People v. Johnson, 146 Ill. 2d 109, 585 N.E.2d 78 (1991).

People v. Eckhardt, 156 Ill. App. 3d 1077, 509 N.E.2d 1361 (1987).

In re Hightshoe, 155 Ill. App. 3d 371, 508 N.E.2d 488 (1987).

People v. Lang, 113 Ill. 2d 407, 498 N.E.2d 1105 (1986).

Koesterer v. Edgar, 143 Ill. App. 3d 832, 493 N.E.2d 702 (1986).

Escalona v. Board of Trustees, 127 Ill. App. 3d 357, 469 N.E.2d 297 (1984).

People v. Gacy, 103 Ill. 2d 1, 468 N.E.2d 1171 (1984).

People v. Parker, 113 Ill. App. 3d 321, 447 N.E.2d 457 (1983).

Iowa

State v. Gettier, 438 N.W.2d 1 (Iowa 1989).

Kansas

State v. Demoss, 244 Kan. 387, 770 P.2d 441 (1989).

In re J.W.S., 250 Kan. 65, 825 P.2d 125 (1992).

State v. Alexander, 240 Kan. 273, 729 P.2d 1126 (1986).

Followill v. Emerson Electric Co., 234 Kan. 791, 674 P.2d 1050 (1984).

Louisiana

Frasier v. Department of Health & Human Resources, 500 So. 2d 858 (La. Ct. App. 1986).

State v. Felde, 422 So. 2d 370 (La. 1982).

Maine

State v. Woodburn, 559 A.2d 343 (Me. 1989).

Cooke v. Naylor, 573 A.2d 376 (Me. 1990).

Maryland

Bricker v. State, 80 Md. App. 532, 565 A.2d 340 (1989).

State v. Allewalt, 308 Md. 89, 517 A.2d 741 (1986).

Massachusetts

Commonwealth v. Tracy, 27 Mass. App. Ct. 455, 539 N.E.2d 1043 (1989).

Commonwealth v. Mulica, 401 Mass. 812, 520 N.E.2d 134 (1988).

Michigan

People v. Allen, 429 Mich. 558, 420 N.W.2d 499 (1988).

Minnesota

Mervin v. Magney Construction Co., 399 N.W.2d 579 (Minn. Ct. App. 1987).

State v. Bouwman, 354 N.W.2d 1 (Minn. 1984).

Mississippi

McInnis v. State, 527 So. 2d 84 (Miss. 1988).

King v. State, 503 So. 2d 271 (Miss. 1987).

Neal v. State, 451 So. 2d 743 (Miss. 1984).

Missouri

Young v. St. Louis University, 773 S.W.2d 143 (Mo. Ct. App. 1989).

McDonald v. State, 758 S.W.2d 101 (Mo. Ct. App. 1988).

Wilson v. State, 813 S.W.2d 833 (Mo. 1991).

State v. Biddy, 748 S.W.2d 794 (Mo. Ct. App. 1988).

Nebraska

Malerbi v. Central Reserve Life Insurance Co., 225 Neb. 543, 407 N.W.2d 157 (1987).

New Hampshire

In re David B., 127 N.H. 772, 508 A.2d 1045 (1986).

New Jersey

In re Vey, 124 N.J. 534, 591 A.2d 1333 (1991).

Baldino v. Baldino, 241 N.J. Super. 414, 575 A.2d 66 (Super. Ct. Ch. Div. 1990).

John's Cocktail Lounge, Inc. v. North River Insurance Co., 235 N.J. Super. 536, 563 A.2d 473 (Super. Ct. App. Div. 1989).

State v. Pitts, 116 N.J. 580, 562 A.2d 1320 (1989).

In re Goldberg, 109 N.J. 163, 536 A.2d 224 (1988).

In re Baby M., 217 N.J. Super. 313, 525 A.2d 1128 (Super. Ct. Ch. Div. 1987).

Saunderlin v. E.I. Dupont Co., 102 N.J. 402, 508 A.2d 1095 (1986).

New Mexico

State v. Bowman, 104 N.M. 19, 715 P.2d 467 (1986).

New York

In re Sanchez, 141 Misc. 2d 1066, 535 N.Y.S.2d 937 (Fam. Ct. 1988).

People v. Taylor, 75 N.Y.2d 277, 552 N.E.2d 131, 552 N.Y.S.2d 883 (1990).

People v. McDonald, 136 Misc. 2d 1047, 519 N.Y.S.2d 628 (Sup. Ct. 1987).

Robinson v. Robinson, 134 Misc. 2d 664, 512 N.Y.S.2d 315 (Sup. Ct. 1987).

People v. Grady, 103 Misc. 2d 211, 506 N.Y.S.2d 922 (Sup. Ct. 1986).

In re L. Children, 131 Misc. 2d 81, 499 N.Y.S.2d 587 (Fam. Ct. 1986).

People v. Gans, 119 Misc. 2d 843, 465 N.Y.S.2d 147 (Sup. Ct. 1983).

Lacomb ex rel. Claytor v. Poland Central School District, 116 Misc. 2d 585, 455 N.Y.S.2d 994 (Sup. Ct. 1982).

North Carolina

State v. Hall, 330 N.C. 808, 412 S.E.2d 883 (1992).

State v. Goodwin, 320 N.C. 147, 357 S.E.2d 639 (1987).

North Dakota

In re Estate of Aune, 478 N.W.2d 561 (N.D. 1991).

Ohio

State v. Tomlin, 1991 WL 161344 (Aug. 21, 1991).

State v. Mccarroll, 1989 WL 155215 (Dec. 21, 1989).

Oregon

In re Adoption of Eder, 312 Or. 244, 821 P.2d 400 (1991).

State ex rel. Juvenile Department v. Ashley, 312 Or. 169, 818 P.2d 1270 (1991).

State v. Moen, 309 Or. 45, 786 P.2d 111 (1990).

State ex rel. Juvenile Department v. Geist, 97 Or. App. 10, 775 P.2d 843 (1989).

State v. Huntley, 302 Or. 418, 730 P.2d 1234 (1986).

State v. Smith, 71 Or. App. 205, 692 P.2d 120 (1984).

State v. Brown, 297 Or. 404, 687 P.2d 751 (1984).

McGarrah v. State Accident Insurance Fund Corp., 296 Or. 145, 675 P.2d 159 (1983).

Pennsylvania

In re Adoption of Stunkard, 380 Pa. Super. 107, 551 A.2d 253 (1988).

Syno v. Syno, 406 Pa. Super. 218, 594 A.2d 307 (1991).

Cohen v. Albert Einstein Medical Center, 405 Pa. Super. 392, 592 A.2d 720 (1991).

Commonwealth v. Terry, 513 Pa. 381, 521 A.2d 398 (1987).

Tennessee

State v. Nnadi, 1987 WL 7695 (Mar. 12, 1987).

Texas

Ex parte Harris, 825 S.W.2d 120 (Tex. Crim. App. 1991).

Fielder v. State, 756 S.W.2d 309 (Tex. Crim. App. 1988).

Schuessler v. State, 719 S.W.2d 320 (Tex. Crim. App. 1986).

Utah

State v. Murphy, 760 P.2d 280 (Utah 1988).

Virginia

Edwards v. Arlington County, 5 Va. App. 294, 361 S.E.2d 644 (1987).

Washington

In re Rice, 828 P.2d 1086 (Wash. 1992).

In re Belsher, 102 Wash. 2d 844, 689 P.2d 1078 (1984).

West Virginia

State v. McCoy, 179 W. Va. 223, 366 S.E.2d 731 (1988).

Wisconsin

State v. Coogan, 154 Wis. 2d 387, 453 N.W.2d 186 (Ct. App. 1990).

State v. Wilkins, 148 Wis. 2d 95, 438 N.W.2d 596 (Ct. App. 1989).

State v. Flattum, 122 Wis. 2d 282, 361 N.W.2d 705 (1985).

State v. Burns, 112 Wis. 2d 131, 332 N.W.2d 757 (1983).

Wyoming

Scadden v. State, 732 P.2d 1036 (Wyo. 1987).

Schmidt v. State, 668 P.2d 656 (Wyo. 1983).

APPENDIX C

INVESTIGATION AND DISCOVERY DOCUMENTS

INVESTIGATION LETTER

Dear ___________:

The following are standard elements I like covered in an AOE-COE investigation in a psychiatric case:

1. If the employee was fired, why.
2. How did employee get along with his or her supervisor or supervisors during the period of employment?
3. How did the employee get along with fellow workers in that period?
4. Did employee indicate that he or she had any personal worries such as children, drugs, police, etc., difficulty with significant other, including wife, financial problems, health problems, parental problems?
5. Very important; information about health history. Can you get medical plan carrier to give you information?
6. Photocopies of complete personnel history and records (everything in personnel file).
7. It is important to determine how long the employee has been employed and during what portion of that period he or she claims stressful events. For example, if there was no change in the type of work or work events throughout the period of employment, but employee says that starting at a certain time things got bad, that is important for two reasons. First, the fact that things were always the same tends to rebut the claim. Second, if non-industrial events which were stressful were occurring around the same time, that is more evidence that it is personal problems rather than job problems that are responsible for mental disorders, if any.

I am enclosing photocopies from the American Psychiatric Association manual "Diagnostic and Statistical Manual of Mental Disorders-III." Almost all psychiatric claims involve claims of either depression or anxiety and the excerpted material summarizes what is considered essential evidence of a clinical condition. I emphasize the word clinical because mere worry, anger, annoyance and irritation are not mental disorders. To be an actual mental disorder, the condition has to have the elements described in the excerpted material. I hope you will find this helpful and I will be looking forward to receiving your report.

Sincerely,

Herbert Lasky

HL:dkg

enc

cc: Insurance Company, ________________,
____

EX PARTE PETITION FOR ORDER TO PRODUCE MEDICAL RECORDS

ATTORNEYS AT LAW

(818) 355-4142
Attorneys for Defense

BEFORE THE WORKERS' COMPENSATION APPEALS BOARD
OF THE STATE OF CALIFORNIA

Applicant, vs. Defendants.	WCAB CASE NO: EX-PARTE PETITION FOR ORDER TO PRODUCE MEDICAL RECORDS

Comes now Defendant, __________, who petitions that the Custodian of Records for __________ Hospital be ordered to produce all medical records in its possession or control without ommission pertaining to Applicant, __________, based upon the following:

1. Applicant has filed an application for benefits alleging psychiatric injury and disability in the above captioned matter.

2. The above named facility has provided care, treatment and/or evaluation of Applicant wholly or partially related to psychological condition, alcohol useage, and/or drug useage.

3. All or a portion of records of the above named facility are priviledged according to the Laws of the Statutes of the State of California and/or the United States of America.

4. Defendant is informed and believes that the records it seeks are relevant to issues in the above captioned matter including but not limited to: Causation; Nature, Extent and Duration of Disability; Liability for Self-Procured Medical Treatment; Further Medical Treatment; Apportionment.

5. Labor Code Section 132 grants the Appeals Board the power to order production of papers to the same extent as a Court of Record.

6. Defendant agrees that all records obtained pursuant to this Petition shall not be disseminated or otherwise revealed directly or indirectly to any person beyond those persons necessary for participation in defense of the above captioned claim.

7. Defendant agrees to provide copies of all records obtained to Applicant's attorney or representative *provided that* said attorney or representative shall not disseminate or otherwise reveal any of said records directly or indirectly to any person who is not necessary for prosecution of the above captioned claim.

8. Present circumstances relating to discovery in this matter dictate that an Order for Production of Records is the most speedy and adequate remedy of law available to Defendant.

9. Defendant respectfully requests an Order to Expediat production of the records it seeks that the Appeals Board allows service of any Order made pursuant to this Petition by mail.

10. Defendant agrees that ___________ should be granted a period of 20 days from personal service of any Order issuing pursuant to this Petition upon the Custodian of Records for said facility. Defendant also agrees that any objection to any Order which issues pursuant to this Petition maybe made within 25 days of service by mail upon the Custodian of Records of ___________.

11. Defendant respectfully requests that an Order issue directing the Custodian of Records at ___________ to appear before a Notary Public at the Law Offices of ________________ and produce, verify, and allow photocopy of all records, without omission which are the subject of said Order. Defendant agrees that the time and place for production of records pursuant to this Petition shall be no less than 20 days from the date of personal service of any Order to Produce Medical Records made upon the Custodian of Records at ___________ and no less than 25 days from service by mail of any Order to Produce Medical Records served upon the Custodian of Records of ___________.

12. Defendant agrees that any objection to production of medical records pursuant to this petition may be accomplished in a reasonable period of time from service of any order issuing pursuant to this petition to be set by the Appeals Board. Defendant respectfully contends that a reasonable period shall be identical to the period of time allowed for production of records depending upon whether service of any order of the Appeals Board is made upon the Custodian of Records of ___________ personally or by mail.

13. Defendant agrees that the Custodian of Records of ___________ may comply with any order issued by the Appeals Board pursuant to this petition by mailing a complete photocopied set of medical records at reasonable charge together with a verification of the Custodian of Records as to the completeness of the photocopies of records provided directly to the law offices of ________________ 20 days of personal service of any Order to Produce Medical Records pursuant to this petition made upon the Custodian of Records for said facility or 25 days for the production of said medical records if service is accomplished upon the Custodian by mail.

14. Defendant agrees that compliance of this order may also be allowed if ___________ makes available through its Custodian to any designated photocopy service of the lawfirm of ___________ and/or defendant within 20 days of personal service of any Order to Produce Medical Records pursuant to this petition made upon the Custodian of Records of ___________ Hospital or 25 days within service by mail of any order made pursuant to this petition upon the Custodian of Records of ___________ Hospital. Defendant further agrees that if compliance of any order is allowed through use of a photocopy service, that said photocopy service shall be limited to making 2 copies only of each writing obtained and shall directly deliver 2 sets of records to the ________________ indicated above without dissemination or revealing of all or any portion of said medical records directly or indirectly to any person. Thereafter the law offices of ___________ shall be bound by the confidentiality provisions in any order of the Appeals Board.

15. Defendant has served a copy of this petition upon attorney for applicant.

WHEREFORE, Defendant, ___________ respectfully requests that the above named petition be granted and that an order pursuant to the same issue forthwith.

DATED: ___________

RESPECTFULLY SUBMITTED

BY: ____________________________

EX PARTE ORDER TO PRODUCE MEDICAL RECORDS

BEFORE THE WORKERS' COMPENSATION APPEALS BOARD
OF THE STATE OF CALIFORNIA

Applicant,	CASE NO:
vs.	
Defendants.	EX-PARTE ORDER TO PRODUCE MEDICAL RECORDS

Based upon verified Petition of Counsel for Defendant and, GOOD CAUSE APPEARING THEREFORE:

The Custodian of Records of ___________ is hereby ordered to appear before a Notary Public at the law offices of ___________ and produce, verify, and allow photocopy of all records of ___________ on a date to be determined by counsel for defendant no less than 20 days from personal service of this Order and no less than 25 from service of this Order by mail.

Any objections to production of any writing subject to this order shall be made no less than 20 days from personal service of this Order upon the Custodian of Records of ___________ and no less than 25 days from service by mail of this Order upon the Custodian of Records of ___________.

It is further ordered that the Custodian of Records of ___________ may comply with this order by photocopying a complete set of records from said facility without omission at reasonable charge to defendant and mailing the same together with a verification of completeness of said records directly to the law offices of ________________ within 20 days of personal service upon the Custodian of Records of said facility or 25 days of service by mail of this Order upon the Custodian of Records for said facility.

It is further ordered that the Custodian of Records of ___________ may comply with this Order by allowing a designated photocopy service of defendant to photocopy two (2) complete sets of records without omission at a mutually agreeable time and place within 20 days of personal service of this Order upon the Custodian of Records of said facility or within 25 days of service by mail upon the Custodian of Records of said facility. If ___________ elects to comply with this Order in the manner prescribed in this paragraph, the Custodian of Records shall provide to any designated photocopy service that the records produced are complete to the extent of his or her knowledge. Any designated photocopy service shall not disseminate or otherwise reveal the contents of records subject to this Order directly to indirectly to any person other than by direct delivery of said records to the law offices of ________________.

Any objection to production of records subject to this order shall be served upon the Appeals Board on less than 20 days from personal service of this Order upon the Custodian of Records of ___________ or 25 days upon service by mail of this Order upon the Custodian of Records of ___________. It is further ordered that any objection to the production of records pursuant to this Order shall be concurrently served upon the law offices of ______________________________.

It is further ordered that defendant or counsel for defendant shall provide a complete photocopied set of records obtained to the attorney or representative of applicant.

No person who is authorized possession of all or a portion of the records subject to this Order shall disseminate or otherwise reveal all or a portion of said records directly or indirectly to any person who is not necessary for the prosecution or defense of the above captioned Workers' Compensation Claim without written approval of the Appeals Board or by Order of a court of record.

DATED: ________________

____

WORKERS' COMPENSATION JUDGE

CONSENT TO OBTAIN URINE AND BLOOD SPECIMEN

I, the undersigned individual, do hereby consent to the collection of a urine/blood specimen for the purpose of providing for a qualitative drug screening test. I consent to this test being conducted on behalf of my employer or prospective employer and do voluntarily waive any claims for invasion of privacy so long as the results thereto are released only to the persons or company designated by me. I acknowledge that I have been advised that the results of this test will be released together with other medical information to:

____

____

____

and authorize release of the above information and results.

____________________	____________________
Signature of Patient	Date
____________________	____________________
Signature of Witness	Date

APPENDIX D

PRIVILEGE BETWEEN PATIENT AND CLINICIAN: HOW TO PENETRATE EFFORTS TO USE CONFIDENTIAL RELATIONSHIPS AS A SHIELD FROM THE TRUE FACTS

Anita Hotchkiss, Esq.
Janet A. Sullivan, Esq.
PORZIO, BROMBERG & NEWMAN, P.C.
163 Madison Avenue
Morristown, New Jersey 07962-1997
(201) 538-4006

TABLE OF CONTENTS

C. Attacking The Relationship Between The Clinician And The Attorney
D. Attacking The Type Of Service Performed
E. Burden Of Proof
F. Waiver Based On Presence Of Third Persons During "Confidential Communications"
G. Challenging The Confidentiality Of The Substance Of The Communication
H. Attacking The Timeliness Of The Assertion Of The Privilege
I. Focus On Exceptions To The Privilege
J. How To Use The Privilege As A Sword

IV. WAIVER OF THE PRIVILEGE

A. Generally
B. Express Waiver
C. Implied Waiver
D. Revocation Of The Waiver
E. Does Waiver As To One Clinician Constitute Waiver As To Others?

V. EX PARTE COMMUNICATIONS WITH TREATING CLINICIANS, ONCE WAIVER OF THE PRIVILEGE HAS BEEN ESTABLISHED

VI. CONCLUSION

I. DEFINING THE PATIENT/CLINICIAN PRIVILEGE

A. State Statutes

1. No privilege against the compelled disclosure of confidential communications existed between a patient and clinician at common law. Communications between a patient and clinician are privileged only by statutory authority. Most states have enacted statutes which create a privilege preserving the confidentiality of communications between a patient and his clinician.
   a. See 8 J. Wigmore, Evidence In Trials At Common Law § 2380 n.5 (McNaughton rev. 1961 & Supp. 1991) [hereinafter 8 Wigmore, Evidence] for a comprehensive listing of various states' privilege statutes.
2. Because the patient/clinician privilege is statutorily derived, its application and scope is defined and limited by the language of the given statute.
3. The common thread of most states' privilege statutes is the protection against the compulsory disclosure of confidential communications between the patient and clinician. However, each statute may have its own particular nuance regarding those to whom the privilege is extended, what communications are privileged, who can assert the privilege, etc.
4. Therefore, the importance of examining the particular state's statute in which the privilege is being invoked, as well as examining how the statute has been applied in that jurisdiction, can not be emphasized enough.

5. For example, states vary in their interpretation as to who has the burden of proving that certain communications between a patient and clinician are privileged. Some states presume there to be a privileged relationship for virtually any communication, while others require the patient to prove the "facts and circumstances" surrounding the communication. See 8 Wigmore, Evidence § 2381.
6. Regardless of whether the privilege is presumed or must be proved, it is, at most, a qualified privilege which can be waived under certain circumstances.
7. Finally, where a state's legislature has been silent on the issue of privilege between a patient and clinician, it will usually be presumed that no privilege exists. That is not to say, however, that general privacy considerations and the general fiduciary relationship between a patient and clinician would not apply to protect the confidentiality of the communication.

B. General Confidential/Fiduciary Relationship Between Patient And Clinician

1. Even absent a privilege statute, the clinician may be bound by other authority to maintain the confidentiality of a patient's communications. For example, the clinician may be bound by certain professional and ethical obligations contained in the Hippocratic Oath, the AMA's Code of Medical Ethics and the Current Opinions of the Judicial Council of the AMA. See Fox & Tatum, What's The Harm In Asking?: A Discussion Of Waiver Of The Physician-Patient Privilege And Ex Parte Interviews With Treating Physicians, 19 N.C. Cent. L.J. 1 (1990) [hereinafter Fox & Tatum]. See also People v. Baker, 94 Mich. App. 365, 288 N.W.2d 430 (1979).
   a. The Hippocratic Oath states:
      (1) "Whatever, in connection with my professional practice or not in connection with it, I see or hear, in the life of men, which ought not to be spoken abroad, I will not divulge, as reckoning that all such should be kept secret." Fox & Tatum at 4.
      (2) See also Crist v. Moffatt, 326 N.C. 326, 389 S.E.2d 41 (1990) (wherein court commented on a physician's duty separate from statutory mandate to maintain confidences).
      (3) See also Petrillo v. Syntex Laboratories, Inc., 148 Ill. App. 3d 581, 589, 499 N.E.2d 952, 957–58 (1986), cert. denied, Tobin v. Petrillo, 483 U.S. 1007 (1987) (wherein the court emphasized the strong public policy favoring the confidential and fiduciary nature of the physician-patient privilege by virtue of the Hippocratic Oath, the AMA's Principles of Medical Ethics, and the Current Opinions of the Judicial Council of the AMA).
   b. Principle IV of the AMA's Principles of Medical Ethics states:
      (1) "A physician shall respect the rights of patients, of colleagues, and of other health professionals, and shall

safeguard patient confidences within the constraints of the law." Petrillo, 148 Ill. App. 3d at 589, 499 N.E.2d at 957–58.

c. Section 5.05 of the Current Opinions of the Judicial Council states:

(1) "The information disclosed to a physician during the course of the relationship between physician and patient is confidential to the greatest degree possible . . . . The physician should not reveal confidential communications or information without the express consent of the patient, unless required to do so by law." Petrillo, 148 Ill. App. 3d at 589, 499 N.E.2d at 957–58.

C. Purpose Of The Privilege

1. The legislative motivation in enacting privilege statutes rests in public policy which favors protecting the patient. Although each state statute is unique in its scope and application, the reason for enacting privilege statutes is relatively uniform. Preserving confidentiality between a patient and clinician encourages the patient to fully disclose all of his injuries and illnesses to the clinician. It is only through full, unfettered disclosure that the clinician can accurately diagnose and treat the patient.

2. Arguably, without the assurances that communications will be kept confidential, the patient, fearing disclosure of information he finds embarrassing or extremely personal, might keep that information from the clinician. That could prove detrimental to the proper treatment of the patient.

3. Thus, while full disclosure of the facts in pending litigation is important, the opportunity of the patient to obtain proper care from the clinician is of paramount importance. The "[p]urpose [of the privilege] is to promote health, not truth. It encourages free disclosure in the sickroom by preventing disclosure in the courtroom." See Cleary, McCormick on Evidence § 102 (3d ed. 1984) [hereinafter McCormick].

II. EXISTENCE AND SCOPE OF PRIVILEGE

A. Under What Circumstances Does The Privilege Apply?

1. The patient/clinician privilege is generally asserted:

a. in actions on life insurance policies where the deceased's misrepresentation of his health is at issue;

b. personal injury actions where the extent of the plaintiff's injuries are at issue; and

c. actions on a will where the testator's mental capacity is at issue. See 8 Wigmore, Evidence § 2385 n.1.

2. The privilege usually only applies to licensed physicians and surgeons, although many state statutes expressly include psychiatrists, psychologists, psychotherapists and dentists. Nurses, optometrists, pharmacists and other health care professionals are generally not included in privilege statutes unless they are present and assisting the

clinician or acting as an agent of the clinician when the confidential communication is made.

3. The privilege may also extend to hospital records that are prepared by the clinician, with the exception of that part of the record which does not disclose diagnosis or treatment information (e.g. name, address, age, etc.).
   a. See, e.g., Kaplan v. Manhattan Life Insurance Company of New York, 109 F.2d 463, 465 (D.C. Cir. 1939).
4. Whether or not the privilege extends to records prepared by a nurse or other "non-clinician" health care provider depends on the language of the statute and therefore varies from state to state.
   a. See, e.g., Weis v. Weis, 147 Ohio St. 416, 72 N.E.2d 245, 252 (1947) (holding that the relationship of nurse and patient not being named in the statute, no privilege is extended to communications between a patient and his nurse).

B. To Whom Does The Privilege Belong?

1. In most states, the patient/clinician privilege is personal to the patient. It is therefore true that in most states, no one may assert the privilege on behalf of the patient unless he is authorized or required to do so. However, in some states it is presumed that the physician is authorized to claim the privilege on behalf of the patient.
   a. See Rev. Unif. R. Evid. 503(c) (1974), which states:
      (1) "The privilege may be claimed by the patient, his guardian or conservator, or the personal representative of a deceased patient. The person who was the [physician or] psychotherapist at the time of the communication is presumed to have authority to claim the privilege, but only on behalf of the patient."
   b. See also Dierickx v. Cottage Hospital Corp., 152 Mich. App. 162, 393 N.W.2d 564 (1986) (holding that the right to assert the physician-patient privilege is personal to the patient).

C. Scope Of The Privilege

1. There is considerable variation among statutes regarding the scope of the patient/clinician privilege. Some states afford the privilege a liberal construction, allowing a variety of communications and circumstances surrounding communications protection from disclosure. Others give the privilege a strict construction, limiting the protection afforded by the statute to very specific patient/clinician relationships and communications.
2. The general scope of the privilege statute in most states, however, is that the patient has a right to refuse to disclose and to prevent any other person from disclosing confidential communications made to his clinician for the purpose of diagnosis or treatment. See Rev. Unif. R. Evid. 503(b) (1974) which states:
   a. "A patient has a privilege to refuse to disclose and to prevent any other person from disclosing confidential communications

made for the purpose of diagnosis or treatment of his [physical,] mental or emotional condition, including alcohol or drug addiction, among himself, his [physician or] psychotherapist, and persons who are participating in the diagnosis or treatment under the direction of the [physician or] psychotherapist, including members of the patient's family."

3. Once it is determined that the privilege exists and is applicable to a particular health care provider or communication, it generally applies to all forms of attempted disclosure, including pretrial discovery and disclosure at trial.
4. Finally, the privilege does not generally expire with the patient's death.

III. WAYS TO ATTACK THE PRIVILEGE TO DETERMINE THE TRUE FACTS

A. Attacking The Existence Of The Patient/Clinician Relationship

1. In most states, the privilege applies only where some sort of fiduciary relationship between the patient and clinician exists. That relationship may be held to arise only where the patient seeks the care of the clinician for purposes of diagnosis and treatment, as distinguished from a simple examination.
2. Just as not every health care provider is included within the scope of certain states statutes, likewise not every person who talks to a clinician can be considered that clinician's patient. In most states, the privilege statute has been applied so as to require that the "patient" at least have been examined by or interviewed by the clinician for the purposes of diagnosis and treatment.
   a. City and County of San Francisco v. Superior Court, 37 Cal. 2d 227, 231 P.2d 26, 27–28 (1951) (holding that "if the person examined is not a 'patient' [within the definition of the privilege statute] then there is no physician-patient relationship and therefore no physician-patient privilege").
   b. See also Rev. Unif. R. Evid. 503(a)(1) (1974) which states:
      (1) "A 'patient' is a person who consults or is examined or interviewed by a [physician or] psychotherapist."
   c. 81 Am. Jur. 2d Witnesses § 239 (1976 and Supp. 1991) [hereinafter 81 Am. Jur. 2d].

B. Attacking The Identity Of The Health Care Provider

1. As previously stated, some state statutes only protect confidential communications between certain licensed clinicians, such as physicians and surgeons, while other state statutes expressly include dentists, psychiatrists, psychologist, and psychotherapists within the scope of the privilege statute.
2. Thus, attacking the privilege based on a clinician's noninclusion within the scope of a particular state's statute may also be successful.
   a. See People v. Baker, 94 Mich. App. 365, 288 N.W.2d 430 (1979).

C. Attacking The Relationship Between The Clinician And The Attorney

1. Attacking the privilege on the basis that the clinician involved was actually employed or paid by the patient's attorney will generally be unsuccessful, provided that a patient/clinician relationship as indicated above is established. However, if the patient submits to an examination by a clinician retained by an adverse party, the privilege generally will not apply.
   a. 81 Am. Jur. 2d at § 244.

D. Attacking The Type Of Service Performed

1. The privilege can also be attacked where the clinician involved simply performs laboratory tests or even a physical exam on a suspected criminal at the request of the police.
   a. See Block v. People, 125 Colo. 36, 240 P.2d 512 (1951), cert. denied, 343 U.S. 978 (1952), reh'g denied, 344 U.S. 848 (1952) (citing Hanlon v. Woodhouse, 113 Colo. 504, 160 P.2d 998 (1945).
   b. But see People v. Decina, 2 N.Y.2d 133, 138 N.E.2d 799, 157 N.Y.S.2d 558 (1956).

E. Burden Of Proof

1. Finally, counsel seeking to penetrate an asserted privilege based on the nature of the relationship between the clinician and the patient must keep in mind that the patient has the burden of showing that a professional relationship existed between the patient and the clinician. Thus, the patient must establish that the "facts and circumstances" of the relationship give rise to the privilege.

F. Waiver Based On Presence Of Third Persons During "Confidential Communications"

1. Generally, the presence of a third person during the alleged "confidential communication" between the patient and the clinician will negate the privilege, unless the third person was present to aid in the diagnosis or treatment of the patient.
   a. See McCormick at § 101.
2. More importantly, provided the third person is not deemed an agent or assistant of the clinician, that third person can be compelled to testify as to the communication. Thus, it behooves the attorney seeking to penetrate the privilege to find out who, if anyone, was present during the communication of "confidential" information.
3. It should be noted, however, that when the third person is a member of the patient's family, or the third person's presence is incidental, the privilege is generally deemed not to be impaired. This is especially true where the family member aids in the exchange of information, e.g., where the family member serves as an interpreter for the patient.
   a. See People v. Decina, 2 N.Y.2d 133, 138 N.E.2d 799, 157 N.Y.S.2d 558 (1956).

b. Rev. Unif. R. Evid. 503(a)(4) which states:

(1) "A communication is 'confidential' if not intended to be disclosed to third persons, except persons present to further the interest of the patient in the consultation, examination, or interview, persons reasonably necessary for the transmission of the communication, or persons who are participating in the diagnosis and treatment under the direction of the [physician or] psychotherapist, including members of the patient's family."

G. Challenging The Confidentiality Of The Substance Of The Communication

1. In many states, the clinician-patient privilege is triggered only when the communication was for the purpose of diagnosis and treatment. If the patient relays information to the clinician for purposes other than diagnosis and treatment, the privilege as to that information can be attacked. For example, information such as the number of times the patient visited the clinician, the fact that the clinician was consulted, who paid the bill, the date on which injuries occurred and the manner in which the injuries were inflicted, arguably does not fall within the scope of the privilege statute.

   a. See McCormick at § 99.

   b. 81 Am. Jur. 2d at § 251.

2. Likewise, facts learned by the clinician prior or subsequent to a relationship having been established between the patient and clinician are not privileged.

3. However, information obtained once the clinician/patient privilege has been established is privileged, even if that information is obtained indirectly through examination or observation of the patient rather than verbal communication.

4. In fact, even where the patient is unable to verbally communicate information to the clinician (for example, where the patient is unable to speak or is mentally incapacitated), the privilege will nevertheless, in most states, protect inferences and conclusions drawn from examination or observation of the patient.

H. Attacking The Timeliness Of The Assertion Of The Privilege

1. If the "patient" does not assert the privilege in a timely manner, the privilege will be considered waived. Thus, if an attempt is made to obtain confidential clinician/patient communications and no objection is made, the privilege in regard to that communication cannot be asserted at a later date.

   a. See 8 Wigmore, Evidence § 2390.

   b. See also Rev. Unif. R. Evid. 608(b).

I. Focus On Exceptions To The Privilege

1. There are certain clinician/patient communications which courts will normally exempt from the privilege, regardless of the existence of a privilege statute. See 81 Am. Jur. 2d at §§ 254, 245.

a. Communications made to a clinician for the purpose of committing or concealing the commission of a crime;
b. Communications made in certain criminal proceedings;
c. Where the patient is deceased (note, however, that many states do not consider the privilege extinguished with the patient's death);
d. Information revealed at autopsy (again, some states maintain that the privilege still applies);
e. Matters as to which reports are required (e.g., a gunshot or knife wound, child abuse, etc.); or
f. Communications concerning the physical condition of a defendant in a personal injury case.

J. How To Use The Privilege As A Sword

1. The clinician/patient privilege is usually asserted where the patient seeks to prevent the disclosure of confidential communications made to the clinician. It is, therefore, often said that the patient uses the privilege to "shield" that information from disclosure.
2. The patient may also attempt to use the privilege as a "sword" to prevent the defense from obtaining certain information, while allowing for the release of other information.
3. Patient/plaintiffs, however, are not the only parties who may attempt to use the privilege as a sword.
   a. For example, in Rudnick v. Superior Court of Kern County, 11 Cal. 3d 924, 114 Cal. Rptr. 603, 523 P.2d 643 (1974), the defendant drug company asserted the privilege as to physicians' reports received by the defendant regarding adverse reactions to its product. The court held that the defendants could "claim the physician-patient privilege on behalf of a patient to bar discovery of the adverse drug reaction report submitted by his physician if the submission of such report was in confidence and was reasonably necessary in order to accomplish the purpose for which the physician was consulted. If, however, such report was not made in confidence or was not reasonably necessary to accomplish the purpose for which the physician was consulted, then defendants cannot claim the privilege on behalf of the patient."

IV. WAIVER OF THE PRIVILEGE

A. Generally

1. Perhaps the best attack on the clinician/patient privilege is an argument that the patient or his agent has expressly or impliedly waived the privilege.
2. In deciding whether waiver has occurred, most courts will make a determination based on the "facts and circumstances" surrounding the communications between the clinician and the patient.
3. While it is true that in most states the burden of proof is on the patient to establish that a privileged relationship existed, the burden

of establishing the patient's intention to waive the privilege is on the party asserting the claim of waiver, usually the defense.

4. In most states, the affirmative right to waive the privilege rests with the patient or his legal representative, rather than the clinician.
5. However, where the clinician has been named as a defendant in a lawsuit brought by the patient/plaintiff, the privilege is usually deemed waived. In fact, as a general rule, most privileges are inapplicable to the extent that the person holding the information must reveal it to protect himself from civil or criminal liability.
   a. See, e.g., Model Rules of Professional Conduct 1.6(b)(2) (1987), which states:
      (1) "A lawyer may reveal such information to the extent the lawyer reasonably believes necessary . . . (2) to establish a claim or defense on behalf of the lawyer in a controversy between the lawyer and client, to establish a defense to a criminal charge or civil claim against the lawyer based upon conduct in which the client was involved, or to respond to allegations in any proceedings concerning the lawyer's representation of the client."
6. Waiver of the privilege is limited to the specific condition at issue.
7. That is, where the patient/plaintiff waived the privilege by virtue of having filed suit against the clinician/defendant, it is only information concerning the patient's health and medical history relevant to matters that the patient placed in issue in the litigation which will be deemed waived.
8. Although generally only the patient or his legal representative can waive the privilege, often a court will compel the disclosure of otherwise privileged information. Where the court does so in error (for example, on a discovery motion), the disclosure is not considered voluntary on the part of the patient and the patient may successfully assert the privilege later at trial.
   a. 81 Am. Jur. 2d at § 147.

B. Express Waiver
   1. While states vary in their interpretation of what constitutes an implied waiver, an express voluntary waiver is recognized in almost every state.
   2. Like most waivers, an express waiver of the patient/clinician privilege must be found to be voluntary and intentional.

C. Implied Waiver
   1. Generally, the mere bringing of a lawsuit by the patient will not constitute a waiver of the privilege. However, many states' statutes carve out exceptions to that rule.
      a. See, e.g., Moore v. Grandview Hosp., 25 Ohio St. 3d 194, 25 Ohio B. Rep. 259, 495 N.E.2d 934 (1986).
   2. For example, pursuant to some statutes, the filing of an action for damages for personal injury wherein the patient/plaintiff places his medical status at issue is deemed a waiver of the privilege.

   a. See, e.g., Caesar v. Mountanos, 542 F.2d 1064, 1068–1069 (9th Cir. 1976), cert. denied, 430 U.S. 954 (1977) (holding that where the patient placed his mental condition at issue, no privilege would apply to communications with patient's psychotherapist).
3. Other jurisdictions have held that there is an implied waiver where, during pretrial discovery, the patient testifies about his injuries or treatment in the course of taking his own deposition.
   a. See, e.g., In re Roberto, 106 Ohio App. 303, 151 N.E.2d 37, 41 (1958).
   b. 81 Am. Jur. 2d at § 271.
4. Some jurisdictions also have held that the patient has waived the privilege if he takes the deposition of his clinician. However, where the deposition of the clinician is taken by the patient's adversary, the privilege is not deemed waived.
   a. See Phipps v. Sasser, 74 Wash. 2d 439, 445 P.2d 624 (1968).
5. When the patient calls the clinician to testify at trial, the patient waives the privilege with regard to the condition at issue. However, simply calling the clinician to the stand is not regarded as waiver if the clinician is testifying regarding only collateral matters.
6. Similarly, where the clinician is called on to give an opinion based on a hypothetical question, the privilege will not have been waived.
   a. 81 Am. Jur. 2d at § 252.
7. In most states, the release of medical reports by the patient constitutes waiver.
   a. See Scharlack v. Richmond Memorial Hospital, 102 A.D.2d 886, 477 N.Y.S.2d 184 (1984).
   b. Loudon v. Mhyre, 110 Wash. 2d 675, 756 P.2d 138 (1988).
   c. Schuler v. United States, 113 F.R.D. 518, 521 (W.D. Mich. 1986).
8. The rule in most jurisdictions is that a patient's voluntary testimony at trial waives the privilege. However, some courts permit the patient to voluntarily testify about his general physical condition or the nature and extent of his injury without loss of the privilege, as long as he is are not testifying regarding matters of treatment.
   a. Giamanco v. Giamanco, 57 A.D.2d 564, 393 N.Y.S.2d 453 (1977).
   b. Mauro v. Tracy, 152 Colo. 106, 380 P.2d 570 (1963).
   c. Unick v. Kessler Memorial Hospital, 107 N.J. Super. 121, 257 A.2d 134 (Law Div. 1969).
9. The key to waiver at trial based upon the testimony of the patient is the voluntariness of the testimony. Thus, the court may find that there has been no waiver of matters to which the patient has testified on cross-examination because that testimony is not considered voluntary.
   a. McCormick at § 103.

10. Also, waiver is generally implied when the patient places his own mental competency at issue; for example, where a defendant raises the insanity defense.
    a. Davis v. State of Ark., 246 Ark. 838, 440 S.W.2d 244, 248 (1969), cert. denied, 403 U.S. 954 (1971).
11. Some jurisdictions have gone so far as to hold that oral discussions of privileged information at a pretrial conference waives the privilege.

D. Revocation Of The Waiver
   1. It is generally not possible to revoke a waiver of the privilege.
      a. In re Alvarez, 342 So. 2d 492, 494 (Fla. 1977).

E. Does Waiver As To One Clinician Constitute Waiver As To Others?
   1. There is a split in authority as to whether calling one clinician as a witness to privileged matters constitutes a waiver as to all other clinicians who have treated the patient for the particular physical condition at issue.
      a. For the various states' opinions, see Annotation, Waiver Of Privilege As Regards One Physician As A Waiver As To Other Physicians, 5 A.L.R.3d 1244 (19 & Supp. 1966 and Supp. 1991).

V. EX PARTE COMMUNICATIONS WITH TREATING CLINICIANS, ONCE WAIVER HAS BEEN ESTABLISHED

A. There is a vast divergence of opinion among the states regarding whether ex parte communications with the patient's treating clinician will be allowed, once waiver has been established.

B. Courts which have considered this issue have weighed the balance between the patient's interest in confidentiality and the opposing party's right to obtain all relevant evidence and adequately prepare the case.

C. The subject of ex parte interviews with treating clinicians has been the subject of many articles and seminars in and of itself. Without getting too detailed, a brief overview of the policy considerations are as follows:
   1. Many jurisdictions refuse to permit ex parte interviews because:
      a. The clinician may have a conflict of interest because the defendant doctor in a medical malpractice action might be covered by the same malpractice insurance carrier as the clinician.
      b. There is a broad privacy interest underlying the clinician/patient privilege.
      c. There is potential for exposing the clinician to tort liability for releasing privileged information.
      d. It is feared that defense counsel may seek to improperly influence the treating clinician.
      e. There exists a strong duty of loyalty between the clinician and the patient which should not be breached.
      f. Discovery rules should determine whether ex parte communications will be allowed. See Annotation, Discovery: Right to Ex

Parte Interview with Injured Party's Treating Physician, 50 A.L.R.4th 714, 717 (1986), cited in Fox & Tatum at 15.

D. Other jurisdictions allow ex parte interviews under the reasoning that:
   1. No party has a proprietary right in a witness.
   2. There is no specific rule or statute prohibiting ex parte interviews.
   3. Interviews are less costly to litigants than formal discovery.
   4. The public interest in the search for truth outweighs the private interest protected by the privilege.
   5. See Stempler v. Speidell, 100 N.J. 368, 495 A.2d 857 (1985). But see Petrillo v. Syntex Laboratories, Inc., 148 Ill. App. 3d 501, 102 Ill. Dec. 172, 499 N.E.2d 952 (1986); Loudon v. Mhyre, 110 Wash. 2d 675, 756 P.2d 138 (1988); Nelson v. Lewis, 130 N.H. 106, 534 A.2d 720 (1987).

VI. CONCLUSION

A. Any effort to attack and destroy the stone wall of privilege must begin with a careful review and analysis of the applicable state statutes. The most successful artillery to breach the wall will likely be armed with the cannonball of public interest.

BIBLIOGRAPHY

Articles

1. Fox & Tatum, What's The Harm In Asking?: A Discussion of Waiver of the Physician-Patient Privilege and Ex Parte Interviews With Treating Physicians, 19 N.C. Cent. L.J. 1 (1990).
2. Aranoff & Hirsh, Confidential Communications Between Physician and Patient in Judicial and Administrative Proceedings, Med. Trial Technique Q. (1983).
3. Thoren, The Physician-Patient Privilege, Med. Trial Technique Q. (1983).
4. Kohlman, Protected Communication Between Physician and Patient, 45 P.O.F. 2d 595 (1986 and Supp. 1991).

Books & Treatises

1. Cleary, McCormick on Evidence (3d ed. 1984).
2. 8 J. Wigmore, Evidence in Trials at Common Law (1961 and Supp. 1991).

Legal Encyclopedias

1. 81 Am. Jr. 2d Witness (1976 and Supp. 1991).

Annotations

1. Annotation, Discovery: Right to Ex Parte Interview With Injured Party's Treating Physician, 50 A.L.R. 4th 714 (1986 and Supp. 1990).

2. Annotation, Waiver of Privilege As Regards One Physician As a Waiver As to Other Physicians, 5 A.L.R. 3d 1244 (1966 and Supp. 1991).
3. Annotation, Commencing Action Involving Physical Condition Of Plaintiff Or Decedent As Waiving Physician-Patient Privilege As To Discovery Proceedings, 21 A.L.R. 3d (1966 and Supp. 1991).
4. Annotation, Pretrial Testimony Or Disclosure On Discovery By Party To Personal Injury Action As To Nature of Injuries Or Treatment As Waiver Of Physician-Patient Privilege, 25 A.L.R. 3d 1401 (1966 and Supp. 1991).
5. Annotation, Physician-Patient Privilege As Extending To Patient's Medical Or Hospital Records, 10 A.L.R. 4th 552 (1981 and Supp. 1990).
6. Annotation, Right of Physician, Notwithstanding Physician-Patient Privilege, To Give Expert Testimony Based On Hypothetical Question, 64 A.L.R. 2d 1056 (1984 and Supp. 1991).
7. Annotation, Admissibility of Statements Made For Purposes of Medical Diagnosis Or Treatment As Hearsay Exception Under Rule 803(4) Of The Federal Rules of Evidence, 55 A.L.R. Fed. 689 (1981 and Supp. 1990).
8. Annotation, Discovery, In Medical Malpractice Action, Of Names Of Other Patients To Whom Defendant Has Given Treatment Similar To That Allegedly Injuring Plaintiff, 74 A.L.R. 3d 1055 (1976 and Supp. 1991).

Note: This bibliography is not necessarily definitive.

BIBLIOGRAPHY

American Academy of Orthopaedic Surgeons (undated). *Manual for orthopaedic surgeons in evaluating permanent physical impairment.* Chicago, IL: Author.

American Medical Association. (1984). *Guide to permanent impairment.* Chicago: American Medical Association.

American Medical Association. (1988). *Guides to the evaluation of permanent impairment* (3d ed.). Chicago: American Medical Association.

American Psychological Association. (1982). *Ethical standards of psychologists.* Washington, DC: Author.

Azzam, B.H., Munroe, M.L., & Richard, M. (1987). How "expert" is your vocational expert? In R. Fry (Ed.), *Third national forum on issues in vocational assessment.* Menomonee, WI: Materials Development Center, Stout Vocational Rehabilitation Institute.

Blackwell, T.L. (1991). *The vocational expert primer.* Athens, GA: Elliott & Fitzpatrick.

Botterbusch, K.F. (1986). *A comparison of computerized job matching systems* (2d ed.). Menomonee, WI: University of Wisconsin-Stout, Materials Development Center, Stout Vocational Rehabilitation Institute.

Brown, C.D., Woodard, D., & McDaniel, R.S. (1991). Differences in workers' compensation settlements using vocational or medical impairment ratings. *NARPPS Journal & News, 6,* 239–44.

Bureau of Labor Statistics. (1984). *News, USDAL 84.* Washington, DC: United States Department of Labor.

Curtis, W.C., & Wilson, L.E. (1976). Determining loss of earnings resulting from impairment or death. *Alabama Lawyer,* 221–29.

Deutsch, P.M., & Sawyer, H.W. (1989). *A guide to rehabilitation.* New York: Matthew Bender, Inc.

DiVivo, M. (1990). Occupational status post-injury. In Stover, S.L., & Fine, P.R. (Eds.). *Spinal cord injuries: Facts and figures.* Washington, DC: National Institute of Handicapped Research.

Dillman, E. (1989). *Economic damages and discounting methods.* Athens, GA: Elliot & Fitzpatrick, Inc.

Dunn, D. (1974). *Placement services in the vocational rehabilitation program.* Menomonee, WI: University of Wisconsin-Stout Research and Training Center.

Ellis, C. (1984). The vocational evaluator as expert witness. In R. Fry & C. Smith (Eds.), *National forum on issues in vocational assessment.* Menomonee, WI: Materials Development Center, Stout Vocational Rehabilitation Institute.

Field, T.F., & Sink, J.M. (1981). *The vocational expert.* Athens, GA: VSB Inc.

Field, T. (1984). *Labor market access* (rev. ed.). Tucson: Valpar International.

Field, T. (1985). *Transferable work skills.* Athens, GA: Elliot & Fitzpatrick, Inc.

Field, T.F., & Taylor, C.M. (1986). *Transferability of work skills.* Athens, GA: VSB, Inc.

Field, T.F. (1989). *Labor market access.* Athens, GA: Elliott & Fitzpatrick, Inc.

Field, T.F., Choppa, T., & Shafer, K. (1981). *Labor market access.* Athens, GA: Elliott and Fitzpatrick, Inc.

Gamboa, A.M. (1987). Assessing capacity to perform work and earn money. *Journal of Applied Rehabilitation Counseling, 18,* 49–51.

Gamboa, A.M. (1987). Introducing VALE: A micro-computer program developed to assess earning capacity. *Rehabilitation Counseling Bulletin, 30,* 278–81.

Gellman, W., Gendel, H., Glaser, N., Dridman, S., & Neff, W. (1957). *Adjusting people to work.* Chicago: Jewish Vocational Services.

Hanke, T. (1981). Present value of future earnings. *Insurance Counsel Journal,* 25–31.

Jones, K.A. (1989). The effect of attorney involvement in the workers' compensation system on time, benefits cost and return to work. *National Forum,* 39–45.

Lynch, R.K. (1983). The vocational expert. *Rehabilitation Counseling Bulletin. 27,* 18–25.

Lynch, R.K., Lynch, R.T., & Beck, R. (1992). Rehabilitation counseling in the private sector. In E.M. Szymanski & R. Parker (Eds.). *Basics and Beyond.* Austin, TX: Pro-ed.

Menninger Return to Work Center. (1986). *Predicting which disabled employees will return to work: The Menninger RTW Scale.* Topeka, KS: The Menninger Foundation.

Moruv, H. (1986). A rehabilitation oriented social security disability system. *Journal of Rehabilitation.* 52, 21–24.

Nadolsky, J. (1984). Social security: In need of rehabilitation. *Journal of Rehabilitation.* 50 (4), 6–8.

Rausch, J. (1985). *Rehabilitation of workers' compensation and other insurance claimants.* Springfield, IL: Charles C. Thomas.

Report on Disability Programs. (1991). *Substantial gainful activity level increased: New social security regulations.* Silver Spring, MD: Author.

Stanton, A.R. (1991). Vocational evaluation in the workers' compensation arena: Guidelines for state and private sector professionals. *National Forum,* 221–25.

Taylor, H. (1986). *Report from Louis Harris and Associates to the Senate Select Subcommittee on the Handicapped.* Washington, DC: Author.

U.S. Department of Health, Education, and Welfare. (1966). *The Vocational Rehabilitation Act as amended through 1965.* Washington, DC: Author.

U.S. Department of Health and Human Services. (1981). *Social security regulations: Rules for determining disability and blindness.* Washington, DC: Author.

U.S. Department of Health and Social Services. (1990). *Vocational expert handbook.* Washington, DC: Office of Hearings and Appeals.

Wainscott, E.B. (1978). Computation of lost future earnings in personal injury and wrongful death actions. *Indiana Law Review,* 647–91.

Weed, R.O., Taylor, C.M., & Blackwell, T. (1991). Job analysis for the private sector. *NARPPS Journal & News,* 6, 153–58.

Weed, R.O., & Field, T.F. (1990). *Rehabilitation consultant's handbook.* Athens, TX: Elliot & Fitzpatrick.

Yankowski, T.P., & Sniderman, R.L. (1991). Return to work: Rehabilitation of the injured worker in California. *NARPPS Journal News,* 6, 245–50.

INDEX